Incurable Blues

The Troubles & Triumph
of Blues Legend

Hubert Sumlin

by Will Romano

Backbeat
Books

San Francisco

Published by Backbeat Books
600 Harrison Street, San Francisco, CA 94107
www.backbeatbooks.com
email: books@musicplayer.com

An imprint of CMP Information
Publishers of *Guitar Player, Bass Player, Keyboard,* and *EQ* magazines

CMP
United Business Media

Distributed to the book trade in the US and Canada by
Publishers Group West, 1700 Fourth Street, Berkeley, CA 94710

Distributed to the music trade in the US and Canada by
Hal Leonard Publishing, P.O. Box 13819, Milwaukee, WI 53213

Cover design by Richard Leeds — bigwigdesign.com
Composition by Maureen Forys, Happenstance Type-O-Rama
Front cover photo © Michael Ochs Archives.com
Back cover photo by Brian White

Library of Congress Cataloging-in-Publication Data

Romano, Will, 1970–
Incurable blues : the troubles & triumph of blues legend Hubert
    Sumlin / by Will Romano.
        p. cm.
Includes bibliographical references (p. 241), discography (p. 223),
    and index.
ISBN 0-87930-833-8 (alk. paper)
1. Sumlin, Hubert, 1931– 2. Blues musicians—United States—
    Biography. 3. Guitarists—United States—Biography. I. Title.

ML419.S85R66 2005
787.87'1643'092—dc22

                         2005000468

Printed in the United States of America

05 06 07 08 09   5 4 3 2 1

Contents

Preface

I remember the first time I heard Howlin' Wolf. I was so frightened by his impossible voice that I was rocked to my very core—the honesty, the simplicity, the fierceness inherent in his words. How could this man speak to a human experience from a place that few dared live?

The music was too outside my immediate element to understand it, perhaps. I had to turn away from it and bury the experience. Later, of course, I would unearth Wolf, swallowing my fear of his vocal prowess, and in the process rediscover a guitar player named Hubert Sumlin.

I was seduced by Hubert's shifting, horn-like, and melodic guitar tones. I couldn't pinpoint the feelings his sound stirred in me, let alone verbalize them. In many ways, I *still* can't. However, I do know that the Wolf–Hubert bond produced a startling result that tinkered with (or did *something* with) my psyche.

There was no way of knowing back then, but to simply focus on Hubert's guitar work is to ignore his personality—the personality that created the heralded idiosyncratic style that proved so integral to Howlin' Wolf's monolithic music. Much has been written about how Eric Clapton, Jeff Beck, Keith Richards, Peter Green, and Jimmy Page reinvigorated America—and the world—with the blues. But it is not said nearly often enough that there would have been no Clapton, no Beck, no Richards, no Green, and no Page without B.B. King, Freddie

King, and Albert King. Without Buddy Guy, Willie Dixon, and Otis Rush. Without *Hubert Sumlin.*

It is mind-boggling how many people Hubert has influenced, how many people love him, and how many people have been touched by his phenomenal guitar playing and that boyish charm.

In 2002 Hubert survived a battle with cancer. Although his entire left lung was removed, he continued to record and tour throughout the world. In 2004 Hubert had another brush with death, one that has forced him to swear off cigarettes and booze, among other vices, forever. When he was more or less back on his feet I spoke with him and he told me, "I saw angels—I thought I was dead—but I'm still livin'. I'm still here."

I was relieved to see him weeks later and to know he was feeling better. And his playing seems to be as inspired as ever. Recently, pop icon John Mayer (whose idol, Stevie Ray Vaughan, learned from Hubert) invited Hubert to perform two songs with him at Webster Hall in New York City. After Mayer's band (augmented by Hubert) executed an adequate version of Wolf's "Killing Floor," I got the feeling that the elder statesman was holding back a bit. Chalk it up to miscommunication, unfamiliarity with one another, voluntary slumber, or Hubert's onstage graciousness, I thought. Whatever the reason, this golden opportunity to win young fans—largely teens and twentysomethings who hadn't even heard of Hubert Sumlin before Mayer introduced him—was not to be squandered. Mayer, to his credit, turned the stage over to the blues master for the next tune, T-Bone Walker's "Stormy Monday Blues." Hubert didn't disappoint. His impossible-to-duplicate runs stuttered, screamed, and squealed as Mayer (whose scorching blues-rock licks were met with resounding applause throughout the night) wisely and unselfishly declined to tread on the path Hubert had blazed. It was clear: this was *Hubert's* moment. Still, fundamental questions kept hounding me. How is it possible for a human body to take this kind of pounding year after year and keep on going? The deeper I studied him, the less I understood, and, in turn, the more questions cropped up.

In the following pages I investigate the Hubert Sumlin experience (intent on highlighting Hubert's nature rather than robotically documenting his life by rattling off a list of arbitrary dates and names in chronological sequence) and how being everyone's best friend—*always finding time for everyone*—has been Hubert's blessing and his curse. It's easy to see a fan's or a buddy's irresistible attraction to Hubert. I admit that I, too, have been caught in the Sumlin spell. Hubert has a way of making even the most mundane conversations intimate, as if this icy world had melted from the warm glow of his friendship.

Even as Hubert expressed to me on separate occasions that he wanted to lay low for a while and get away from the constant demands of his professional life (which included my probing questions, of course), I felt this inexplicable bond between us. "You'd be the onliest one who would know where I was, Will," he once told me. "People be looking for me and you'd say, 'Wait a minute, I'll bring him up for ya.' They'd say, 'You mean to tell me *you* got him?'"

Once I was driving Hubert to a show and we had been on the road a while. My eyes were watery and I was tired. We were both tired. Realistically speaking, it was of little consequence in the grand scheme of things whether I kept my eyes opened or closed once we got to the venue. But Hubert had to perform that night and was feeling winded. I knew he would need a little shut-eye once we got to the hotel. After checking in to his room, Hubert noticed that I could have slept with a rock as a pillow at that point, and he turned to me and said, "If you want, you can rest in this bed. Hell, we'll sleep head to toe. You take that side and I'll take this side."

First thing I thought was, *Who the hell would offer up his bed?*

I declined his offer, but not because of any phobia or social mores. *I just couldn't take the man's bed.* It was classic Hubert: he would've given me the shirt off his back, even if it were the last stitch of clothing he had. How and why he shows this almost boundless generosity is confounding to a sometime cynic like me.

During the research process for this book I spoke with guitarist Robert Cray, a legend in his own right. When Cray first heard Howlin' Wolf he asked himself *why* Hubert played the way he did and why he played *what* he did. Cray still asks himself those questions even after hundreds, maybe thousands, of spins of classic Wolf sides. Mr. Cray, I can say with certainty that the answers don't come any easier the longer and closer you examine Hubert Sumlin.

To me, Hubert personifies a phrase that actor Joe Pesci, portraying alleged CIA operative David Ferrie, delivers in Oliver Stone's movie *JFK*: "…a mystery wrapped in a riddle inside an enigma."

A beautiful enigma, that is.

Will Romano
Long Beach, New York
December 2004

Chapter 1
Birth of a Mythical Bluesman

"**H**ubert! Hubert! Remember me?" says an enthusiastic voice deep within the wooded area cloaking the entranceway to Brookhaven National Laboratory (BNL)—a hub of scientific and governmental defense research in Long Island, New York. BNL is a seemingly unlikely place for a blues show, but tonight it hosts co-headliners Hubert Sumlin and 89-year-old folk-blues legend David "Honeyboy" Edwards from Greenwood, Mississippi—Hubert's hometown.

Blues fanatics will be coming out of the woodwork, I'm sure, and Hubert, having just moments earlier left the comfort and safety of his hotel room, seems to have encountered a rabid one. Dusk masks the approaching man's face—it's hard to get a read on who he is. Still, Hubert continues to walk toward the stranger, without regard or perceived danger. This *fan*, it turns out, is actually Willie Steele (not the famous Chess-label drummer), a New York blues guitarist who is playing rhythm guitar to Hubert's lead tonight. "You called me once a while back, and we spoke for two hours on the phone," says Steele, as his cheerful, bearded face lights up. "It's Willie Steele. Do you remember, Hubert?"

Hubert nods his head and says, "Sure. I remember you, Willie." Steele is exuberant and escorts the legend to Berkner Hall's backstage area—a solitary, glowing yellow crevice that seems to occupy its own space and time in the wooded darkness.

As Hubert enters the dressing room, his pickup band perks up. Hubert will be backed by guitarist Bill Casey (aka Willie Steele);

bandleader Doug "Harmonica" McLean, a grizzle-faced, tall, and slender harp player who cites Louisiana Red as his mentor; Don Celenza, who doubles tonight as a pianist and guitarist; drummer Tom McGraph; and Al Levy on bass. They are local blues vets who have played with such greats as Son Seals, John Lee Hooker, and Lightnin' Hopkins.

Smiles all around: royalty is holding court. Everyone is brimming with excitement at the prospect of grabbing his own piece of history by playing with the man who, as a member of Howlin' Wolf's band for over 20 years, helped create and shape the legendary electric Chicago blues sound. Out of respect, Steele tunes Hubert's guitar. Tonight Hubert plays "Momma"—the name he gave to his pinkish/red-faced guitar in the style of a Fender Stratocaster. Scrawled in Sharpie ink on the back of the guitar is a note—more like a fire-and-brimstone threat—from friend and fellow guitarist Jimmy Vivino. The note implies that if one should find him- or herself in possession of Hubert's property, he/she should give it back directly to its rightful owner. If he/she does not, Vivino wrote, "…you WILL burn in hell!!" (Hubert has had a number of guitars go missing over the years, most recently in 2000 when his 1955 Gibson Les Paul Gold Top, serial number 51005—given to him by Vivino—was reportedly stolen at a show in the Milwaukee area but retrieved soon after.)

Doug McLean, who spent time carefully picking the right songs for tonight's gig, hands Hubert a set list: all Wolf standards. Hubert studies the list, folds up the piece of paper, and lays it down by his guitar case. Hubert is quiet for a moment, then barks, "We'll do one of my numbers, a song called 'Chunky' from my *Heart & Soul* record."

With that, the tone of the evening is cemented: it's a Hubert Sumlin night. And that could mean any number of things. Hubert is a grand wizard, sometimes playfully commanding and spinning elaborate practical jokes on unwitting musicians, the punch line of which perhaps only he gets—a kind of erratic, albeit genius, musical "catch me if you can."

The band seems unfamiliar with the song, so Hubert describes its percussive, rubbery, and "clucking" nature. McLean pinpoints the vibe via a reference to Tex-Cal blues jumper Lowell Fulson, and the crew is locked and ready to go. McLean beseeches Hubert to call out the opening chord of each song and not let the band hang out to dry. "You're gonna let me know the chords, right? You're gonna let me know the chords?" McLean repeats as he tilts his beret-topped head, cups his harp in one hand, and points at Hubert. Smiles. Hubert just nods his head and promises, "Yeah. I will. I will." They decide on a cue as to when Hubert will take the stage during "Chunky."

Despite the ease McLean's band will have in adapting to the curve Hubert throws them, it gnaws at Hubert that more people don't know his music. Pickup bands mean well when they present Hubert a set full of Wolf "hits," but their unfamiliarity with Hubert's solo material is a lingering, career-spanning problem. Hubert is known as Wolf's guitar player—first and foremost—despite the fact that he has been recording his own music since well before Wolf died in 1976.

Seated in the middle of the room wearing a dark blue suit, glasses, and a brown safari hat (one he purchased during a recent swing through Australia), Hubert observes the band milling around. The night air is getting muggier and heavier by the minute. Simply put: it's getting hot backstage as more and more people crowd in to see Hubert. One unexpected face, blues great Sam Taylor (DJ and Blues Hall of Fame member who has written songs for Elvis Presley, Freddie King, and Sam and Dave, among others), pops in to say hello to Hubert, his friend for over two decades. Taylor's amiable presence seems to act as a relaxation pill. Everyone is having a good time, bullshitting, sharing stories, and trying out each other's instruments. It's a regular party, and the noise level grows—nearly rivaling the sounds emanating from Honeyboy's brilliant acoustic set in progress. Some of the guys don't seem to know what to do with themselves (Hubert's accessibility seems to have floored them), yet they show restraint. But you can almost read their minds: once this set is over they will call their wives, girlfriends, and all of their friends in a euphoric panic to say, "Yeah, I played with Hubert Sumlin tonight. Can you believe it?"

McLean picks up a harp from his gig bag, blows a few bars, puts the harmonica down, and tries the next one. His bag seems bottomless as he spot-checks each and every one of them. He then slots several of the harmonicas into his belt holster—à la Sonny Boy Williamson II (though McLean admits it is one of the few things he does that is *not* an homage to the greats but out of practicality). He looks like a cowboy preparing for a bloody gun battle. From the bag he also pulls out a book on the history of Chicago blues (which features Hubert) and an LP relic: a 1980 album of the American Folk Blues Festival. "I learned how to play by listening to these records," McLean insists as he displays the LP flap to reveal a black-and-white photo of Hubert passionately playing his Les Paul.

"This guy's a regular walking encyclopedia," Taylor says with a laugh. Hubert laughs, too, but he seems anxious, and the nervous energy and humid air backstage saturate the senses, creating a kind of uneasiness. It causes him to bolt from his chair, strut through the backstage door, and pace on the lawn, now nearly black in the dark night.

Earlier in the day, as Hubert and I had surveyed the tree lines and expansive foliage on the BNL campus, he had remarked on its familiarity: "It reminds me of home." I took this to mean his Milwaukee home, the one he bought with his beloved wife, Willie Bea. "Well, that, and *home*, home," referring to his childhood home in Arkansas where he grew up, where he first met and played with the Mighty Wolf.

It's clear now that Hubert wants—yearns—to commune with something greater than himself, something outside this musical arena. Honeyboy's rootsy, acoustic music in the background and the soupy, embryonic humidity recall a time in the South when the Great Migration was in its infancy. Tonight's audience may be comprised of Northerners, but they are lulled by the warmth of communal experience that we, as Americans, understand. Hubert is homesick (and perhaps a bit more).

In a flash, Honeyboy has finished and McLean's crew invades the bandstand. Hubert, having returned from his jaunt, waits patiently for his cue, and…there it is. The band has captured the yo-yo feel of "Chunky" perfectly. Hubert takes the stage, waves to the crowd, then straps on his guitar. He soon bursts into a stinging, fiery solo, rife with signature double-note attacks that push the boundaries of the song's meter limit. Hubert's handle on the song is precarious, as if it will all fall off the table and splatter, making a terrible mess. You're unsure that Hubert is aware of (or even cares) how—or if—he will come out of his foray unscathed, and where this will leave the other musicians. To their credit, the band is right there behind Hubert, and the bluesman's tightrope act raises a smile from pianist/guitarist Celenza.

The band is energized and blows through blistering takes on "Smokestack Lightnin'"/"I Asked for Water" and "300 Pounds of Joy." At points, McLean and Hubert share impromptu brilliance as lyrical A-A-B call-and-response patterns ensue. McLean's harp moans and unleashes a sad beast, slithering and wallowing in a kind of sonic-psychic muck, as Hubert's 6-string antics float high above the action, waving good-bye to the earthbound players onstage, who can only look up, slack-jawed, wishing they had wings.

Just as the energy level climbs, Hubert lays Momma down on his stool, as if the guitar is a burden too heavy to carry, and walks off prematurely. He waves good-night to the audience and heads backstage. I ask Hubert if he is okay. "Yeah, son. I'm just resting." (Hubert recently had a lung removed in order to stem the spread of cancer throughout his body.) His breathlessness could easily have been mistaken for a health problem (the kind he has learned to live with since the surgery) instead of something that rocked him to his very core. Visibly out of breath, Hubert stares off into the distance—his eyes an

This classic 1956 side is a close sister song to Wolf's signature tune, "Smokestack Lightnin'" (1618).

impenetrable wall, blocking unwanted and invading questions. There is silence between us for several minutes, though music reverberates throughout the building. Then, a split-second decision: Hubert rockets himself off his chair and returns to the stage to raucous applause. His final song, "All I Can," is dedicated to Willie Bea, who passed away in October 1999.

For a moment Hubert almost seems on the verge of tears, speaking through the hazy mists of time. The hushed crowd realizes that they are witnessing an epiphany—the exposure of Hubert's soul. This confession is more than poignant or beautiful; it is cataclysmic and timeless. Whether the crowd realizes it or not, a joyous yet painful emotional powder keg has exploded deep within Hubert. The implosion burns its way to the surface and out of the legendary bluesman. It spreads through everyone like wildfire, until the entire auditorium is charred with Hubert's burning memories.

When the song is over, Hubert leaves Momma on his stool and slowly swaggers backstage. As the crowd cheers for an encore, the 440-seat theatre comes to its collective feet and claps. There's momentary confusion as to what will happen. Will Hubert take the stage again? He darts back and forth for a few seconds and doesn't disappoint: he shuffles back onstage. Now both Honeyboy and Hubert are illuminated by stage light, seated and tuning up. While no one would deny the historic significance of this performance, there is actually something far greater, and deeper, at work. Hubert's catharsis seems unresolved and stunted. Strangely, he seems to want it that way—it's perhaps the only way he can connect and reconnect with his past, the love(s) of his life, his audience, and even himself.

As we head down Route 112 after the show, shrouded in early morning fog, Hubert quietly tells me why he walked off the stage earlier in the evening. "I got too emotional. I was overcome. I saw Wolf's face up there, man. I saw him. He was looking at me and I just couldn't go on. I just couldn't do it." That statement hangs in the air. Hubert's bond with Wolf went way beyond a musical connection, or a connection perhaps spawned by proximity that five or six musicians experience sharing a stage on a nightly basis. Hubert had reached a part of himself that no one else—save for the Wolf—could ever identify with. As we

turn into his hotel parking lot, Hubert gets out of the car and retires for
the night. He says he'll be okay and that I should "go on home and give
me a call when you get in."

"I was born—1931," Hubert says in a soft voice. "I came up in a little
ole town, Greenwood, Mississippi. That's where my people come from."

Hubert Sumlin, who has lived the majority of his life as a gentle,
soft-spoken individual, came kicking, screaming, and crying into this
world on November 16, 1931. He couldn't have been born at a worse
time: the South was experiencing a debilitating depression that wiped
out entire life savings, setting the US economy on a dizzying descent
(the effects of which would be felt throughout the 1930s). The country
was divided by prohibition; the economy was devastated by the stock
market crash of 1929 (by 1933, nearly 30 percent of the work force was
unemployed); and the Southern farmer would again be tested and frus-
trated by the annual enemy: the boll weevil beetle, which burrows its
larvae into unripe cotton bolls, causing widespread destruction of crops.

The Mississippi Delta region was like an agricultural spigot that
could not be shut off. Like other Delta regions in the world (Nile and
Ganges rivers, for example), it is a fan-like strip of fertile land formed
by deposited silt and sediment at the river's mouth. The Delta pos-
sesses rich nutrients that are perfect for agriculture, and its treasures
were well known to the indigenous peoples of America hundreds and
hundreds of years ago. But in the 1930s, the region's most valuable
commodity was, ironically, hurting the nation's economy and threatening the well-being of Delta farmers: farm products, especially cotton,
were being overproduced.

Mississippi's weather, virtually unpredictable, bounced from one
end of the spectrum to the other. Less than a year before Hubert was
born to John and Claudia Sumlin, the very earth of Leflore County,
Mississippi, was scorched by sun and drought. Just two months after
Hubert's birth, Leflore County's Greenwood saw one of the worst floods
in the state's recorded history. God was smiling if crops could be har-
vested and sharecroppers (or farm tenants) could live off them for the

next season. If floods washed away everything, or drought dried up the earth, or the boll weevil rendered crops useless, the devil's handiwork had marked the poor people of Mississippi. Hubert couldn't have been born in a worse place at that time: it was a land of extremes. Mississippi was the site of intense creativity that represents the best of the human spirit, and it was the site of extreme hatred and racism—arguably the worst anywhere in the country.

As had been the tradition since before the American Civil War, singers from work camps and churches sang about their troubles and the hard-luck hand that life had dealt them. Ma Rainey first sang "Bo-Weavil [sic] Blues" in 1921, and a version was recorded in 1929 by Delta country blues giant Charlie Patton (under the pseudonym "The Masked Marvel") as "Mississippi Boll Weevil Blues." That was life in the Delta and the Delta region: there was always a vocal guide—a running musical commentary—that informed listeners and lamented the major events of the day.

At the end of the 1920s and in the early '30s, the devil's hands were quite busy. Between the stock market crash and the fall of cotton prices, the South had seen its worst agricultural economy since the beginning of the Civil War. In 1931, the year of Hubert's birth, the production of cotton was at a five-year high, but prices were at their lowest in the 20-year period between 1920 and 1940. By 1939, the carryover (overproduced cotton supply in reserve) exceeded annual production.

The Delta's traditions were steeped in folk arts and history, which gave the region its inner strength. The Delta and its people have been nurtured by a confluence of three distinct cultures: Native American, African-American, and white European-American. The very name Greenwood was derived from a Native American chief (Greenwood Leflore) of the Choctaw Nation Native American tribe. (It should come as no surprise, then, to find that Hubert's sister Maggie Watkins claims her grandfather was white. "My daddy's dad was a white man," says Maggie. "Back in time…they had people cookin' for 'em, you know?")

Greenwood experienced a surge in population, nearly doubling in the 20-year period from 1910 to 1930. For 100 years prior, Greenwood was the shipping point for the land between the Yazoo River (in the west) and Tombigbee River (in the east), and it was Mississippi's largest cottonseed market. But by 1931, that was all in the past. The country, the South, and the Southern farmer had seen better days.

President Franklin Delano Roosevelt's New Deal attempted to help the Southern farmer with the three "R"s—relief (offering loans at low rates), recovery, and reform—to preempt any future catastrophic events like the 1929 crash. By 1935, the Works Progress Administration or Public Works Administration (known as the WPA) was established to help unemployed farmers. One program, the Agricultural Adjustment Administration (AAA), restricted the production of cotton in the hope of driving up the price per bale. When the AAA law was enacted in 1933, millions of acres of cotton were destroyed; the government enticed farmers to destroy it by paying them benefits per acre. The AAA did little, initially, to stem the output of cotton.

As if echoing his environment, Hubert (or "Hubeh," as his mother used to call him) was a cranky, restless soul as an infant—the youngest of 13 children. Sister Maggie (now 88 and living in Memphis, Tennessee) remembers Hubert as a baby. "I was a teen when Hubert was born—15 pounds—and I remember him cryin'. Lord, he cried so much. My mother, she didn't have no learnin'. I sat up all night with that boy when he was born. He was howlin' all night."

Hubert and his family lived as sharecroppers on the Pillow family plantation. Maggie recalls working long hours in the fields of Mississippi. "My daddy worked the fool out of us. We really worked hard, but we didn't do too bad." Truth be told, there wasn't much else for many African-Americans in the rural South to do but work in the field. "We had over 100 acres of cotton and my brother, A.D. [Smith], could pick a bale of cotton a day," Hubert brags. "My daddy could pick a half a bale. Oh, lord! My daddy had 25 acres of tobacco, too. We used to pick the leaves off the tobacco."

Sharecroppers would typically give landowners a large percentage (half, usually) of the crop's yield for their boarding. While on the surface this seems equitable, it was a vastly unfair system. The sharecropper had to pay for everything he needed for the year (clothing, food, tools) from half the harvest's yield. In some cases, sharecroppers had the ability to trade on credit. Plantation owners would pay sharecroppers in chits (paper money) or brozine (coins)—a form of money that was good only for use at the plantation commissary. This plantation money was worthless if a sharecropper wanted to travel to a more densely populated area where US currency was accepted. Was this the Emancipation that Lincoln had promised in 1865? Some sharecroppers would beg to differ. But it was the landowner's goal, one would suppose: to keep the sharecroppers down on the farm.

Nonetheless, the Sumlins did rather well for themselves. Hubert tells why, at least in part, this was the case: "When we were growing up we had shoes, me and my sister. We were the only kids who had shoes, and I used to wonder why we had shoes and nobody else did. When I was young, Daddy would—there was a swamp out behind the house—and I'd see Daddy go out behind the house, go off toward the swamp and disappear. One day after I seen him do this a number of times, I snook out and followed him. But my dad saw me coming, and I got close to the swamp and suddenly there's a door laying on the ground and this door opens and an arm comes out that grabs me by the shirt. It's Daddy and he pulls me down into this cave that is covered by a door. My daddy is making moonshine down there. He locked me in there for a day. My dad said, 'I'll teach you to follow me,' you know? So then I said, 'But boy, I figured out about them shoes.'"

While John Sumlin provided for the family any way he could, Claudia made sure that the children always had good, home-cooked meals. According to Hubert, Claudia cooked so well that the plantation owner would often plead with her to cook for him. "My momma was supposed to be taking a break from work, you know what I mean? And the owners said, 'Miss Claudia, Miss Claudia, please don't leave us,'" Hubert says. "The plantation owners were cryin', you know? Momma said, 'How about we just make it to the end of the month?' 'Yes, ma'am, you got it. We pay you for it.' Let me tell you something, that whole month Momma was on vacation she was working for the plantation man. She was cookin' for this one and that one. She was a good cook. Goats, hogs, sheeps, cattle. Everything. She ain't here anymore, but they gots the best food you ever eaten in your life. When I go down South, I don't stay long—I wouldn't stay a week to save my life. I'll tell you why: when you leave there, brother, you gonna have some weight on you, number one. Number two? You gonna feel good. Then you are gonna, maybe, stay another week. This is what the South is all about. They known for good food. Home-cookin' food."

Claudia's cooking was so tasty that Hubert would typically risk physical harm to eat it. Hubert remembers one dinner fraught with danger. "With 13 of us in the family, my daddy had to build this long wooden table that would take up the room and stick out the door," Hubert explains. "The end of it would stick out the door, it was so large. There were 13 of us and we all had to get around this table. He added a piece, too. Here come the preacher. My daddy built another space in the table for the preacher. We didn't figure we would use the table for the preacher that often, maybe a couple of Sundays for the preacher. Every holiday or something he would come and every Sunday, whether it rain or shine, he was there—that was our preacher. That was the chicken-eating-est preacher I ever seen in my life. My momma would make 14, 15 chickens at once.

"So this guy got there, [Claudia] had to add two more chickens just for him. One morning my daddy sat down in front of the preacher. All the way down along the table there was a bowl of chicken—four bowls of chicken, each as beautiful as a flower. This preacher eat the first two bowls of chicken. Then, he ain't through yet. He had that for a starter. A starter! They brings four more. This dude got the last bowl on the table and then I caught his hand. I reached over there and I got his hand. I said, 'Hey, preacher, I want that piece.' My daddy said, 'Oh, you. What is the matter?' I said, 'Oh, no. I done messed the preacher.' But I done messed myself up. I said the best thing for me to do is to shut up and get out of there.

"Before I left there, since I knew I was gonna get it, I say, 'Hell, I'm gonna get me some chicken,' and I got the last piece," Hubert continues. "I had four halves. My daddy said, 'Where you goin'?' I said, 'Good-bye.' I went into the oat patch where they used to feed the cattle. They grind the oats like flour right in front of our house. The oats was up over my head, the stalks. But I could run. My daddy got on a mule, name Pearl. He could run like a horse, this mule. My daddy got on the mule and I saw him. I'm watching him. But I was in the middle of the patch, hiding in the stalks. My daddy said, 'Where are ya?' I see he is getting closer and closer to me. Then I see that he is going the other way—the wrong way.

But then this old mule, he could smell, man. I heard him. My daddy say, 'I knew you in there. My mule tell me you is.' Sure enough, I was. 'There you is. Don't you know better?' He hit me twice…before I made it back to the house. When I got back to the house, and the house we had was on cement blocks, I could get up under there and crawl around and be safe. But a big dude couldn't. I was a little ole dude. I made it. I ran up in there so he couldn't hit me a third time. Then he got off the mule and he put his head in the hole and looked up and said, 'I know you are up in here. I'll come get ya.' I said, 'Hey, come on. Come on. You can't get up in this house.' Then he said, 'I will wait here until you come out. I'm gonna kill ya.' I said, 'Uh-oh.' I knew I ain't coming out now. After a while he got on the mule and went on to his woman's house. He had a woman on four corners of the plantation."

As usual, Hubert stops himself before saying any disparaging words about another human being. I attempted to ask what his father was doing with women "on four corners of the plantation" and Hubert simply said, "Oooooh, I better quit now."

Maggie wasn't so shy. "Oh, god. My daddy was a rollin' stone," she declares. "We got about I don't know how many children in our family. I didn't even see them all. My brother A.D. had another dad. His name Smith. My momma left my daddy…one time she was done so bad…and she came back pregnant. He got the gun and was gonna shoot Momma. He didn't. But I think he was the meanest one in the family."

Life on the farm forced Hubert to grow up quickly. "My daddy had this little shack out the back of our house where he did all of this chewing of the tobacco," Hubert says. "Shit, man! I learned how to smoke at seven years old. Before I got my guitar even. And drinking coffee? Yes, sir. I did this for 60-some years. That will show you how God is, man."

It was around this time that Hubert began taking an interest in stringed instruments. His brother A.D. would spend hours tinkering and plucking the one-stringed instrument called a diddley bow. It simply mesmerized Hubert. The diddley bow is made of a plank of wood that is nailed to the wall of the house. (Sometimes the house itself would be used as a resonator, instead of a plank of wood.) A bottle, usually a snuff bottle, is put beneath the single string at each end (these act as surrogate bridges), raising the string a few inches off the wood. A third bottle (which acts as a slide) is moved across the string with one hand for melody, while the other hand picks the string to create a bassline.

"Listening to what he was doing, I was in a flower bed of ease," Hubert reflects. "It sounded so good. He'd take this baling wire and wrap it around these two bottles—he put bottles up there against the wall, one on top, one on the bottom. Then he would take another bottle and use it as a slide. He could make that thing sing, man. One string. He could make it sing. I tell ya, he is a better guitar player than me!"

A.D.'s overzealous younger brother decided to try his fingers on the instrument. One can picture a beady-eyed Hubert plucking away with abandon on the one string, smiling. Smiling—until his aggressive playing snapped the wire. A big mistake. "It was soundin' good," Hubert explains. "But when it was time to change the tune of the song, I had to slide that damn bottle up and I broke the bottle and the string. Boy, he got mad. I thought he was gonna whoop me, man.

"Since our house was set on cement blocks, A.D. was gonna hit me with a stone, right on my head," Hubert says. "He started saying, 'I hope you die.' My momma was coming from Greenwood; she had to walk four miles to get to her job. She worked at this funeral home, making eight dollars a week. She stopped him from whooping me. She told me, 'Next week, you are going to have something to play on. He ain't.' Sure enough, a whole week's pay…she got me a new guitar. It didn't even have a name, but what a guitar. My first guitar I ever had. I still have the neck of that guitar."

Many of the tales Hubert spins have reached mythical proportions. He is one of the twentieth century's most influential blues guitarists (guitarists, period!), and although many people know a little about him and his playing, few know the man. The best analogy I can make is to say that Hubert is like the Shroud of Turin. The seemingly fresh wounds are on display for everyone—its very image the representation (or approximation) of human divinity in the real world. And, like the Shroud, just when you've carved it up, studied it diligently under the microscope, and tracked its origins, another piece of information crops up and makes you say, "How does this fit?" Inspecting the fibers of the details of Hubert's life to uncover all the shreds of facts and secrets only leads you into a maze of unanswered questions and conjecture. And as with any good mystery, you are left with a body of evidence, puzzling questions, and few answers.

Attempting to find documentation to corroborate information or answer some lingering questions about Hubert's early life proved fruitless. Hubert claims that there is no record of his birth in Leflore County, Mississippi. "I have no birth certificate," he maintains. "I was birthed by a midwife. The place burned down there in Jackson, Mississippi. There is no birth certificate." Maggie backs up Hubert's assertion. "I don't have no birth certificate," she says. "I tried to get it, but they said that the place or something had burned up in Jackson. That is where mine's supposed to went to. Momma had midwives to birth me—I couldn't get a birth certificate. But I tried."

Hubert was reared in a land fertile with mythical musical figures. Greenwood, Mississippi, is nestled between Highway 55 and Highway 49, which intersect and skirt such musically potent cities as Memphis, Tennessee, New Orleans, Louisiana, Clarksdale, and Jackson. Greenwood is also the site where Chester Burnett (aka Howlin' Wolf)—Hubert's future employer and a man who would define Hubert's very existence—played with "King of the Delta Blues" Robert Johnson. And Greenwood (or just outside it) is where the suave, free-spirited Johnson met his demise in 1938 (as his death certificate reads) by what many speculate to have been poisoning. "The original Pillow Plantation included the ground on which was constructed Three Forks juke joint where Robert Johnson was probably poisoned," explains Steven LaVere, Mississippi and blues historian and producer of the box set *Robert Johnson: The Complete Recordings*. "This is the third Delta blues generation that has farmed here now."

A young guitar player named Eddie Jones was born in Greenwood in 1926, and would make his mark on New Orleans—one of the few Delta musicians to do so—as Guitar Slim. Slim recorded his much covered "The Things that I Used to Do" in late 1953 for the Specialty label, climbed to the top of the *Billboard* R&B charts in 1954, and had a profound effect on many of Hubert's contemporaries. Hubert was well aware of the country folk-blues of Mississippi, even though he never got a chance to see many of its major proponents perform in person. "Charlie Patton, Robert Johnson, I didn't get a chance to see these fellas," Hubert laments. "I was a little too young. You know what I'm talking about? But I remember the first time I heard Charlie Patton. I got this little ole record out of the garbage or something man. The record sounded like it was warped and I started playing it. I just heard this man moaning and whining, you know? That was Charlie Patton. I said, 'Oh, yeah! That's the stuff. This is where it is at for me.'"

Inspired by people like Patton, Johnson, and Peetie Wheatstraw, Hubert carried his guitar wherever he went. But one day that guitar got him in trouble when he picked more strings than cotton. "That farm man caught me playing that guitar in the field one day—I was supposed to be workin'," Hubert admits. "He just took it and cracked it—he broke it." When Claudia found out about this, she raised holy hell. Cowed by Claudia's strong will and love for her son, the plantation owner apologized to the family. "He bought me a new guitar and handed it to me and just said, 'Here you go. Don't play it in the field no mo','" Hubert says with a smile.

Claudia was supportive of Hubert's creative outlet, but she believed that Hubert's proper place—as a young man and as a musician—was in church. "My grandmother was very religious," confirms Charlene Higgs, Hubert's niece and the Sumlin family historian. "She didn't approve of him playing guitar. She only bought him the guitar because she knew he could play, and then it was only so he would play in church. She wanted him to be a church-going person, not a bluesman. She did not approve of that 'boogie-woogie music,' that 'wild music,' she called it. She was a sanctified person."

A bluesman's life, which encompassed much more than just singing songs in a juke joint, was the fast track to hell. After all, the blues was "the devil's music." It wasn't so much the singing as the amalgam of drinking, womanizing, fast living, and the musicians' wanderlust that helped to formulate such hatred and dread in the religious community. That being said, perhaps there was a grain of truth in what was being preached from the pulpit. Bluesmen could be unfocused, violent, and unreliable, and their crazed facial expressions resembled a man possessed or sex-starved. Either way, what these devils were doing was tantamount to heresy and paganism. It was voodoo; voodoo that was better left to prison camps; voodoo that bemoaned the time of slavery and backbreaking labor.

Although the thread that ran through the blues (and always has) was to exorcise fear, heartache, shame, and anger, the music's not-so-subtle sexual innuendo and power to attract female attention were to be degraded, not praised. "…No truly respectable Delta woman was supposed to sing the blues, even in private," wrote Alan Lomax in his book *The Land Where the Blues Began.* "All women of repute belonged to the church.…On the other hand, women were attracted to these devilish blues musicians because these gents with guitars and harmonicas usually had a little money in their pockets."

And, of course, Claudia had said, "No way you're gonna play the blues. No way!"

When the Sumlins moved to Hughes, Arkansas, in the late '30s to early '40s—Hubert was eight, possibly nine years old—Claudia, now a member of the local Sanctified Baptist church, convinced Hubert to play for the congregation and learn from a deacon there (whose name Hubert doesn't remember). Hubert was still young and painfully shy, and would turn his back to the congregation when he played because "it sounded better that way." (Hubert would continue this trend even after he joined Wolf, but that would have as much to do with protecting his techniques from competing guitarists as with his shyness.)

Hubert's guitar continually got him in trouble with his elders. One day, he admits, he "messed up. I hit a bad note—I was playin' the blues. She [Claudia] pulled me down from the bandstand there in church and when we's got home, my momma beat me. Blues was devil music. And here I was playin' it. She thought she'd put a stop to that, but I kept on playin', man." There was nothing Claudia could do to stem the tide of Hubert's musical inclination. "Heaven know," Hubert notes, "music is all I ever wanted."

Music was the number one priority, though there was still work to be done. According to Hubert, the Sumlins most likely left Mississippi for economic reasons. "What happened, when I was eight years old, my people got tired of cotton," he explains. "Arkansas was just like, they had cotton all over. We were going to go down there. But it was changing. Finally cotton was giving out there. They want rice." (Data shows that US cotton production was far exceeding demand. Prices per bale were up nearly $.04, and production per bale was on a steady decline for the third straight year.)

At that time, the South's populations were on the move. Three million African-Americans would jettison themselves from the South in the years between 1940 and 1960. Major northern, midwestern, and western cities such as Chicago, Cleveland, Detroit, New York, Newark, Los Angeles, and Seattle were beacons of hope. "The onset of the Depression dampened the prospects for economic opportunities up North, but still a steady stream of black workers made the trek anyway," wrote blues authority Robert Santelli in *Martin Scorsese Presents The Blues,* the companion book to the PBS series.

Three major forces were at work to help kick-start the Great Migration to the North: the AAA's program to cut production of cotton (fewer acres to farm, fewer workers needed), the Great Depression, and mechanization (often cited as the main reason for African-American and white migration to the North). It was the landowners who stood to make the most money and benefit in any way possible from the land—not the sharecroppers, who were simply stymied by the will of the farmers, the government, and Mother Nature. Some sharecroppers were soon evicted. It was inevitable: farmers (non-landowning farmers) had to leave to seek a better job, a better economic climate, and a better life. "Prior to mechanization, everything in Greenwood was based on cotton," notes historian LaVere. "The banks were here because the money was here, and the money was here because of the cotton. All the businesses were here to support the plantation owner of the plantation worker."

The farm had a stranglehold on the South and the sharecroppers, who were nothing more than doomed dependents of this failed capitalistic experiment. The South was forced to become modernized, and in doing so began the long road to recovery from its many ills (including racism). Farm machinery became more efficient, driving the number of farmhands down considerably. In a larger sense, as more families got out of their repressed situations, factors like mechanization, government programs, perhaps infertile or barren fields, overpopulation, and selfish landowners (who virtually enslaved African-Americans even after the Great Emancipation of 1865) all helped to free sharecroppers from an economic system: the plantation. "You can still find cotton down there today," Hubert says. "But they use electric cotton pickers and the cotton is government cotton. Shit, man! They got dudes operating the equipment that know how to do it. They can pick eight rows at a time where that would take you a month. You know? More so, rice country. Rice country."

"The popular belief that people were chased from the South because of mechanization is not altogether true," offers Donald Holley, however. A history professor at the University of Arkansas and author of *The Second Great Emancipation: The Mechanical Cotton Picker, Black Migration, and How They Shaped the Modern South,* Holley explains: "There were no commercial pickers before 1950, for example. Millions of people had already moved north. Migration to the North was happening long before mechanization was widely used on the farm."

Whatever the impetus for the Great Migration, by leaving Mississippi the Sumlins forced Hubert to take one step closer to his ultimate goal of becoming a musician. The musically fertile corridor from West Memphis, Arkansas, down through Hughes and Helena, Arkansas (not to mention nearby Clarksdale, Mississippi, right on the Mighty Miss), was home to such legendary musicians as Aleck "Rice" Miller (aka Sonny Boy Williamson II), Howlin' Wolf, Johnny Shines, and Robert Jr. Lockwood (a companion and sort of stepchild to Robert Johnson). "All these Arkansas 'Delta' towns had one or two blues singers coming out of 'em, if they had any population at all," explains Terry Buckalew, director of the Delta Cultural Center in Helena, Arkansas.

Hubert was more alive with music than ever before.

Though much has changed since Hubert lived in Arkansas (a considerable amount of money has poured into Hughes and adjacent areas in recent years), the primordial elements of the countryside still exist today. The overgrowing foliage in the shapes of prehistoric monsters dwarf the brush underneath. Snakes slither in front of your automobile on a backwater road, turtles have the right of way, and the sun beats mercilessly on the surface of any parched earth that is not shaded by a thick forest of mixed hardwood trees. Eerie silence is broken only by distant bird cries or buzzing insects. You know you are alone in the wilderness, yet you take every step with caution, as though you are trespassing. Perhaps you are. The very soles of your feet tread on eons of human history. There is an indescribable, indiscernible, and inexplicable energy here. It's unnerving, as though someone—or something— has its eyes trained on you. "Eastern Arkansas can be spooky," admits scholar David Evans, music professor at the University of Memphis. "It can be scary."

Like so many aspects of Hubert's personal history, evidence and documentation of eastern Arkansas's history are scarce. The area holds

The Sumlins moved from Greenwood, Mississippi, to Hughes, Arkansas, circa 1940. (Photo taken in 2004.)

much mystery for those who dig deep into its past. Going further back, long before plantations, it may have been a playground and hunting ground for Native American tribes. But no one is certain. "That part of Arkansas, while we couldn't call it a no-man's-land, has not yielded any real evidence as to who lived there," explains Dr. Jeff Mitchem, director of the Arkansas Archeological Survey in Parkin, Arkansas. "Perhaps some tribes, like the Osage, hunted there, but there is no solid evidence to point to that."

What remains is an energy, spirits and ghosts if you will, that prey on your psyche. Driving a circuitous route that winds around Horseshoe Lake (once a channel of the Mississippi River), I approach Seyppel, a place of considerable import for Hubert. I expect to find something here, some marker of significance, something that would denote an historic event occurred here.

I roll through a stretch of farmlands for a mile or so and see no flag, no sign that reads "Seyppel." Thinking that perhaps I've gone too far up Highway 131, I double back and enter a store in Horseshoe Lake. The owner is having a cigarette, talking with a local in the dark and dank shack. When I say that I am looking for Seyppel, the local backs away from me as if I were a wild animal, and the owner, puzzled by my question, thinks for a minute.

"Say-ple?" She pauses. "Oh...you mean Sigh-pell," she says, correcting my pronunciation.

She explains that there is nothing left of Seyppel except a small farm industry—an E.H. Clarke cotton company. The area was once heavily populated with sharecroppers, but now has faded into virtual nonexistence. Seyppel is not a proper town, is not incorporated, and, as my research revealed, never was. It exists in name only, and only because mapmakers choose to continue identifying it.

Ironically, Seyppel is home to rich historical legends. One legend has it that this area provided a Jesse James hideout, another that it was the location of light skirmishes during the Civil War. Still another has significance in blues history. Seyppel was the first place that Hubert Sumlin claims to have seen Howlin' Wolf play, at a juke joint called Silkhairs. Like so many legends, its verbal mythology has spread throughout the blues world with slight variations on a theme:

Horseshoe Lake, Arkansas: Where Hubert's world collided with the Wolf universe.

"When Hubert was about ten, he sneaked out to the local juke joint and stood on a pile of Coca-Cola crates to see Howlin' Wolf," explains Bob Margolin, guitar player for Muddy Waters in the 1970s. "Drawn in by the music, he fell through the window and landed right on the stage. The club owner tried to throw out the underage boy, but Wolf insisted that Hubert stay and sit on the stage while he played. He later took Hubert home to his momma and asked that he not be punished."

"There's a very funny story my Uncle Hubert tells about a tavern—that is what some called them in those days," confirms niece Charlene. "My uncle pulled up all of these Coca-Cola bottle crates to see through the window of this establishment and he fell through the window."

But Hubert recounts the tale in his own words: "Wolf was playing this little ole honky-tonk right on the Mississippi called Silkhairs. I was young. It was this place they had up on blocks, cement blocks, you know what I mean? So, I was able to get up under the house. They wouldn't let me in, they kept throwing me out. I'd try to get in and run between people's legs and everything, but they threw me out. So, on account I wanted to see, I climb up on these crates, Coke bottle crates, and start leaning over into the window to see. And his band is playing. I'm looking down at Wolf and Matt Murphy, who was playing with him at that time. Willie Steele was on drums. Then all of a sudden—blam!

The crates crack and I land right on top of Wolf. Right on top of 'im. They were going to throw me out, but Wolf stopped them. He stopped them, man. He said, 'Let him stay.' He asked someone to get a chair for me and sat me down right next to him. I wasn't going to do nothing on account I was with Wolf."

Hubert sat next to the gargantuan musician, listened to the band, and stayed to the end of the set. After the show, in the early morning, Wolf took Hubert back home. "He said, 'Where you live, boy?' So he took me home and he begged my parents not to beat me, not to punish me; that I was just wanting to hear the music. 'Please don't whoop the boy,' Wolf said." Charlene adds, "My grandmother Claudia argued with Howlin' Wolf about his playing and argued with Hubert, but Wolf told them, 'I don't want you to spank the child. Don't whoop 'im. He just wanted to hear the music.' He was maybe twelve or so when that happened."

Hubert has told this story a few different ways, and in one variation both his mother and father do, indeed, "whoop" him. Regardless of whether there was any physical contact, Hubert had made up his mind about playing music. "I didn't stop going [to shows]," Hubert affirms.

Some relatives seem to think Hubert was a preteen at the time of this incident. This may not gibe with the dates of other sources. Wolf was in the army, stationed in Seattle, in the early '40s when it is thought that Hubert had this fateful meeting with him. And it wasn't until later in the 1940s that Wolf had put a band together—he was playing solo acoustic and harp (thanks to lessons from Sonny Boy Williamson II) before that time. "After the war...I did some farming of mine own," Wolf told Pete Welding in a 1967 *Down Beat* interview. "I made two crops [in Penton, Mississippi], and then I moved to West Memphis, Arkansas. It was there, in 1948, when I formed my first band to follow music as a career."

By the time Hubert reached puberty, he wanted the chance to play in front of people with his no-brand acoustic guitar. Boyhood friend James Cotton, born in 1935 in Tunica, Mississippi, would bring his harp over to Hubert's home and the two would jam. "Cotton was younger than me, man, couple years, or so he'll say," Hubert jokes. "That man, he looked like a man when he got me from my momma's house, you know what I'm talkin' 'bout? My momma let me play with him."

Cotton would play with Hubert regularly, and although Claudia was becoming more lenient with "that devil music," she refused to invite it into her house. "Being sanctified," Hubert explains, "she didn't like no blues. She'd tell us to get the hell outta there."

If Claudia couldn't completely stop Hubert from playing the blues, she'd try a different tactic to sway him from his guitar playing: good, old-fashioned motherly guilt. "My momma said, 'Y'all are kids, you ain't gonna be nothing. You ain't gonna do nothing. So go on. God bless ya.' Sure enough, man, we learnt. We played with a lot of people. I played with a lot of people in my lifetime."

Guitarist Pat Hare and drummer Willie Nix would join Hubert and Cotton occasionally. "We got Pat Hare," Hubert says. "[He] was looking for a job with Cotton. Pat Hare would fight you if you wasn't right. He killed a policeman in Minneapolis. He killed that woman. He got three hundred years. That's the way he was." (Hare was convicted of murdering his girlfriend and a policeman in 1964 in Minneapolis.)

Those days of playing, sometimes on the street and sometimes in juke joints, making a little money, created a strong bond between Hubert and Cotton. "I lived with James Cotton," Hubert says. "Other words, me and Cotton had a little band goin'. We was too damn young to drink and be messin' around in clubs. But they would let us play anyway. Maybe we'd make a quarter a night. Or maybe we'd make ten cents, but that was a lot of money back then, too. Fifty cents, you could, shoot, you could do whatever you want. But we didn't know shit. Cotton couldn't blow no damn harp. But I know I had a tune. I had my shit. But I wasn't shit, neither. I was still learnin'. I still is. Hey."

Cotton and Hubert formed one stream in the flow of a new wave of musicians who were experimenting with electrified blues, which began back in the 1930s. Electric guitar masters like T-Bone Walker and Charlie Christian had both stepped into jazz territory after having a big hand in developing the electric blues sound. T-Bone possessed a suave command of blues guitar chords. His start-and-stop action riffs in combination with his vibrato finger style, fluid, weepy runs, and subtle, jazz-inflected chords became the standard for any electric blues guitarist in the World War II era, influencing B.B. King, Otis Rush, and Buddy Guy as well as Hubert.

By the late '40s and early '50s, amplifying instruments with electricity became a necessity. Population shifts to the North meant more people frequented full-scale nightclubs—not tiny juke joints where acoustic instruments could be heard easily. As other instruments increasingly became amplified, the electric guitar player became essential to keep the sound uniform—and to be heard (Little Walter's amplified harp could send sharp, sonic spikes through your skull).

Before too long, Hubert and Cotton had drifted to West Memphis, Arkansas, where they had heard the money was good and radio broadcasts were playing blues. KWEM, established in February 1947 and broadcast with 1,000 watts, pumped blues and other popular forms of music of the day from its tower and transmitter on the west bank of the Mississippi River. KWEM was only the second legal station in the state (Arkansas granted WOK a broadcasting permit in 1922).

Riley "B.B." King had performed first on KWEM, where Sonny Boy Williamson II took the young guitarist under his wing. (In the early '40s, Sonny Boy had performed on the "King Biscuit Flower Hour" for 15 minutes every day on KFFA in Helena, Arkansas.) After meeting Sonny Boy, B.B. soon had his own daily ten-minute show on WDIA in Memphis, Tennessee, and gave himself the name "Beale Street Blues Boy." "I got my first break, I guess you'd say, at KWEM, when I performed with Rice Miller, Sonny Boy Williamson II," King says. "He gave me the opportunity to perform."

Howlin' Wolf, now Hubert's idol, had grown up and bounced around in Mississippi but made his way to Arkansas, where he continued to farm and play music. Known as "Bigfoot Chester" or "Bull Cow" in those days (due to his enormous frame), Wolf had his own 15-minute program six days a week on KWEM (though he occasionally broadcast on KFFA).

"…I had a steady job on [KWEM]," Wolf told *Down Beat* magazine. "It came on at three o'clock in the [afternoon]. It was in 1949 that I started to broadcast. I had been lucky enough to get my own spot…

I produced the show myself, went around and spoke to store owners to sponsor it, and I advertised shopping goods."

Eventually, Hubert and Cotton also got a regular spot on KWEM. "We had 15 minutes on the air, behind the Wolf. I'll tell ya, this was great. We—Cotton and I—played together about two years. We were having a good time."

Though Hubert had been exposed to Wolf as a child, in his late teens he found something magical, almost mystical, about Wolf's radio shows. "I know the guy," Hubert says, "but his voice scared me. His voice was so powerful. I knew that this guy was it! I heard Muddy, too, and then I said something to myself, man. I said, 'Someday, I'm gonna play with them.'"

Cotton offers his recollection of how Hubert's "someday" came to pass: "When Willie Johnson was drinking too heavily to play with Howlin' Wolf I suggested Hubert, so he played with Howlin' Wolf for one night. I had played with Wolf for a few years and knew him well. A week later, Howlin' Wolf went to Chicago…and later sent for Hubert."

If places like Chicago, Illinois, and Memphis, Tennessee, were to become hotbeds of electric blues, then West Memphis, Arkansas, was the incubator of the form. If Memphis was the "uptown," the sophisticated place for nightlife, then West Memphis was its seedy, no-curfew, after-hours, ugly little sister. Today, West Memphis is a fairly quiet suburb separated from its larger and better-known cousin by four miles and the mighty Mississippi River. A police station stands guard on the invisible yet tangible line separating one side of West Memphis from the other (read: middle class, and the combined lower-middle and ghetto). "You'll see a cotton field, a soy field, that is what lies on the river bank— really nothing," explains local Arkansas musician Mark Sallings. "There is a subculture of society that lives along the river bank in campers and school buses and stuff. The only time you see them is when the river gets over its banks and they all have to fire up their buses and move on to the access roads."

In the late '40s and early '50s West Memphis didn't look like much to outsiders viewing the town from the banks of the Mississippi River on the Memphis side. Indeed, it was a second-class city well into the 1940s. All one could see was cotton fields and plantations. Not much has changed. "If you want to see a Third World, you want to drive from West Memphis to Helena, Arkansas," offers Wayne Jackson, legendary trumpet player on countless Stax records and one half of the Memphis Horns. "If you want to see Tobacco Road and Ethiopia all in the same day, go there. It is heartbreaking poverty back there."

But amid the rural components of the area, a thriving, throbbing nightlife seduced many on the Memphis side to cross the river. West Memphis and its airwaves were brimming with activity, and anything you wanted or needed—prostitutes, alcohol, gambling—was all there. Traffic on Saturday nights was at a standstill from several blocks south of Broadway as African-Americans flooded the area. One handbill for a West Memphis nightclub printed at the time read: "Ed and his boys will be there, waiting for a head and head gambler. James will take care of pitty-pat games. Old Silk Hair and his boys from ragged Front will be there. Buster and George of Crawfordsville will be there betting on 10 and 4. All peace breakers, leave your guns and knives at the door."

Eighth Street in West Memphis, sometimes referred to as "Little Chicago," mirrored its cousin—the bustling, uptown sophistication of Beale Street in Memphis—and then some. The hotspots were Eighth and Sixteenth streets: places like Terry Payne's Café, James Triplett's High Chaparral, Sarah Strong's Café, David Suggs's Chicken Shack Café, the Square Deal Café (aka Miss Annie's Place) where B.B. King played as a young professional blues musician, and many others. "West Memphis was more open than Memphis," King says. "Memphis closed down. So you had people coming over to West Memphis when Memphis was closed."

More and more, Cotton was playing with guitarist Pat Hare, who hailed from Cherry Valley, Arkansas. (Hare was in Howlin' Wolf's first band in 1948 and eventually recorded with Cotton for Sam Phillips's Sun Records and with Muddy Waters for Chess Records.) One night Cotton went to pick up Hare for a scheduled date at a hole-in-the-wall venue in Howell, Arkansas, but couldn't find the guitarist. "I had a gig and went to Parkin, Arkansas, to pick up Pat," Cotton remembers, "but Pat was nowhere to be found. I thought he went to the gig, but it turned out he wasn't there either."

Cotton became skeptical about Hare showing up for the gig. "Word soon got out in the club that I needed a guitar player, and that I couldn't find Pat. Someone yelled out, 'There's a guitar player!'"

That player was Hubert, who by now was over at the craps table, shooting dice. As would be the norm throughout Hubert's career, he found himself without a guitar and musical equipment.

"Hubert borrowed a guitar from the man who'd pointed to him, grabbed a pencil and a piece of twine, and made a capo," Cotton continues. As he recalls in the documentary *Hubert Sumlin: Living the Blues,* "[Hubert] looked up at me, he said, 'I'm ready now.' I didn't know what to play! He hit it just like Pat Hare. I couldn't tell it wasn't Pat Hare."

Hubert gratefully recalls Wolf's generous gift of a 6-string electric Kay guitar in 1954 when the two first started recording together in Chicago.

One Hubert legend tells of him leaving Hughes, Arkansas—more like fleeing—when a mule died while he was working on the plantation. The landowner, Hubert believed, would certainly blame the animal's death on him. He knew he had to get out of the area as fast as he could.

Hubert became one of the few in his family to break free of a life of hard labor on the farm. "Muddy and them worked in the field. Wolf, he turned out to be the second man in command at his plantation—the second boss to the guys at the plantation," Hubert notes. "He used to do a lot of stuff and did a lot of work. Also Muddy. They worked. They didn't want to do it—just like me. They loved the music as much as I do. I was the only somebody in the family who did what I wanted to do and what I loved to do. And this is what it was: guitar, man. [Brother] A.D., he play better than me, but he didn't want to leave Arkansas. He never went professional."

It was around this time that Hubert found his first love. When he was 14 or 15 he "wed" (perhaps only promised to wed) a young girl from Arkansas. When asked about the situation, Hubert simply says, "I don't even remember her name. It was so long ago. It was a cute name. [It may have been Bertha.] I remember seeing her. Her mother would drive her to school. I met her in the same school." As soon as the two future families-in-law got wind of the alleged marriage, Hubert and his young "bride" had to part ways. "We stayed together not even a year. I took her home. I told her momma, 'Here she is.' She said, 'Son, thank you. You know what, son? You'd have been a good husband.' I was. I would have been. I believe I would have. We was just too young, that's all."

Hubert may have lost a deep and lasting love, but his first love was still by his side: music. He maintained his interest in playing and continued to learn the guitar inside and out. (Hubert did not have any formal training, though he did take classes at the Chicago Conservatory of Music, paid for by Wolf. The lessons were with an "opera guitarist" Hubert believes was named "Gowalski or something" who taught him "all the chords and stuff," he clarifies. "But he died about six months after I started." Hubert would eventually leave the school with no regrets.) Hubert even expanded his musical horizons with the drums when he was playing with Cotton. "Cotton had a little drum set," Hubert explains. "It was a kit, man. Not a lot of people know that. He can play, man. He don't want that to get around. So, I played his set. I played with Wolf one week while we were fresh out of drummers, you know? But my feet swelled up and I needed an injection of somethin' from the doctor to stop it from swellin'. Hey, I didn't just try the drums—I tried everything. I even tried piano. I played one down in Arkansas. I played [Hubert mimes a hunt-and-peck motion]. Just picked it up in places that I've been around."

Just as Hare was playing with Cotton more often, Hubert—whom Wolf had seen play and remembered as a young boy from the Silkhairs window incident—got the call from Howlin' Wolf. It was the beginning of what would be a major turning point in Hubert's life.

Wolf had recorded for both RPM and Chess at Sam Phillips's Memphis Recording Service (Phillips would later record such luminaries as Elvis, Carl Perkins, Roy Orbison, and "The Killer" Jerry Lee Lewis) and soon found himself in the midst of a bidding war between the two labels. Chess ultimately won, and put out Wolf's "Moanin' at Midnight," a true haunter with an eerie, closed-throat intro and featuring dirty and distorted guitar tones spun by Willie Johnson. The song reached *Billboard* magazine's Top Ten jukebox chart. A few weeks later a second song, "How Many More Years," shellacked with Johnson's rust-like amplified washes, was released and also had great success, remaining on the *Billboard* R&B charts for three months.

Chess Records, owned and operated by Polish immigrant Jews Leonard and Phil Czyz (aka Chess), also recorded tracks at its South Cottage Grove address in Chicago. At the time, the label had a string of R&B hits with Little Walter & His Night Cats' "Juke" and "Sad Hours" and Willie Mabon's "I Don't Know." (In 1950 at Chess, Muddy Waters recorded "Walkin' Blues," a version of the Robert Johnson song of the same title; Muddy would record the regional hit "Rollin' Stone" later that same year.)

Wolf was playing with Willie Johnson, Pat Hare, Tommy Bankhead, and Matt "Guitar" Murphy—confident, aggressive, and distinct guitarists who faded in and out of his band. They were fine players, even great. But the middle-aged Wolf knew what he wanted, what he needed: a young man with ideas, with a true creative approach; someone who had the chops, the fire, the musical vision; and someone who could be loyal. He needed Hubert Sumlin.

The night before he officially joined Wolf, Hubert—barely in his twenties—was treated to a crash course in the older man's powerful music. "I went [to Louisiana] the last night before he went to Chicago to see his band," Hubert remembers, "to see what was going on [wrong]. I saw it and I said, 'I don't see nothin'. Wolf, you got a good band.'" The imposing figure would hear none of it as he glared down at the youngster and said of his band, "'They don't want to come to Chicago, and they think I'm leaving them, stabbing them in the back. But I'm going to Chicago—fuck 'em. And when I get there, if I send back for you, will you come?' I said, 'Yes, sir.' I really didn't believe him. I didn't believe he was right. I figured he was just talkin' on account that he was mad at them and everything. But he wasn't mad, man. Cool ass, man. So, then I asked Cotton, 'Should I go with 'em?' Cotton says, 'Sure, you'll make more money with him than you will with me.'"

That's the way Cotton remembers it, too: "I told him he should go, 'cause he'll make more money with Wolf than he was with me." Hubert's departure spelled the end of James Cotton's band. "Everybody in that band just broke up," Hubert admits. "We all just went our ways, you know? I ended up with Wolf, and Cotton and Pat Hare ended up with Muddy."

It seemed all those days spent picking his guitar in the fields against the landowner's orders (and eventually his mother's) had saved Hubert from a life of hard labor. His talent had won him a gig with his idol, and there was nothing holding him to Arkansas—except his own decision.

He accepted.

Hubert took to Wolf immediately, and vice versa. It seemed as though these cats had known each other for decades. Hubert told me about an explosive incident from his early days with Wolf now burned into his memory.

One night, after a late gig, the band retired to Wolf's residence in West Memphis where he lived with his wife, Katie Mae. "I'm coming out the wagon and I'm looking up at this woman in Wolf's apartment," Hubert says. "She said, 'Hi, Hubert.' I say, 'Yes, ma'am.' She say, 'Go to bed, you just got here.' I go to bed. But on Sunday morning, Wolf's wife wanted to make a nice meal before we all had to go to work. She sent him on foot to the store for some tomatoes, potatoes, and some other stuff."

It seems the night before someone in the band had taken Wolf's wagon and had some fun. The car was returned before daybreak, just in time for breakfast. While Wolf was at the store, Katie Mae took it upon herself to clean (perhaps inspect?) the band's touring car and she stumbled upon a startling discovery: several pairs of ladies' underwear. Katie Mae assumed the worst: this wolf (a monogamous animal in the wild) had strayed. So she kept the "hardware," didn't say a word, took a double-barreled shotgun that Wolf kept in the wagon, and waited for Wolf to return.

Striding down the street comes Wolf, grocery bags stuffed into his folded, humongous arms. "I saw them barrels," Hubert recalls. "I didn't know really what it was, and I really didn't care. But I said that it really seems like a shotgun to me, you know? I hear something—BOOM!" Wolf let out a bloodcurdling shriek. "Shot him right in the ass, man,"

Hubert says. "They was pulling pieces out of his ass for what seemed like two years, man. Probably more like two weeks. I still think they left some in 'im."

The air was never cleared between Wolf and Katie Mae. Ultimately, Wolf would leave his marriage—just as he would leave West Memphis—in a smoke cloud of intensity. Through the ashes and the haze, Howlin' Wolf and Hubert Sumlin were about to enter into what would become one of the greatest partnerships in Western music history.

Chapter 2
Father and Son

The second half of the twentieth century was home to many famous and successful musical partnerships. These distinct personalities fused to become one musical entity. Whether it was Lennon and McCartney, Coltrane and Elvin, Simon and Garfunkel, Mick and Keith, or Hubert and the Wolf, the juxtaposition of these creative minds produced a powder keg of inspiration.

Hubert and Wolf shaped each other's music and lives. Hubert's very existence and place in the world took a dramatic turn when he was called to Chicago in 1954. "When I came to Chicago, Wolf had my union card paid up," Hubert says. "I mean, I didn't have to do nuthin'. All of this shit, goddamn kitchenette I had. It looked like my house. The whole fuckin' thing paid up. I was still down in Muddy's house. Otis Spann picked me up, Illinois Central, Twelfth Street Station—old smokestack to Chicago. We go back to Muddy's and Muddy was looking at me. He wanted to know who the fuck I was—Wolf give me the keys to [Chess's] daddy's building and it was a big mansion. Maid in there.

"I was about 20, somewhere around there; early twenties. I knew one thing, he wouldn't let me have no booze; Wolf wouldn't let me drink nothing," Hubert complains. "I went to a store on the corner just to get a bottle of wine, I said, 'Muthafucker, let me have some wine.' Then two muthafuckers walk in and say, 'Don't sell him nuthin'.' Wolf had done hit the entire city, you understand? He wouldn't let me have nuthin'. They say, 'He don't get nothing.' I said, 'Fuck it. I don't need to have it in the first place.' Water is what they brought me. I never was a dope guy. I believe Wolf and Muddy did, but I didn't see 'em. But I know they drink. Wolf had bottles in one of his pants pockets. I may be wrong. As long as you don't see, you don't know. You could tell by how they act. And with Wolf, you couldn't tell if he was drinking, or if he wasn't. He kept his cool, man."

Alcohol flowed freely in the 1950s; it was high times for the blues. Alcohol was everywhere for everyone—except Hubert. Jody Williams, Chess Records studio guitar ace (who'd cut songs with Bo Diddley), remembers an incident involving Hubert attempting to buy alcohol. "I remember one time we went into this corner store where Hubert was trying to get liquor and I was buying a pack of cigarettes. They saw Hubert and maybe they thought he was underage, so they threw him out—just threw him out. They just said, 'Get outta here.' He was thrown out...but I got my cigarettes," Williams laughs.

The blues "stars" of Chess Records were living large. Little Walter was one of the first (along with Muddy Waters) to bring success to the Chess labels through the blues. Born Marion Walter Jacobs in 1930 in Marksville, Louisiana, Little Walter was a volatile character who nonetheless was a steady hitmaker from 1952–1958. He cut such songs as "Juke," "Blues with a Feeling," and "Sad Hours." ("Juke," originally titled "Your Cat Can Play" and released on Chess's Checker Records label, was recorded by Little Walter & His Night Cats and featured Muddy Waters on guitar.)

Money was flowing, too—from the cash register to the label, from the label to the artist (sometimes with a little help). "Chess is the one who pushed his records," Hubert admits. "But he thought he was owed more than he was getting paid, understand? He came back and made the muthafuckers pay. Even with no gun on. He...just a snap, and he'd kill yo' ass. Onliest muthafucker I see have that much money in his life. Little Walter had a brand-new Cadillac. Rust colored. He parked the muthafucker in the street, on State [Street in Chicago]. [Chess] gave him a suitcase full of money. Police was running around trying to figure out whose Cadillac that is. Little Walter's in the bank. He took his time and got his car. Police said, 'Do you know whose...' Walter didn't say a fuckin' word. It was getting-off time and there was plenty of traffic."

Muddy, too, had had great success with Chess, producing a string of hits that included "Mannish Boy," "I'm Ready," and "Hoochie Coochie Man." He was the label's King Bee, so to speak. High on the hog, Muddy was not shy about his hits, money, women, and booze. Hubert remembers it clearly:

"Muddy? He didn't give a fuck. Muddy drink 100-proof Granddad. He had a whole houseful. He didn't care. When I got to his house, he and Wolf [were drinking]. I'm telling you the truth. I didn't drink nuthin'. But Otis Spann was so damn drunk when he picked me up, I thought he was going to go down the wrong street. Goddamn, I saw them cars coming at us. I knew he was high as a muthafucker. He say, 'Hubert, we made it home.' He was right. He and Wolf sitting up there playing cards. You understand? 'You made it, huh? Glad to see ya. Here're the keys.' I didn't say nothing. Otis Spann showed me to my apartment.

"Otis stayed with Muddy in the basement. He lived in the basement and had a big old apartment down there: bedroom, kitchen, he had everything. The piano was right in front of his bedroom. That was where they, you know, before they record, they went down to the basement to rehearse."

It was a glorious time for music, and a time of social breakthroughs and upheaval. In 1954, in the case of *Brown v. Board of Education* the US Supreme Court overturned the decision to segregate state schools, partly due to a strike organized by students at the Farmville, Virginia, school—the flashpoint of the hot-button issue. Segregation in the educational system was ruled unconstitutional. Hubert, too, was unshackled and vindicated. At an early age (not much older than those striking students), he had already realized a dream. He had made "the big time" with a new boss—one of the new kings of Chicago. Just as he had predicted back home in Arkansas, "I was playing with the man. Beautiful."

Wolf achieved success quickly, Hubert tells me. "As soon as I got there, man, Wolf had everything in Chicago sewn up. He had it all. He was playing every night." Rock 'n' roll hadn't taken full effect. Yet. Blues was still the order of the day. "You could walk out of one place and go to the next place and everybody was different—I'm talking 'bout the people playing," Hubert says of the Chicago scene in the mid-'50s. "A lot of them dudes was coming up, you know, when I got to Chicago. Wolf was already there and he sent for me. The shit, Muddy Waters and Jimmy Reed, every sonofagun you wanna name that was in this business was there. You just go down to one street and you don't have to go anywhere else to see anyone."

In March 1954, Hubert and Wolf recorded together for the first time in Chicago. The sides they cut were "No Place to Go"/"Rockin' Daddy," "You Gonna Wreck My Life," "Neighbors," and "I'm the Wolf." Two months later, Hubert and Wolf would cut the hits "Evil" and "Baby, How Long."

Guitarist Jody Williams remembers Hubert's first time in the Chess studio. "Leonard Chess introduced me to 'the Howlin' Wolf,'" Williams notes. "Chess said that he needed a band because he was here in Chicago to stay, so I was a Chess guitar player, and we got together. I was one of the guitarists who worked there in the studio. I remember when Wolf called for Hubert. He sent for him in the West Memphis area. Wolf had this big car go down to pick him up; Hubert was coming from the station. When he first got there, I knew he was a good guitar player. I remember him doing real good and being real young."

The two guitar players (often playing matching Kay electrics with thumbpicks and wearing similar suits onstage) were not competitive and worked well together during the recordings. "We got along fine," Williams says. "I don't remember the exact words we used, but we were very friendly toward one another. We were on the street together a lot. There was no conflict or nothing like that. Sometimes I'd play lead, sometimes Hubert would play the lead."

Hubert has a different recollection of the sessions. Phil and Leonard Chess, being slight perfectionists in an imperfect business, pushed their studio players and stars to the limits. They needed the best out of them to make the best records—and the most money. Quality meant payday. That being said, Hubert recalls that during his first recording session with Wolf, Phil was peering through the glass window of the console booth and making sure Wolf's band was shipshape. Things were going along well when, somewhere, Hubert hits a bad note. Not a bad note as in a "blues note"—a *bad* note! Chess stops the recording session, the door to the studio flies open, and he immediately berates Hubert for his obvious mistake. "He didn't do that right. You have to take it again," Chess said. "You muthafuckers have to get this right!"

Hubert looks at Chess, a bit shaken, then looks at Wolf, then lowers his head thinking, "I ain't gonna like this." Wolf holds up his hands as if to say, "Truce!" Sensing his young friend's trepidation, the six-foot-four, nearly-300-pound giant bluesman glares down at Chess and says, "Don't talk to him like that no more. You want something done, you ask me and I'll tell him what to do."

When a man that big tells you something, you tend to listen. "He was a serious kind of man when he wanted to be, and everybody knew he meant business," says Diane Sanders, stepniece of Howlin' Wolf (her mother, Lucy, was Wolf's stepsister). "We known him as Uncle Wolf. When he say something, we pretty much do it."

Wolf expected superior conduct and musicianship from his band while performing onstage.

Wolf was an impressive man-mountain, a fear factory of passion and integrity. "Wolf was a very scary guy," says Jimmy D. Lane, son of the late, great Wolf and Muddy guitarist Jimmy Rogers. "Not mean—scary, from a kid's perspective. He'd be singing and shaking in my house. I just remember, as a little kid, Wolf being this animated, large man. His shoe size was about as big as me. I remember saying, 'Look at this big man.'"

"I remember he shook my hand one time and his hand literally covered mine," notes Richard Ramsey, program director of the Howlin' Wolf Blues Society in West Point, Mississippi. "Every time I would watch him play harmonica, I couldn't even see it in his hands."

"That cat…he shake hands with you, I mean, I'd think, 'I don't mind shaking hands with ya, but you oughta take off that catcher's mitt,'" drummer Sam Lay says. "He was supersized."

One can visualize Wolf in the studio recording a haunting track like "Smokestack Lightnin'." The shimmering echo of the song evokes images of a late-night, dark studio where this larger-than-life, vein-poppin', sweaty troubadour jerks the mic stand as his raspy voice belts out one punishing line after another. His harp is forced to suffer wind gusts, coming damn near close to being swallowed up. This commanding performance and personality has the other musicians cowering in the corner, looking down at their instruments or the floor, concentrating on their own performances—anything to avoid looking into the eye of the hurricane—because when this storm blows through, better take cover.

The often-quoted words of Sam Phillips (who went on to discover Elvis Presley) testify to Wolf's greatness: "When I heard Howlin' Wolf, I said, 'This is for me. This is where the soul of a man never dies.'"

If we say that Wolf was Mount Everest (a virtually unattainable height with dark, hidden crevasses), then Hubert is the Grand Canyon, formed by a river of talent and boasting broad and beautifully layered creative expressions that reveal an understanding of timing and superior musical instinct. Where Wolf had a massive, iron-fisted hold on a song—punching it in the stomach and leaving it for dead—Hubert could keep the music on life support, keep it from being devoured by his subtly spicy guitar lines. Hubert could easily strangle the music—

bring it to the brink of breathlessness—but his power lay in always allowing it to flow, in never overpowering the tune.

Hubert was a faithful companion and musical foil to Howlin' Wolf on and off for nearly 23 years. Some of their tracks together, such as "Smokestack Lightnin'," "300 Pounds of Joy," "Louise," "Shake for Me," "Killing Floor," "Hidden Charms," "The Red Rooster," and "Sitting on Top of the World" defined the very sound of electric Chicago blues in the mid-'50s and the 1960s. In varying degrees, Hubert had a hand in arranging, playing on, contributing to, and writing all of these songs. (A full investigation of Hubert's precise involvement with these tracks is offered in Chapter 3, "More Than a Sideman.")

The musical partnership between Wolf and Hubert comes down to one thing: Wolf would never have made the same memorable music without Hubert. And in reality, Hubert never would have had the same longevity without Wolf.

Hubert's only male role model of his younger years was his father. But John, who died in 1960, just a few years after Hubert went to Chicago, was forced to work his children in the fields. Hard physical labor was all Hubert learned about from his father. He never had a true teacher to take him under his wing and show him a secure path for his burgeoning talents—that is, until he met Wolf. "Wolf was like a father to me. I wouldn't have stayed for so long with him if he hadn't have been. I put it like that," Hubert declares. "He was one of them guys, hell, he was the Wolf. And what a man he was. He loved me so much."

Wolf had plenty of great guitar players at his disposal (most notably Willie Johnson, whose T-Bone Walker-ish jazzy chord progressions and distressed amplified sound supplied a rugged sophistication to Wolf's music), but there was something about Hubert. Wolf believed in Hubert and let him develop in his own time. Wolf saw the latent, potent prowess Hubert had. He was patient with him, and suffered through the young man's painful stage shyness. "One night, I'm playing there with my back turned to the audience and Wolf says, 'Ladies and gentlemen, I'd like to introduce you to Hubert Sumlin's ass,'" Hubert laughs.

After learning to face the audience square on, and having picked up on Wolf's vibe, Hubert found an opportunity to take the lead guitar seat. It was what Wolf was waiting for. "Wolf didn't take me but twice on tour with him," Hubert explains. "When he went out, I was there. One time was the *Shindig!* television show [with the Rolling Stones]. He left me in Mobile, Alabama, when he went to L.A. I was back in Mobile with the band. The other time he took Jody Williams with him to New Orleans. Jody had got into some kind of trouble with firecrackers or something. And it wasn't even the Fourth of July. He wasn't able to play, so when Wolf got back to Chicago, that's when I got my chance to play with him—lead."

Hubert was perhaps the opposite of Wolf in every way. Hubert would be completely subdued—a "Bizarro Wolf"—onstage. He'd typically stare down at his hands while playing the guitar, perhaps bob his head to the rhythm, not draw too much attention. Where Hubert was reluctant to be out front, Wolf relished the attention. Perhaps the single most important thing Wolf learned from Charlie Patton (even more than Spanish tuning or how to use a slide) was to always entertain the

Wolf on the prowl, with Hubert second from left.

folks. Patton was a showman; he would twirl the guitar, turn it "over backwards and forwards," and "throw it around his shoulders, between his legs, throw it up in the sky," as Wolf described it. Wolf took the immediacy and attention-grabbing qualities of Patton's kind of magic show, put his own touches on it, and evolved it into a musical monster.

Crowds that showed up at clubs like Chicago's Key Largo, Silvio's, Pepper's Lounge, the Big Squeeze Club, and, later, the 1815 Club were treated to shows of immeasurable and unparalleled live achievement. "It was packed every night," remembers Wolf pianist Henry Gray. "Wolf'd get up there, crawl around, and put that handkerchief in the belt of his pants, right in the back," Williams says. "Just like the tail—just like a wolf."

Even if Hubert's demeanor was understated as compared to his boss's, the musical playing field that connected him and Wolf was level. Performing tunes like Robert Johnson's "Dust My Broom" Hubert would double Wolf's harmonica lines to the note. A young, curly-topped Hubert, with his lips sucked into his face and his fingers crawling across the fretboard, was a force of nature. Wolf's harmonica work would shriek through the music like a speeding silver-bullet train, and Hubert, without batting an eye, would extend his musical arm, as it were, latch on to the caboose to hitch a ride, then jam the accelerator. Pretty soon, Hubert would operate the steaming hulk of screaming music.

It's easy to see what Wolf saw in Hubert—it's no secret that band-leaders like their players young and impressionable. After all, eager, gifted musicians who are malleable are easier to control. But Wolf was pulling for Hubert. "I play some guitar, you know," Wolf told *Living Blues*. "Sometime I always let Hubert play, because he is a young man and I want him to be seen. I partly raised him, you know. Always keep him out there to the front and I do the singin'."

If there was one thing that got Hubert in trouble with Wolf, it was his drinking. Despite Wolf's attempts to keep the band completely clean, Hubert did dabble. That's not a major scoop, considering that Hubert was a young, good-looking bluesman in the 1950s who liked to have a good time when he played in the clubs. But Wolf didn't stand for people to be drunk on the bandstand. Oftentimes Hubert would be on the business end of Wolf's strict policy. "That is what Hubert got in trouble with," explains chitlin circuit legend Bobby Rush, who has known Hubert for more than 40 years (he knew Wolf very well, too). "He would [drink], try to stand up straight, and still get in trouble. Wolf fired him many times about those many things, about not being where he should be or doing what he is supposed to do. Wolf would fire him and fine him. But then that wouldn't make too much difference to him. I think [Hubert] thought deep down inside that Wolf needed him. He did. And Hubert used that to his advantage. Still, Wolf loved him as a person. They loved each other." Hubert admits that Wolf fired him often. "I was fired more than anybody. Sometimes it was five minutes, sometimes ten minutes. You fired, you hired."

Still, Wolf respected his players. He fed them and bought them clothes. If someone didn't have a suit, Wolf gave him money to get fitted. If someone needed money to get through hard times, Wolf reached into the pockets of his tuxedo trousers. But Wolf also fined band members for conduct unbecoming a musician, like fooling around and getting drunk. No nevermind: Wolf gave the band members a Christmas bonus, effectively erasing whatever fine was issued earlier in the year. And he was one of the few blues bandleaders in Chicago who offered musicians unemployment insurance.

Wolf could be very hard to please, though, and he was tough on the musicians in his employ. Wolf had his moods—and a reputation on the line. Hubert saw this clearly. No matter how volatile Wolf was, Hubert rarely, if ever, speaks disparaging words about his former boss. Their connection went way beyond business, even if their arguments were precisely about the business of music. "That old man, when he came to Chicago, no one knew that he couldn't write his name: he had to put an 'X,'" Hubert reveals. "You know what I'm talking about? For a lot of years. But he could hear you, man. He could tell you that you were out of tune—tell you what string is not in tune—he said, 'Hey, you messed up. Get it together.' Then the musicians, they knew. If you didn't, he'd warn ya. He said, 'Look, I allowed you a chance. I can't get you guys to know. You are not interested in this stuff. Maybe I'll see you in a couple of years when you get your stuff together.' The Wolf had to satisfy these folks."

"Wolf was all business. He was *all* business," explains Gray, who was in Wolf's employ for 12 years. "You can't play drunk. Wolf didn't want nobody up there drunk. It was all tuxedos, shoeshines, and sobriety. But

I drank, Hubert drank, Wolf drank, but nobody drank onstage." "He'd fuss and raise hell about something," Lay says. "Could have been a song that we was playing and it wasn't to his satisfaction. I do that, too. If you don't play it right, you are going to hear from me. Maybe not on that stage, but you will hear from me."

Legend has it that Wolf's temper would fly uncontrollably—sometimes right onto Hubert. One myth tells of Hubert losing his front teeth in a terrible fight with Wolf. The story has been circulating in blues circles for decades, but Hubert reveals to me the real culprit: "No, Wolf didn't knock out these teeth," he insists, peeling back his upper lip and pointing to his front teeth. "It was Evelyn, my former wife. She did it. She did it with a hammer." Pointing to a tooth on his upper right jaw he admits, "Wolf knocked out this one here. Wolf and I only had two major fights—that was it."

"Wolf had his ways," Detroit Junior, Wolf's last piano man, says. "You had to know how to handle Wolf. Wolf told me about the fight he had with Hubert before I joined. Hubert was in all kinds of trouble, his wife had him in a bad way, and Wolf would try to bring him out of it." "I heard about that fight, too, but ain't nobody prove it," Lay points out. "Hubert has never said it before to me. I know him just as well as anybody. I heard Wolf cuss out everybody on that stage before, but I ain't never seen him hit nobody. Another thing: I ain't seen nobody hit him, neither."

"People say a lot of things," Gray notes. "A lot of it ain't true. I never seen nothing like that ever happen." Chico Chism, Wolf's last drummer, agrees. "People always talk psychological bullshit, but they wasn't there. I was. They were close. We all were close—we'd be together, riding in the bus—everything."

There is no denying that Hubert was the workhorse of the band for many years. He was a young man who could act as bandleader, rhythm guitarist, solo guitarist, creative director, and tour bus driver. Yet, despite the closeness between Wolf and Hubert, some in Hubert's family thought Wolf took advantage of him—forced him to be the unquestioning, tireless team player.

"We had some lazy fellas with us," Hubert points out. "They didn't do nothin'. They just played. They could play, for sure. Play…and eat. That's all. I had loaded the top of the bus with drums, big upright bass on top. All the heavy stuff. Never had an accident. God was good to us." Niece Charlene notes, "Hubert used to drive for Wolf and my grand-mother said she was concerned about Hubert." "She'd say, 'I'm worried about Hubert. He's always driving.' The rest of the band would sit back and relax. Howlin' Wolf maybe took advantage of Hubert because of his youth when Wolf took him under his wing. He may have taken advantage of him. Hubert was not educated and Wolf took him out of school. My grandmother used to say that Wolf made him do things. Howlin' Wolf was a demanding person. My grandmother knew that." Adds Marshall Chess, son of the late Leonard Chess, "I saw him hit, slap Hubert on the arm onstage in some blues club, just to get him to do the song right."

If Wolf was angry with Hubert it was because he knew the young man's unrecognized potential. And no one can deny how close he and Wolf were. "Wolf sent for him and let him stay at his house," Bobby Rush says. "[Wolf and his family] knew a lot about Hubert. They would buy his clothes, wash his clothes. They were Mom and Dad for him. There was genuine love there. And Wolf needed a guitar player who knew his stuff so well he could play the material with his eyes closed. [Someone who could play it] straight up or upside down."

Wolf made sure that Hubert was taken care of on the road, too, even if he had to resort to force to do it. "At that time, you could get a bag o' cookies [for five cents]," Hubert recalls. "You could live two days off those cookies. So, I wanted cookies, but I didn't have but four cents. I thought I had five cents—the cost of the cookies. I'm in the store and I wanted those cookies, so I get the cookies, pull out four cents. This guy [behind the counter] needed a penny. I told him, 'I don't have the money.' The guy said, 'You don't get the cookies.' But then he took my money and didn't give the four cents back. I told Wolf that there was a guy in there and…anyway, man, Wolf got mad! He went behind the wagon and got this hatchet. This brand-new hatchet. He took out a penny, split the penny right in two in front of the guy, so now there is five cents—maybe more. This guy is looking at him, man. And Wolf is standing in the door with my cookies. 'Muthafucker, there's your one cent.' The guy, man, he locked the place. I'll tell ya, man, that old man knew how to pinch a penny."

Wolf and the band would frequently head down South in the bus. Doubling as the band's driver, Hubert got to know his boss in the stillness and darkness of those countryside jaunts. "This guy [policeman] came out the cornfield, man," Hubert says. "It was a big cornfield, and he got me. Wolf said something to him, man, and that guy didn't give us a ticket. Wolf told him something and he went back. We were the only ones awake in the bus, you know. It was like magic. We'd be driving and talkin'. I remember once he said to me, 'I was born 30 years too late.' He said, 'I should have been where I am now, 30 years ago.' I knew what he meant. I said, 'But...' And he said, 'Yeah, it's true.'"

Hubert remembers another incident fraught with peril that nearly got someone hurt or, worse, killed. "I remember one time with Wolf, we were on our way from Memphis, coming out of Memphis, to Chicago," he explains. "We had to come through Tennessee to get back home. Wolf was drivin'. Wolf never really drove, I did. Other words, it was the first time he did, and probably the last time. All the guys in the back, asleep. It was a Dodge station wagon. We had just as much stuff in the back of the car as we did on top. We had the drums and everything up top. It was six guys on the tour. There was this freight train blowin'. The other guys hadn't heard it. I know they ain't heard it. We stopped short. Hit the brakes. Coming across the road, it looked like the train was coming. But it was [a good distance] away from the road and Wolf put on the brakes, man. And all that shit come crashing down into the river. One guy got his neck almost broke. I said, 'Hey, Wolf. That is it, partner. I'll take over.' He said, 'That train was comin'.' I said, 'Look, man, where is the track and where is the train?' From then on in, I drove."

While Wolf was gallivanting around the small stages of Chicago and the juke joints of the South, Hubert was quietly galvanizing the band—and beginning to get a name for himself as a guitar player. Hubert had been with Wolf two years, and the new kingpins of Chicago were starting to take notice. Guitarist Jimmy Rogers had just left Muddy's band, and Muddy, a close friend (and growing rival) of Wolf's, had had his eye on Wolf's young Sumlin from the day he hit Chicago. According to Hubert, it wasn't an argument, as some suggested, that drove him from Wolf to Muddy in the fall of 1956. It wasn't creative differences—or even indifferences. It was good, old-fashioned green.

"Muddy triple the money I was making with Wolf," Hubert admits. "He offered me so much money to leave. I had enough money to do me five years, if I had the sense, at that time."

Muddy sent his driver to pick up Hubert at the Zanzibar Club where Wolf was playing one evening. Stunned, Wolf saw Hubert—and Muddy's driver—hauling out his gear and loading it in a car out front. Hubert had said nothing to Wolf, and leaving right in front of his boss made him nervous. Hubert wanted to explain, but just couldn't get out the proper words. Regardless, Wolf would hear none of it. "Wolf say, 'After what I done for you….Get the hell out of here,'" Hubert recalls the scene. "I put my head down and walked out the place. I knew what I was doing—but then again, I didn't know what I was doing, you follow? I was young."

Hubert coupled with Pat Hare (from his West Memphis days) to play on a Muddy recording session that yielded the song "Don't Go No Farther." On the track, Hubert makes his presence known immediately: he plays a dirty wash of chords, then beeps along, sliding up the neck of the guitar. (It's a signature sound that would be echoed in Wolf's "Killing Floor" in 1964.) Frosty guitar riffs hit points on a curve, as Hubert's note placement forms sonic rings that are etched into the track. Less is more here, and Hubert lets his lines breathe. The spaces he allows have no ill effect on the fluidity of the song—in fact, they mysteriously create something more solid.

It stung Wolf more than a little to see his young friend cross over to his Chicago competitor. But from Muddy's perspective, Muddy had shown Wolf the ropes when he came to the Windy City in 1952: gave him a place to stay, "learned" him the ins and outs of the Chicago club scene, even had Wolf fill in for him when he was on the road. Now for Muddy to have Hubert, Wolf's prized player, arguably the best band musician he ever had—his "son," no less—was more than a coup; it was a necessity. Wolf, it seemed, cared little about this. He quickly went to work dismantling Muddy's reputation as Chicago's blues king, playing a kind of one-upmanship with him.

"Oh, lord, I quit Wolf and went with Muddy," Hubert moans now, half laughing and half regretting the entire incident. "These guys, they was rivals. They were really rivals—and they was really actors. We thought they had a thing going on. Well, they did, but the thing they had goin' on was, 'I'm the Wolf.' 'Yeah? Well, I'm Muddy, dammit.'"

Hubert enjoyed recording with Muddy, but the touring took its toll. During a Southern package tour that went through Georgia, Florida, Mississippi, and Louisiana, Hubert's morale hit a speed bump. He wanted to go home; he knew he had made a mistake, and there was no backing out now. "Here I'm coming with a little bag with one suit, and Muddy say, 'What is in the bag?' I said, 'I just bought a brand-new suit.' Muddy said, 'New suit? You only got *one* suit in there? Goddammit, we got to play 41 nights. You need more than one suit.' I said, 'You didn't tell me 41 nights when I joined.' 'I didn't tell you how many nights then, but I'm telling you now,' Muddy said. I pulled the money out of my pocket and started thinking about it. Shit. All of this money. 'I'm young. Okay. Forty-one nights. Let's go.' But those 41 nights almost killed me. We played the shows and we had to play for Ann Cole—she was doing 'Got My Mojo Workin'.' She stayed with us two weeks."

The last leg of the tour was grueling. Hubert could barely stand it. "The last night I had to drive from Miami to Chicago in one night," Hubert says. "We had to drive 1,000 miles from Miami to Chicago. I did it. I was sober, see? Those muthafuckers, drunk, sitting back there. I'm driving like a muther…four o'clock in the morning. Muddy had a chauffeur; he had his own car. The sonofabitch driver, he was driving 80, 90, man—taking the curve. I was driving that muthafucker on two wheels, man, to get to the other job. We had 800 miles [to go], I said, 'We ain't gonna do it in one night. Why don't we take it easy?' Muddy said, 'Muthafucker, we got to get there. I got to have rest.' Big ole Cadillac, two womens. The Cadillac was so big it was like a bed. That was Muddy."

Before the band went to Chicago's 708 Club to perform that night, they recorded "Got My Mojo Workin'"—an idea that Muddy and Chess had hatched. Having backed Cole on the tour for weeks, the band was comfortable with the arrangement. Of course, Muddy's version was different (he was, after all, the Super Stud), as he put his own twist on the lyrics. Hubert's twangy, jangly tone answered Muddy's line, "Got my mojo workin'/but it just won't work on you," similar to the hypnotic groove he stroked in Wolf's "Smokestack Lightnin'."

"Chess wanted this record out so fast," Hubert remembers. "You gotta know—Ann Cole had sung this song with us backing her, but she didn't have it copyrighted, and they knowed it and everything. The onliest thing she got out of it was, they give her $20,000. They say, 'Keep quiet.' When she heard that goddamned record—they were playing it in Nashville—she called Muddy every goddarned thing. 'All of you, you no good.' I felt bad. But I couldn't do nothing about it. Chess paid for us to [record]. She did not have it copyrighted and they went through all this shit to find out. I've seen a lot." (Cole had based her performances of "Mojo" backed by Muddy's band—and later her own 1957 recording of the song—on the original composition by Preston Foster. Muddy, however, credited himself as composer on his Chess recording and a legal battle ensued between Foster and Chess Records. The suit was settled out of court.)

After the session, the band headed down to the club on East Forty-Seventh Street. "We got to the job and God was in the plan, man," Hubert says. "My ass hangin' out. I had the hemorrhoids so bad, I had to sit on pillows from Miami to Chicago. Then I had to go on the bandstand. I was not able to sit down. I had come back sick. Before we went to the bandstand, I told Muddy I was sick. Muddy, he didn't give a damn, you know what I am talkin' 'bout?"

Though Hubert was ill through most of the set, it was the wonders of electricity that snapped him out of it, he says. "The bandstand couldn't hold but three people—the piano player, the guitar player, and the drums were on the floor behind the bandstand, next to the bar where the whiskey was and everything. This was the way it was made. It was hot in there like a sonofagun and the fan was directed at the band. I had my hands on these here strings and I touched the fan. It lit up. I saw it and I felt it. I said, 'Shit.' When I turned the fan loose…I think the fan turned *me* loose…I got well! I felt like a new person. I got shocked. Shoot! But that didn't keep me from calling Wolf. I called him from a public telephone. I spoke with him. Wolf said, 'I'll be there in two minutes. I know why you are calling me. I'll be there in three minutes.'" Wolf showed up in short order, perhaps because he had been waiting for Hubert to come off the road with Muddy. Call it telepathy.

When Wolf arrived, "Muddy was already fucked up, Muddy was high," Hubert says. "He was drinking five quarts of Granddad 100. That is what he drank. Wolf told him to forget [about me], man. Wolf said, 'I came to get my son.' Muddy thought for a few minutes," Hubert pauses, then cries in a high-pitched voice, "'But, he…bah bah bah.' Wolf said he would give him his guitar player, the one who was there in my place."

And that was it. "Wolf said, 'Get your shit.' He took my stuff down from the bandstand and loaded it up. He went to take me to eat, man. I felt so goddamned good, man. 'I'm back home.' Muddy wouldn't speak with me for a year, but he came out of it." (Hubert would leave Wolf again in the mid-'60s for a brief tour which lasted only "a few months," Hubert notes.)

You can hear it in Hubert's voice: he loved Wolf. He calls him "the old man." And it would be Wolf's love for Hubert that would propel the guitar player into a realm where he had his own style and feel—a player who would be impossible to copy or reproduce. Slowly becoming an idiosyncratic genius, Hubert would soon be bestowed with the ultimate title: the guitarist's guitarist.

Chapter 3
More Than a Sideman

Our eyes are trained on Hubert Sumlin at the Cape May Jazz Festival on the New Jersey shore. It is a raw, early spring evening in 2004, and Hubert—ever the professional and the gentleman—is wearing a dark beige suit, slightly smoky glasses, and a kind of *Crocodile Dundee* safari hat that he purchased on a recent tour through Australia. (I learn that he just returned from the land down under and has spent nearly three hours in the car to get here. He's tired, but the saving grace is that he gets to play his guitar.)

The pickup band tonight is incredible: native Billy Hector (of Fairlanes fame) on second guitar; singer Eric Mingus (he of the extemporaneous lyrics and wild, uncontrollable stage dances); the bearded, barrelhouse-style keyboardist Brian Mitchell; former Fairlanes bassist Tim Tindall; and versatile drummer Sim Cain, a onetime member of Henry Rollins's band. Still, it is Hubert who is nearly translucent—he shines brighter than anyone else. He is truly the "star."

Tonight, Hubert is playing softly. His fingers caress the strings and the body of the guitar, as if coaxing the notes from his instrument. He's not using a pick: he leads with his index finger, almost scratching and clawing the string, while his thumb and his middle finger complete a triumvirate digit attack. Hubert's fingers move quickly, and it is unclear if every touch of the fretboard is garnering an amplified note. (Hubert has a way of spidering his fingers across the guitar's neck that gives the appearance of playing, though sometimes you'd swear he isn't playing at all.) The attack is percussive as much as it is melodic. Hubert has the ability to play staccato notes and then a glissando run, easily flipping back and forth between the two. You always hear of someone's guitar playing being "unique," but it is often a euphemism or a downright lie. With Hubert, it is the truth. No one plays like this cat.

After working with Howlin' Wolf for a number of years, Hubert was forced to develop a style that would forever define him as a guitar player. Hubert recalls: "Wolf said, 'Son, it has been so many years that you have been with me already. Don't you think you better think about slowing down a little? You have been running over me for years. You've been getting by. I love you. Right now you are fired. Don't come back until you get it together.' I never will forget that I got fired for playing 'Smokestack Lightnin'' too darn fast.

"I said, 'Lookithere, I am fired,'" Hubert says. "The Key Largo club in Chicago was full of people. There had to be about five hundred, almost six hundred people there. That was the worst thing that ever happened to me. That was the worst whooping I ever got in my life. I went home that night and prayed to God. I said, 'I must be doin' something wrong. God, please show me.' I went to sleep at some point. This is the god-loving truth. In the middle of the night, man, it was like God came to me. A voice said, 'Put them picks down, man. Put 'em down and try your fingers.'

"Wolf spoke with me before the band went to work that next day. He said, 'Hey, son, how you doin'? You all right? I'll see you tonight.' He did see me that night, and he kept me to the last number. He had me wait until the laaaaast number. That music sounded so good to me and I got to sit there, understand? He punished me.

"He told the crowd, 'Ladies and gentlemen, this little ole boy I brought here, my son, he's gonna play tonight for you.' That made me feel good. I went to that bandstand. I ain't missed a note. I couldn't. My great God was guiding me, man. I had my tone, I had my own sound. I had everything. Wolf said, 'You did what I asked ya.'" It was a rare moment of life-altering self-discovery. Hubert had delivered what Wolf

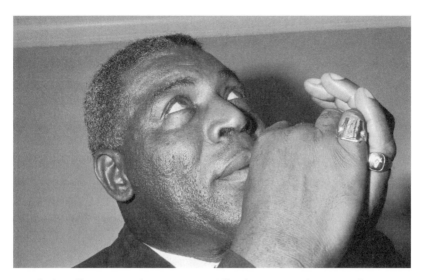

Howlin' Wolf, 1964, at the American Folk Blues Festival in Manchester, England.

wanted and in the process he arrived as an individual musician, spawning legions of admiring guitarists for generations to come. Because Hubert doesn't play with a pick, and because no one can truly cop his style, he has assured his place in the pantheon of blues legends.

"When Hubert picks with the soft part of his thumb, while the guitar is up loud," explains Muddy Waters guitarist "Steady Rollin'" Bob Margolin, "there is a fullness with nuances that convey a certain feeling. When he plucks and picks notes with his fingers, there's a percussive snap that's also very dynamic and expressive. He doesn't sound like anyone who uses a pick, and his personality in his sound is his trademark."

"I had been listening to Hubert for years before I knew he was playing with his fingers," says eclectic musician Corey Harris, who picked up a thing or two about African fingerstyle technique during the making of PBS television's *Martin Scorsese Presents The Blues.* "Hubert's got such a great tone, but his attack is not sacrificed either. It is so sleek, and he plays with speed. His playing reminds me of African fingerstyle and has those qualities: nice attack, beautiful tone, and expressiveness that I don't hear as often when someone is playing with a pick."

"Hubert uses all his fingers on his right hand," notes guitarist Steve Freund (who first played with Hubert in the mid-'70s and was Sunnyland Slim's guitarist for over 15 years). "It is a very meaty, percussive sound and he knows how to get an out-of-phase tone. He also uses his fingers on his right hand sometimes as a drummer would to play syncopated beats. It is like a drummer using a stick."

Colin Linden, the Canadian producer/guitarist who met Wolf at age 11, explains, "The thing that was really cool about the way Hubert plays that I discovered from watching him, is if you think about the way you hold your hand on a guitar, your thumb is closer to the neck than the bridge—your fingers are behind the bridge, most of the time. Hubert is almost the other way around. His fingers are closer to the neck and his thumb is closer to the bridge. So, he gets more attack on the side of his index finger that is closer to his thumb. He is the only guitar player I have ever met or heard who has this way of attacking the guitar—not just with his right hand but his left hand, too. His left hand has a tremendous amount to do with tone production as well."

The band presses on at the festival. Hector's volume creeps up and Mitchell's low-end runs are challenging Hubert to play a more rhythmic bottom end. Hubert stops for a moment and it looks as though the wheels are turning. His fingers flex over the strings, attempting to come up with the appropriate solo run. Then, like an airplane on a runway, Hubert readies for takeoff, revs his fingers, raises his nose in the air, closes his eyes, and braces himself for the liftoff. Then...it's off: Hubert plays a breakout, propulsive, single-string lead.

The explosion is brief but inspiring and the crowd applauds, sensing the significance in it. The band is pumped now and the song has some legs. Soon, however, it's over, and Hubert appears pleased with himself. He raises his ringed fist in triumph as if to punch a hole in the meandering depression of international travel lag that had engulfed him. If Hubert looked winded or weak earlier, there are no signs of it now.

It is guitar lines like these that made such a major impact on generations of electric guitar players—from Eric Clapton to Peter Green,

Keith Richards, Stevie Ray Vaughan, Robert Cray, Jimmy Page, Jeff Beck, Carlos Santana, John Mayer, Derek Trucks, and Jack White. Hubert Sumlin was recently named No. 65 in *Rolling Stone* magazine's 100 Greatest Guitar Players of All Time.

"Hubert's tone is astounding," says Jack White of the White Stripes, who covered an old Howlin' Wolf song for the *Cold Mountain* film soundtrack. "It's perfect. At times it is very thin and trebly, with a lot of slinkiness. I sound like some guitar shop idiot now! You can't deny his tone."

"It doesn't matter what type of music you play—jazz, blues, or any kind," notes guitarist Derek Trucks of the Allman Brothers Band and the Derek Trucks Band. "His side of the fence is the one I want to be on. Some sounds are just so pure and immediate. We'll be listening to Nusrat Fatah Ali Khan, Stravinski—everything. Still, when Hubert comes on, it is just as powerful. It's amazing that way."

Hearing Jimmy Page's fingers bend, slide up, and stammer over the third and fourth strings of his Danelectro electric guitar on a solo number like "White Summer" (circa 1970), one can only think of Hubert. The vibrato, the out-of-phase tones, the muzzled, nearly horn-like sound—it has as much to do with Hubert as Page's imagination and Indian music influence. "I often thought that in the way the Stones tried to be the sons of Chuck Berry, we tried to be the sons of Howlin' Wolf," Page explained to Robert Palmer for the liner notes to the Led Zeppelin box set released in 1990.

To really understand what Hubert Sumlin has done to deserve this reverence, we should examine some of Wolf's major tracks and analyze the significance of Hubert's work on them. Let's start with Hubert's choice of tools.

Hubert has played an assortment of guitars over the years: Gibson Les Paul, Fender Stratocaster, Paul Reed Smith, Gibson ES-335, Fender Telecaster, Rickenbacker, Harmony, semi-hollowbodies Kay and Gretsch, and a Bartolini. The Bartolini, an Italian-made guitar, was equipped with accordion-style plastic facing, as well as push-button selector controls (popular in 1960s European models) that afforded the

Hubert Sumlin with Bartolini guitar in 1964, Manchester, England.

use of preset tones such as "twang" and "jazz." Hubert claims to have played Wolf's 1961 classic "Goin' Down Slow" on the Bartolini, but the guitar's current location is anyone's guess. "I've lost so many goddarn guitars over the years, I can't keep track," Hubert admits.

These days Hubert usually sticks with one of two guitars: a Fender Stratocaster-type or a Gibson Les Paul. The Les Paul, a blonde wood double-humbucker, was to have been auctioned off, but Hubert thought better of it; the guitar is signed by such stars as Bonnie Raitt, Keb' Mo', Steven Tyler, Buddy Guy, the Neville Brothers, and many more.

Hubert has also played using a variety of amps. "…I had an old Wabash amp that held the biggest speaker I ever seen in my life," Hubert told *Guitar Player* in July 1998. "I believe it was one of the first 15s. I let Freddie King borrow it, and he blew the speaker right out. So, I played a big [Sears] Silvertone amp for three or four years before Wolf bought me a Fender Twin." Hubert used the Twin for years. As of this writing, when it is feasible Hubert plugs into a custom, handmade, 30-watt Louis Electric HS M12C Porthole tube amp with an LEL ceramic speaker. As anyone who has ever played with Hubert can tell you, while the arsenal of guitars and amps he has used is impressive, it matters little in the grand scheme of things.

As Linden notes, "I remember [Hubert] playing a Rickenbacker one night, a 335 another night, a Strat another night—totally different-sounding guitars—and Hubert sounded absolutely identical on whatever instrument he played. I remember noticing that he would turn his amp up or turn the guitar down, or play lighter when he wanted to be quieter, which, ergonomically, is such a beautiful way to look at it. Hardly anybody plays like that."

"Every gig Hubert would have a different guitar or different amp," recalls guitarist Curtis Obeda of the Minneapolis-based Butanes. "I saw him playing Les Pauls, I saw him playing Harmony guitars, Fenders, you name it. And he didn't have an amp, either. Hubert was using a backup amp that I kept at home, mainly because it was too heavy to carry to gigs. But once it was known that he did not have an amp, we started bringing it with us. And the thing was, Hubert sounded exactly the same no matter the guitar or the amp. I mean, literally, I've seen him play a ukulele through a no-name amp and make it sound the same as he would with brand-name stuff. It still sounded like Hubert. It's all in the hands."

This is what critics and fans have been saying about greats like Jeff Beck, Jimmy Page, and Eric Clapton for years. The truth is, they were influenced by Hubert. It was Hubert who demonstrated the basics (and not-so-basics) of playing a blues electric guitar solo. "Killing Floor" (partially covered in Led Zeppelin's "The Lemon Song") is as good a place to start our Wolf/Hubert tracks examination as any.

Written in the key of A, "Killing Floor"—one of the most recognizable Hubert riffs in the entire Wolf catalog—is centered on one galloping chord vamp that features Hubert's slide up the neck on the fourth string (using the two middle fingers of his left hand, which go as far as the guitar's neck allows). Simultaneously, Hubert plucks the open, high E string with the fourth finger of his right hand. Hubert's tone is harsh and cold here—almost like the crackling brass sounds that dovetail into his notes. It's fitting, given the theme of the song. ("Killing Floor" is partly based on "Hard Times Killing Floor Blues" by Skip James. The "killing floor" is the slaughterhouse where animals were killed before being chopped up and sold for human consumption.) After playing a solo in which his left hand bends the fourth string, Hubert returns to the rocking chord vamp punctuated by low thumps of stutter notes played on the A string. Buddy Guy, on second guitar, maintains the rhythm part throughout. If there ever was a signature Hubert Sumlin song, "Killing Floor" is it.

"One of the things Hubert told me in the times we performed together was that he didn't like people stealing his licks," explains guitarist Robert Cray, a professed Wolf and Hubert fan. "He would turn his back to the audience and put his hands on the neck of the guitar in such a way that you couldn't tell what he was doing. He might not be playing anything. The thing is, and Hubert knows this, is that it is not so much what or how he plays, but *why* he plays what he plays. It's amazing. I find myself asking the same questions of the old Wolf records. [Hubert was] out of this world—he was drawing on something that is somewhere else." "Killing Floor" was an urban song, with urban themes for urban people. As nine-to-five workers had adjusted to the ebb and flow of city life (far from the field work some had known), so, too, had the music adapted to its new surroundings. Country-blues didn't cut it in the bustling streets of Chicago. Instead, Wolf and friend/ sometime rival Muddy Waters had to change the blues to suit this shift in mentality, psychology, and geography—by creating a more raucous, immediate, menacing, and "big" sound. It was the sound of grinding industry, bustling traffic, and the beautiful cacophony of city life. Chicago blues had to be more than amplified Delta grooves.

However, many of the African rhythmic/European melodic influences found in Delta music slipped through to the Chicago sound. "Wolf was doing this Delta country feel and Hubert was all over the place," Cray says. "[He] was taking it to another level. Hubert was the perfect foil for Wolf's voice. Hubert's piercing, high-pitched tone was opposite to Wolf's down-home country voice and feel. Wolf would be down in the pocket and Hubert had this electric sound that was city—it was 'street.'"

The electric blues was a collective effort, unlike the sounds coming from Delta bluesmen such as Robert Johnson and Charlie Patton who, lacking bands, used polyrhythmic patterns to counter their vocal lines and create a full sound. "It was [Patton's music] what started me off playing," Wolf told journalist Pete Welding in the mid-'60s. "...I asked him would he learn me, and at night, after I'd get off work, I'd go hang around."

It makes perfect sense that both Wolf and Hubert should be influenced by Patton. Although the three performers are each separated by at least one generation, they all hail from Mississippi and had similar lifestyles shaped by harsh surroundings. After working in the cotton fields, Wolf would sit with Patton for hours and learn how to play guitar. Patton's work was seasonal, following the money from the North to the South. Just as he roamed, so did his art. Adding a meter here, extending a meter there, adding a note or two where one might not think appropriate, created subtle intricacies in his music.

"...Patton plays fast and loose with the commonplace of blues structures (you won't find a standard twelve-bar anywhere in Patton's recorded output)," wrote Ray Templeton for the liner notes of the British label JSP Records box set *Charley Patton: Complete Recordings 1929–1934*. Instead, there are triplet feels, finger-tapping techniques, and a polyrhythmic sense that seems at once both nurtured and instinctual.

"If you really listen to what those cats were doing, they were able to sing in one time and their hands seemed to be playing in another," points out Colorado-based bluesman Otis Taylor. "How did they do that? All of that feel, all of that sadness, all the moaning and rhythm really comes from Africa. People like Hubert."

It is ironic, on the other hand, that Wolf and Hubert should find each other and then take Patton's collective influence to create a totally electric urban blues sound. One of the most seminal songs in the Wolf canon is Patton's "Forty-Four." Partly based on Roosevelt Sykes/Lee Green's "44 Blues," "Forty-Four" is a good example of how Hubert brought "street" to the blues—and to Wolf's band.

Jody Williams's boogie bass pattern on "Forty-Four" resembles the left-handed boogie-woogie groove of Otis Spann. "I started that bass-line," Williams says. "Hubert then came in with the 'dabba dabba dah/ dabba, dabba dah.' When I was a kid I used to love to look at the cowboy pictures—the shoot-'em-ups. That line was similar to something

I had heard on the soundtrack to one of those old shoot-'em-ups. So I made it my own."

Hubert uses what is known as "blues box" riffing patterns (in the key of *F*) for solos and rhythm/background guitar work. (A guitarist uses "blues box" to create tension by playing notes in both the major and minor keys of a scale—fluttering back and forth between them. It was used by T-Bone Walker and other electric blues pioneers.) On many tracks he recorded with Wolf, Hubert juxtaposes a minor sound against a major sound in his solos, as the rest of the band struts its stuff. In short, that juxtaposition is what gives the song and the solo its "blues-ness" and electricity.

All of Hubert's left-hand fingers (except the thumb) press down on and quickly release the strings of the first, second, and third frets on the neck, producing the classic trill riff in 4/4 time. But don't let the time signature fool you. The vocals enter the song at a weird angle (Wolf yelps like a possessed, lonely man who is going mad without his woman) and extra bars crop up in unexpected spots. It all sounds smooth, but it really isn't.

The song "Forty-Four" is one of those quirky electric blues tunes that even seasoned performers have trouble tackling. "Some of those blues songs depart from the standard twelve-bar blues," explains piano ace David Maxwell, who counts Otis Rush, Freddie King, Muddy Waters, Bonnie Raitt, and Buddy Guy among his playing credits. "There may be an extra beat and a half every four bars after every phrase or something like that. With '44,' when the phrase 'I wore my 44 so long…' and then there's a lick after that, there's a little hesitation for about a bar and a half. Then the vocal comes in. Sometimes musicians pick it up, sometimes they don't. Sometimes the singer picks it up, sometimes not."

"When you are trying to cover 'em, you can pretty much tell right away if you are pulling it off," notes Paul Barrère of Little Feat. "Lowell [George] was a Wolf freak and we used to do 'How Many More Years.' We stopped doing it, haven't done it for years, because Lowell thought he wasn't doing it justice. That is what we poor white kids try to do when we play the blues: not butcher them too bad."

"In March of 2004, we did ten shows at the Beacon Theatre in New York City," says Derek Trucks. "Hubert was the highlight of the last year or so with the Allman Brothers, at least for me and [bass player] Oteil [Burbridge]. We played '44' and 'Who's Been Talkin'?' Hubert's got a groove that is so dark and deep. He is such a positive spirit to be around. When he came out, it broke down. Everyone onstage got real quiet and subtle. There was a reverence that I really haven't seen with any of the people that have sat in with the Allmans. He is a great human being. He is one of those people you want to root for and you want to be around. He is a rare spirit."

In "You'll Be Mine" and "Just Like I Treat You," Hubert's light strumming and human-voice-like vibrato (added to Sam Lay's double shuffle—more like a tap dance across the snare drum head) make for uptempo, enjoyable listens, despite Wolf's unnerving rants, particularly in "You'll Be Mine," in which he repeats over and over, "you'll be mine…you'll be mine."

"Commit a Crime," a romp based on one chord (very much like a Delta song), shows how Hubert's effortless fingering serves as hypnosis for the listener. Hubert vamps on the same progression over and over (with slight variation), throwing in commentary as he sees fit. This is where Hubert's true genius is shown. Being creative with your riffs is far easier when you are not required to build the structure of the song. Yet Hubert buzzes and flutters about—thumbing his nose at convention. He cares not about playing a full polyrhythmic (some might even say staid) structure. In short, his playing is very "rock guitar god" before there was such a thing.

On "Hidden Charms," recorded in August 1963, Hubert vamps in the key of *D*. The rhythm is based on Wolf's "My Mind Is Ramblin'" (a variant on Wolf's 1952 jumper "Mr. Highway Man," itself based on Robert Johnson's "Ramblin' on My Mind"). Much like "Commit a Crime," there are no chord changes, but somehow Hubert is able to sustain the song's thrust without the slightest feeling of repetition through chordal vamps and brassy melody lines. His right hand whips around the strings, playing a combination of upstrokes and downstrokes. Even more impressive is the way Hubert bounces along the strings—he virtually scats with his fingers. Though he does not hit many notes, his fingers touch the strings, producing a percussive "click" (albeit a subtle one) that can be heard and, more importantly, felt. "In 'Hidden Charms,' Hubert was playing with the rhythm section and he essentially finishes the solo before it is through," Cray elaborates. "That man knew where he was going, didn't map anything out, and you had no idea where he was going to go to."

Perhaps the best example of Hubert balancing control and propelling the band is the classic "Smokestack Lightnin'." Even today, nearly 50 years later, the song still holds magic and intrigue. "That is my favorite song," Hubert once revealed backstage at a New York gig, singing lines between bites of his Chinese food. (One would suppose "Smokestack Lightnin'" should be etched in his memory, given the fact that it got him fired and forced him to find his own sound.)

"Smokestack Lightnin'" simply is the crown jewel in Wolf's catalog. The Yardbirds (featuring a young Eric Clapton), Soundgarden, and the Grateful Dead, among others, have taken a shot at covering the tune, perhaps more out of respect than a feeling they could top Wolf's electric blues masterpiece. At its fiery core, the three-plus-minute song is about a train. But it is far, far more than that. Wolf tied his hopes of a better life—of any life beyond the brutal plantation life given him by his Uncle Will Young—to trains he'd see pass through White Station, Mississippi, just outside West Point. Having been cast out by his mother Gertrude and worked to the bone by Young, Wolf saw in these trains a way out of his personal hardship.

That smoke-spewing, lightnin'-fast train was not just a people mover, but a raging fire igniting the hopes and dreams of a young man. "I wholeheartedly believe that the song "Smokestack Lightnin'" came from Wolf's younger years living out there by the railroad tracks," notes Ramsey of the Howlin' Wolf Blues Society, which is located not far from Wolf's birthplace. "He wanted out from that oppression and that mean uncle…who used to run him in the ground, plying the mules and cotton fields, and not feeding him right. While [Will Young] was in there eating chicken, Wolf had milk cornbread. He got tired of it, he was 16, and went out, with the old man chasin' him on a mule. The song says that there's this little boy wearing a derby—he's wanting to get out. That in and of itself is so powerful."

For all of its dark beauty, "Smokestack Lightnin'" starts off innocently enough with a jazzy one-chord pattern (in E) that varies slightly throughout, plus a strong backbeat from drummer Earl Phillips—nearly rock in nature (or what would become known as "rock music") with a twist of swing. But Wolf's mournful hollers (echoing to his country days) color and coat the track in a deeper shade of blue. It stops you dead in your tracks. *Billboard* magazine in 1956 called "Smokestack Lightnin'" a "hard-driving, primitive chant."

Based on an earlier track that Wolf cut in 1951 called "Cryin' at Daybreak," "Smokestack Lightnin'" has many tentacles that grab you and pull you in many different directions. It seems Wolf is at once dreaming of a faraway life yet imploring his woman to tell him what is happening with their relationship. He's begging her to tell him where she stayed last night. The song is a revelation and forces the singer to look at how he got here, and why he's here.

One of the reasons why Wolf's songs are so fluid and haunting (and haunted) may have to do with the fact that the band could record only on off-hours at the Chess Studios at 4750 South Cottage Grove (the label would move to the world-famous 2120 South Michigan Avenue address in 1957). "We'd record about three or four in the morning," Hubert says. "After we did the gig, we had to leave the job and come to the studio. That was the only available time that they had at the studio then. Chuck Berry and the Moonglows would be cutting a record in there—and sometimes it would take days for them to do it. By the time they were through, it would be nearly two in the morning. They knew we were playing in Chicago so they'd invite us in, right after we played the gig, to cut the record. We were all warmed up."

"Smokestack Lightnin'" also reveals how much of an impact Patton's country-blues had made on Wolf and Hubert. It's evident upon listening to Patton's seminal "Pony Blues," considered a masterpiece by some, "Pea Vine Blues," "High Water Everywhere," and "A Spoonful Blues," that a connection existed between Patton's gravelly voice and Wolf's similar sandpaper tones. And while Hubert's guitar playing tends to be more linear (doubling similar notes or soloing on a single string), "Smokestack Lightnin'" comes from country-blues. Hubert keeps a bouncing bassline going as he soars above it with higher-stringed melodies—straight out of country-blues.

The song's propulsive, one-chord vamp stroked by guitarists Sumlin and Willie Johnson creates a continuous, unbreakable, rolling feel of a locomotive screaming at high speed, taking its passengers beyond the horizon—to someplace else. The rising sea of violence in Wolf's voice (that settles to a near yodel à la "The Singing Brakeman" Jimmie Rodgers— a personal hero of Wolf's) nearly threatens to derail this train, but it stays on its tracks. Simply put, this fierce yet contained ultra-passion is beyond compare and reproach by most, if not all, blues artists working in the genre today.

What made Hubert so groundbreaking was his willingness to free himself from Delta phrasings. While unquestionably influenced by them, he goes in another direction (some would say another dimension) in songs like "Louise," "Tail Dragger," and "300 Pounds of Joy." Like a wild animal starving for nourishment and never quite getting it, Hubert twists, gnaws, suckles, and bites the "hard blues nipple" until it bleeds. He doesn't let go. In "Louise" and, to a degree, "Tail Dragger," Hubert's horn-like tone and spiraling licks ensnare Wolf's menacing but tongue-in-cheek words. Hubert doesn't sit still, yet his very lines define and give shape to the song (with the help of Donald Hankins on baritone sax and Arnold Rogers on tenor sax). While Chester Burnett spouts off about being "the Mighty Wolf" going on a "midnight creep" where hunters won't find him, Hubert defiantly, boastfully sounds the alarm with his guitar, alerting all that the Wolf—and he—have arrived. (And they ain't leavin', neither, makin' fools of everyone 'cause they'll wipe out their own tracks.)

"Tail Dragger" (an anthem for anyone who can't get his ass in gear, including Wolf) no doubt served as an influence for Clapton, whose single-note bends and slippery, fluid solos defined blues-rock guitar. Pick up a record by Cream (check out "Strange Brew" for a reworked classic "blues box" or "Outside Woman Blues" for double-stop action—the kind Hubert perfected), or Blind Faith, or Derek & The Dominos, and you'll hear that same Hubert stamp you hear on this track. "Hubert is extremely important in music history," the Stripes' White says. "His tones and technique were copied by everyone, copied by the Yardbirds and the Rolling Stones across the Atlantic. It would be ignorant to not realize that the music being made today is indirectly influenced by Hubert Sumlin." "300 Pounds of Joy," written by Willie Dixon, wouldn't be half as catchy if it weren't for Hubert's mercurial, brassy, out-of-phase, muzzled tone (due to the pickups fighting each other for supremacy). Hubert's

musical touch is the bold, unmistakable stamp on this musical profile—
the belly button on the song's bloated stomach. While Sam Lay clicks
out a Latin beat on the rim of his snare (a variation on a traditional
mambo-clave pattern), the horns (J.T. Brown on tenor sax and Hankins
on baritone) soak up the foreground, only to be challenged and brushed
back by Hubert's licks, which slice through the horns' haze. It sounds
very much like an African call-and-response—a duel, even.

"Hubert's playing on '300 Pounds of Joy' completely kills me," says
Freund. "Some guys are able to craft a solo and they can play it the
same way again and again. You can almost memorize it. With Hubert,
he plays it spontaneously, but it comes out crafted."

It's a given that Hubert made immeasurable contributions to these
songs, but why was he never credited with writing any of them? It's
obvious that he was laying the groundwork for much of this music for
years. "He never got no goddamn accolades or royalties or nothin'," complains Band drummer Levon Helm, who has also often suffered from
misconceptions involving songwriting credits. "He never got nothing but
another kick in the ass from life. [People like Hubert] put up with more
goddamn bullshit and abuse and shit and never had a fucking break in
their lives. They don't hold it against nobody. They keep pushing on. It
is a wonderful inspiration. It is hard to try to be that way." Milwaukee
guitarist Perry Weber agrees. "It is almost like hearing about those old
boxers, prizefighters, who were getting their money chiseled off from
them. That is basically what happened to guys like Hubert all of their
lives: they got their heads beat in and didn't get paid for it."

Why Wolf never shared the writing credit, we'll never know. One
reason may have been Hubert's absolute, trusting loyalty to Wolf. He
was Wolf's guitar player, and if that meant he had to chop a good deal
of the wood to keep this fire going, so be it. "I've been doing things
behind people my whole life," Hubert says. "Especially with Wolf. I
thought he would live forever. I thought Muddy would live forever. I
didn't know those peoples was going to…you know. But I know my guitar must have done something for somebody. A lot of somebodies."

It was not uncommon in the 1950s for musicians to be unde-
servedly credited or, conversely, uncredited. And with payola being the
rule of the day, it was obvious that independent record label owners,
especially those who were spinning out blues, would do anything to get
the music to the masses—even if it meant the artist himself got somewhat of a demotion. Legendary DJ Alan Freed, for instance, was credited with co-writing such songs as the Moonglows' "Sincerely" and
Chuck Berry's "Maybellene" merely for agreeing to play it on the radio.
"Many like Chess and Atlantic and the big companies—Columbia and
RCA—paid the [disc] jockeys by check and noted the sums on their tax
returns as business expenses," wrote Nadine Cohodas in her book *Spinning Blues into Gold: The Legendary Chess Brothers and the Legendary
Chess Records*. Some see the payola scandal as a necessary evil, however. "If it wasn't for disc jockeys who were willing to play the music—
whether they were paid or otherwise—we might not have this great
music today," says blues authority and author Bill Dahl. True, but all
of this meant it was harder for people like Hubert to not only gain exposure but, perhaps more importantly, royalties. What should also be considered is the fact that Wolf undeniably thought he was the boss, and
this boss brought Hubert into his successful band. Why share? Some
bandmates, though, have witnessed Hubert's importance within the
band dynamic. "Wolf would have Hubert tell us what to do," Lay says.
"Hubert was there the longest, so he was the boss, you know?"

Some of the confusion lies in the players' credits. Depending on the
compilation, there is some debate as to what Hubert actually plays on
key tracks—sometimes he plays lead, sometimes he plays second guitar. That is especially true for the Willie Dixon–penned "Spoonful,"
which MCA/Chess credits (possibly) to the great Freddie King and
Hubert. (Hubert confirmed in an interview for *DISCoveries* magazine
in 1995 that it was, indeed, Freddie King who played on the track. King
himself confirmed this in a 1977 *Living Blues* interview, but others have
speculated it was Freddy Robinson.)

"Spoonful," about betrayal and getting what you need to live, is a
minimalist masterpiece. Wolf's gut-wrenching delivery of "that spoon,
that spoon, that…" (Wolf drops the last "spoonful" from the song when
singing) is an open invitation for Hubert to pick up where the boss

leaves off and create a moment of sheer electrified, bottom-end joy. The entire band—including Otis Spann on piano—locks into a guttural seven-note, immaculate groove. You feel the very ground quaking as the forcefulness of the line grows more acute. If Hubert is not playing lead on "Spoonful," does it matter? It only underscores his importance as a support player.

Are we to believe that Wolf, Dixon, and Hubert never sat down and worked out the song? In so many cases, the three (or just Hubert and Wolf, though that would be unlikely on a Dixon-penned song) would run through the tracks and work out the arrangements. (Ironically, the song has its origins in Charlie Patton's 1929 wheezing slide-guitar tour de force "A Spoonful Blues.")

Dixon's knack for writing hooks helped Wolf deliver many "hits," though perhaps not in the traditional, chart-topping sense. (In retrospect, Dixon's collaboration with Wolf was nothing short of pure magic. Many Dixon-penned Wolf songs were later popularized by British rock stars, and these covers have themselves become blues-rock classics, such as Cream's "Spoonful" and Jeff Beck's "I Ain't Superstitious.") Wolf, however, always felt that his own music was being passed over by Chess, forcing him to record Dixon's songs. Wolf was never happy about this. So, perhaps, when he could, he took full credit for everything that was not Dixon's. Regardless, Hubert was there for all of it. "When Wolf was writing music, he let me write some numbers, put music to the songs," Hubert says. "I got a lot of stuff that nobody has ever heard yet. This is *me*. You are going to hear it. You'll know this is Hubert. Nobody else."

Hubert is consistent on this point. In a 1987 radio interview he explained in detail the transformation some of the Wolf tracks went through. According to Hubert, he had a big hand in every step of the writing process. "What we did, when I was with this guy [Wolf], we rehearsed. We got it together two or three months before we even recorded—nobody but me and him. So, really, the band had to come in. We weren't worried about the band. The band really didn't change anything. [When they did] change, [the band] would say, 'I don't think this is right, and this and that.' Then, what happened is, we'd end up coming right back to what we originally did. One of those things."

Only someone with intimate knowledge of the inner workings of the music could have such a handle on Wolf's songs. "Hubert could listen to the old Wolf records and play and sing every part of the song," remembers Obeda. Some, however, are unconvinced that Hubert is anything more than a credit on a CD booklet. "As far as Hubert is concerned, he is the Great 'B' Player [sideman]," Marshall Chess says. "He was making mistakes. He played well, but even to Wolf, it was not the way Chess treated him, it was the way Wolf treated him. We all thought Hubert was great and there was something that we knew that Hubert added to Wolf, but I am not sure Wolf looked at it that way. He might mess up and Wolf might slap him in the arm onstage."

"The very term itself—'sideman'—is just a goddamn putdown," counters Helm. "Hell, everybody knows who Muddy Waters is. Everybody knows who Howlin' Wolf is…and they should. But damn, not enough people know who Hubert Sumlin is. Not enough people know who Pinetop Perkins is. People don't know who James 'Peck' Curtis is. The players—they don't even get a dance book. They don't even get to go to the dance. Muddy and Wolf get to go and they get fucked while they are at the dance, while the rest of us have to hear about it."

It's true that Hubert's "sideman" work with Wolf has been better known than the rest of his career, and at one solo performance it was that very sideman status that dogged him. Before the set started, the announcer butchered Hubert's name, and various mispronunciations ensued: Herbert Sumner, Hubert Sumner, Herbert Sumlin—all of whom, apparently, were playing that night. (The stage wasn't that big!) It was an embarrassing display, but an undeterred Hubert Sumlin jetted out of his stool, buttoned his suit jacket, and took the stage.

When you watch Hubert backstage, you see that pickup bands admire him and often urge him to sing. Hubert soldiers on, more out of duty to his band and the fans than out of a passion for singing. It seems he would just as soon sit on his stool, play guitar, and keep his mouth shut. "I ain't no great singer," he declares. "I never wanted to be, I'll tell you like it is. I never wanted to come out of the background."

But this is a business. Hubert understands that. He knows the difference between a Hubert Sumlin performance where he doesn't step forward, and one where his guitar alone propels the band. And on many nights he is billed as Hubert Sumlin, not Hubert Sumlin "and band." He must be the focus and he acts as people expect; Hubert can't let people down.

In all fairness, Hubert never really had the *chance* to develop into a lead man when he was with Wolf. Why would he need to? "I am used to being a boss," explains Bruce Iglauer, founder of Alligator Records in Chicago. "I like the fact that people who work for me don't want to be the boss. I've never seen Hubert in a situation where he wanted to be the boss of anybody. Whereas Wolf, of course, wanted to be the boss of everybody."

I'm watching the band tackle the eight-bar blues of "Sitting on Top of the World" at the Cape May festival. It's a song Hubert loves to play live (perhaps because it's in his vocal range and he was the only guitarist on the original recording). Hubert's energy level seemed to rise during the latter part of the evening, and that fire has now lit the enthusiasm of the crowd and the band members. A bandana-wearing biker and his cycle queen move to the sounds of the music at the center of the dance floor. Soon more couples and even singles follow. They groove to the sounds onstage and the place is feeling great. The band is smokin' and the music bounces—people are forgetting their troubles. A little bit of Arkansas juke joint has found a home in New Jersey. People are performing dance moves that most Southern black ministers 50 and 60 years ago would have forbidden their parishioners to do.

After the set I run into a fan by the bar, an ex-jock who has been sidelined with a knee injury. He was happy he got a chance to hear "real blues from a real bluesman." Well, Mr. Ex-Jock, you got Hubert's best. But there were times that would demand he give more. Much, much more.

Chapter 4
Goin' Solo

The sight of the hillbilly-rockin' Chuck Berry chicken-walkin' across stages and TV and movie screens throughout the country was an ominous sign of things to come for some bluesmen.

By the mid- to late '50s, rock 'n' roll was king. Berry had taken precedence over many of the blues artists on the Chess Records label and increased its bottom-line expectations. Berry and such hitmakers as Bo Diddley (who had propagated what would be known as the Bo Diddley beat) and the Moonglows were helping to support most of the blues artists on the label's roster. "In those days, selling 20,000 copies of a blues record was a lot," Marshall Chess says. "After a while I think the blues artists realized that a record could help get gigs, not royalty checks."

Chess Records believed in using the best players they could find. Through the cross-pollination of talent, blues guys had recorded with rock 'n' rollers—Willie Dixon, Fred Below, Otis Spann, and Jimmy Rogers all played with Chuck Berry. This gave Chess the opportunity to do what Elvis Presley did for Sun Records—in reverse. Elvis (who recorded "That's All Right" just months after Hubert first recorded with Wolf) became "the King" by being a white singer who could convincingly cloak himself in the aura of R&B, blues, and gospel music. Berry, on the other hand, could seemingly reach white audiences with his strand of bluesy hillbilly-rock. Chess recorded Berry's hit "Maybellene" (or "Mabellene," as the original sheet music read), based on the Bob Wills & His Texas Playboys song "Ida Red," in 1955 and it galloped to the top of *Billboard*'s R&B charts and climbed into the Top Five on the pop charts.

In 1957 Hubert, too, was tapped to play with the rock 'n' roll sensation. Having gotten the nod from Wolf to branch out and play on other musicians' records, Hubert cut "School Days" and its B-side, "Deep Feeling," with Berry. (Ironically enough, just as Berry was breaking through with an upbeat school-themed hit, President Eisenhower went head to head with then Arkansas Governor Orval Faubus, who had called up members of the National Guard to block integration. Eisenhower was forced to send US troops to Little Rock to desegregate Central High School. The National Guard stepped down and integration was restored to Central. Forward motion.)

"I remember that session now," Hubert tells me. "I walked right into the recording room and Berry pulled $35 out of his pocket and gave it me. You know, $35, back then, was some money. I said, 'Thanks,' and we just got to playin'."

Berry had gained confidence in his two years as a recording artist, and his playing was now more solid and sure. In a way, the Berry record was also a shining moment, if not a defining one, for Hubert (he, too, would soon get a boost of confidence). He was nearly as unspectacular and unobtrusive on the track as he could be. In other words, he did his job: supporting the star, even in rock 'n' roll. Hubert proved that he could move with impunity through different musical styles.

By 1958, having played with bluesman Muddy Waters and rock 'n' roller Chuck Berry, Hubert was gaining confidence by the boatload. He felt he was a key player at Chess, not only for Wolf but for other artists. That resounding confidence came through, for example, on the song "I Better Go Now." It had all the hallmarks of what would make Hubert a grand maestro of the 6-string: furious doubled notes, sonic dips, and a sympathetic (and point-counterpoint) sensibility to whatever Wolf was doing—whether singing or playing his harp. Hubert not only weaves around Wolf's harp lines, but his intermittent intersections of Wolf's husky harp dives and flights give the illusion of the two players being in sync, even if they are only part of the time (think daredevil flying aces in action).

In a similar fashion, "Change My Way" reveals a kind of call-and-response involving Hubert and Wolf. Hubert's glassy, jazzy tone punctures holes in the roof of the song just as it scrambles the time and space, squeezing his sonic vision into the allotted structure. Like two dolphins jumping up from the sea, one arching over the other, Wolf's harp and Hubert's guitar nudge one another playfully, then plunge down inside the melody again for the chase.

Though some Chess label artists (i.e., Muddy Waters) were sorely hurt by Berry and the rock 'n' roll movement, the seemingly ironclad Howlin' Wolf continued making music—perhaps his greatest ever. As the 1960s evolved and society became increasingly tolerant of diversity, it seemed Hubert's playing became more free, confident, and adventurous. For example, "Goin' Down Slow" showcases how Hubert's musical radar was set to "attempt anything." Written in 12/8 by James Oden, the song is about a soul sliding down to die; the singer beseeches someone, anyone, to write to his mother and tell her of his hopeless condition. The song has special meaning for Wolf because his mother never accepted him or his profession as a blues singer.

"See, Wolf's daddy died when he was young," Hubert explains. "His mother, she put him [Wolf] out. I met her once…for the first time and the last time. She put him out of the house because he wouldn't make fifteen cents a day. She said, 'Get out of here, you son of a bitch.' She thought it was the devil's music. She didn't like it. So, he walked to his uncle's after." Hubert, of course, could understand the sentiment; his mother was dead set against him playing the blues for a living. (Later in life, Claudia Sumlin accepted Hubert's choice and career path.)

"Goin' Down Slow" has an interesting composition. It is really made of two parts: an intro that features Willie Dixon speaking lines about a man reflecting on his life, explaining that he has spent more money than a millionaire (which doesn't make him a millionaire now), and a slow, sonic descent that begins with Wolf's vocals.

As Wolf cries for help, Hubert dies a slow death—sonically speaking. The rising then falling lines in his solo (Hubert rummages through notes on an A-*minor* scale) and his darting commentary offer visuals of a man in distress at sea. Hubert's intermittent licks are gasps for air as he rises to the surface and flails about, desperately grasping at anything to save his soul. There is no hope: Wolf, Hubert, and the tune are "goin' down slow."

"For a long time I'd really wanted to meet Wolf's guitarist, Hubert Sumlin, because he did some things that freaked me out when I was picking up the guitar," Eric Clapton told *Guitar Player* in 1976. "'Goin' Down Slow' is just the weirdest playing. He is truly amazing."

It was in the early and mid-'60s that Wolf and other bluesmen were beginning to get noticed overseas. In England, Wolf and John Lee Hooker were experiencing renewed success; they both landed on the charts in 1964. Hooker's "Dimples" and Wolf's "Smokestack Lightnin'," both recorded back in 1956, had charted in the Top 50 in Britain— eight years after they were recorded.

A force was building in Europe, led by groups like John Mayall's Bluesbreakers, the Yardbirds, and the Rolling Stones, who in 1964 made a pilgrimage to Chicago to record their *12 x 5* album at the Chess studios on 2120 South Michigan Avenue (that address was the title of an instrumental on the record).

On the Stones' second trip, they would inspire and galvanize many young, white rock 'n' roll fans: the group that was building its reputation as the world's greatest rock 'n' roll band refused to appear on a television rock music show called *Shindig!* unless the mighty Howlin' Wolf also performed. It was an historic moment, but a bittersweet one for American music. "I sometimes think that if the John Lee Hookers and the John Coltranes and the Howlin' Wolfs of the world would have gotten the respect they deserved in the 1950s and 1960s, the Stones would have come over here and we would have said, 'Oh, cute. These English guys are trying to play like Muddy Waters,'" says guitarist/harp player extraordinaire Jon Paris. "That would have been the end of it. The fact that the Stones brought Howlin' Wolf on *Shindig!* was a milestone. That was very heavy that they did that." (The Stones also covered Wolf's/Dixon's "The Red Rooster" under the title of "The Little Red Rooster," which appeared on *The Rolling Stones, Now!*)

By 1964, Wolf commanded great respect overseas. The American Folk Blues Festival (AFBF), an annual European tour promoted by German music businessmen Horst Lippmann and Fritz Lau, culled the best of the best that America had to offer. Wolf, riding high on the British charts, was asked to join. Rosters included John Lee Hooker, Muddy Waters, T-Bone Walker, Sonny Boy Williamson II, Wolf, Willie Dixon, Lightnin' Hopkins, and many others.

"The first tour behind the Iron Curtain was in 1964 and that was only five or six people I took, namely Wolf, Hubert Sumlin, Willie Dixon, Sunnyland Slim, and one or two more," Lippmann said in *I Am the Blues: The Willie Dixon Story.* "We toured East Germany, Poland, and Czechoslovakia. We played South Galicia, in the Polish country-side, which looks like Russia." "It was wonderful over there," Hubert says. "My first time in Europe, and first tour. We didn't want to leave. And we stayed on for weeks after—we kept doing shows." The tour also included such stalwarts as Sonny Boy Williamson II, Mae Mercer, Clifton James, and Sleepy John Estes.

There was a brief time when it appeared as though Hubert wouldn't make the AFBF—a trip that would unknowingly prove vital to his career—due to a technicality with his paperwork. "Since I didn't have my birth certificate, I had to have my sister vouch for me, tell them that I was who I was, you understand?" Hubert says. "I almost didn't get there."

"Hubert just seemed like a really nice, quiet, respectful guy," says Delmark Records founder Bob Koester, who filmed the 1964 AFBF.

In the 1960s, Hubert's distinctive musical voice became more defined.

"He was not at all the image of a typical, fuck-anything-and-everything bluesman. I always got the impression that it was good that Hubert was playing with Wolf. I don't think Wolf was that great a guitar player."

As the recently released DVDs of the AFBF from 1962 to 1966 reveal, Hubert could take command of a song, fade into the background, and stoke the embers of the very essence of the song, keeping them red-hot. Introduced by Sonny Boy Williamson II as "Li'l Hubert" (after Sonny Boy pats Hubert on the back of the head), Sumlin sits on a chair next to Sunnyland Slim and teases the Chicago piano great by injecting phrases here and there—never letting the rhythm be reduced to ashes but never forking over anything too meaty, either. His jazzy side comes through on "Come on Home Baby."

While on the European tour, Wolf appeared on *Jass Gehort und Gesehen* (*Jazz Heard and Seen*), produced by a German television station in Baden-Baden. Hubert isn't in the frame during his entire solo on "Shake for Me"—his head just catches the corner, playing hide-and-seek with the camera. The filmmakers, while presenting invaluable footage to blues fans, missed an opportunity to get up close and personal with Hubert's playing. It is a loss. From the evidence of the other tracks shown, Hubert is a twitching pile of rhythm. All of Hubert's fretboard acrobatics of "I'll Be Back Someday" and "Love Me Darlin'" are also heard but not seen. Regardless, Hubert's guitar is the backbone and musical leader of the band. This is especially true on "Shake for Me," when his playing complements Wolf's vocal phrases—never running over them, but weaving around them.

After the AFBF, Wolf, Hubert, Dixon, Sunnyland Slim, and drummer Clifton James stayed on to do the first extended tour of any blues artist in socialist countries Poland and the German Democratic Republic. It was great for the European fans, but Hubert remembers friction among the musicians. "We was playin' songs that [Dixon] wrote on this tour," Hubert notes. "He figure on since we playin' the songs he write he wanted money, you know what I mean? Ten percent. Wolf told 'im, 'Get out of here.' He was mad. You didn't do those things to Wolf." (Dixon stayed on through the extended tour, but the 1964 AFBF became his last. He chose instead to remain in the US to book the festival.)

"I used to have to get Wolf off the stage and take him back in the alley and talk to him," Dixon reveals in his book *I Am the Blues,* co-written with Don Snowden. "I've threatened him and even had him in the collar a couple of times, but I don't remember actually coming to blows with Wolf."

Because these American bluesmen were in Europe—and now for longer than they had planned—a unique opportunity arose. "Wolfgang Kahne of VEB Deutsche Schallplatter and myself [Horst Lippmann] decided that an album should be recorded," read the original liner notes to a later LP, *American Folk Blues Festival '80.* "Therefore, on the afternoon of November 1, 1964, we went into Amiga studios. It was to become the first album ever recorded of American post-war blues in a socialist country.

"Howlin' Wolf was unable to make the session because of his exclusive contract with Chess Records and it was just impossible to reach Leonard Chess from Berlin (East) to get last-minute telephone permission. However, you will find more 'firsts' on this album. It was the first time Hubert Sumlin stepped out of the shadow of Howlin' Wolf and not only appeared as a co-leader, [but he] also did unaccompanied solos on acoustic guitar. It was also the first time Willie Dixon and myself would convince Hubert to sing two songs he usually did riding the bus during the tour."

The record would become *Blues Anytime!,* Hubert's first solo record (of sorts, since he is sharing the spotlight with Dixon and Sunnyland). One song on the record, Hubert's "Love You, Woman" (for which he straps on an acoustic and sings), is perhaps the single most impressive vocal performance he has ever given. His words are dense, though not complex. He simultaneously, and impossibly, manages to sound bitter and blasé: he keeps hearing things about his woman, but he loves her anyway (though he won't be no fool). In the acoustic guitar solo "When I Feel Better" Hubert taps his feet to the beat, lets his fingers roll and hammer on the strings. His notes bounce, bob, and swing as he flirts with and runs roughshod over Mississippi Delta blues, Chicago blues, rock 'n' roll, and jazz genres. He loses no ferocity by being unplugged.

What makes Hubert so astounding and timeless on *Blues Anytime!* is that the songs, recorded in 1964, could easily have been made in

2004. Unlike some rock 'n' rollers who were influenced by and drew from the same emotional well as the blues artists, Hubert never went for the cheap sell or quick gratification.

The title track, sung by Dixon, showcases Hubert's muffled and silky-metallic tone. It is in sharp contrast to yet another Hubert acoustic number, "I Love," a song chock-full of ringing strings, simmering basslines, dynamic runs, punchy melodies, and breathy vocals. In fact, Hubert's acoustic guitar playing rivals the ballsy quality he is used to getting with his electric guitar. And once again, Hubert proclaims that love is a double-edged sword: He loves his woman, but she seems to be killing him by degrees.

As Hubert would do for future records, he went into the studio for *Blues Anytime!* without doing pre-production. Everything was spontaneous—the words and his guitar licks.

Things were looking up for Hubert in the 1960s. He appeared to be a rising blues artist (both as a soloist and a member of Wolf's band), and he was building a relationship with the woman who would become his wife, Evelyn Cowans, from south central Arkansas. Hubert had met her in the late '50s, but his shy nature made it difficult for her to get to know him. "She was a waitress—she came from Pine Bluff and moved to Chicago a little later on. She worked for Silvio's, 708 Club. Every place we played, she got a job," Hubert tells me proudly.

Hubert continued to explore sonic possibilities. His progressive approach to blues guitar was fitting for the new urban soul/R&B sounds that now flooded the airwaves. And Wolf and Hubert (and other black blues musicians) were about to get a boost at home. White kids were starting to discover the blues (both electric and acoustic), and blue-eyed bluesmen like Michael Bloomfield and Paul Butterfield seemed to be on a mission. They wanted to, basically, blow away the old guys and prove that they could play the blues just as well as any African-American.

One way Paul Butterfield got credibility (besides his out-of-this-world harp blowing) was to lure greats into his budding band. "Butterfield was welcomed to play with us," Hubert says. "A lot of people were.

[Butterfield] then asked Sammy Lay to play with him. Of course, how could Sammy turn it down, you know? He went and they had a couple of hits." Koester recalls, "When Wolf left for Europe with Hubert, in October, I believe, he left his bass player and drummer behind— Sammy Lay and Jerome Arnold. They were unemployed. They wound up playing with Butterfield. Wolf knew all the good musicians."

It didn't take long before curious white blues fans were flocking to Chicago's ghetto taverns to hear this music. "We used to go to Maxwell Street on Sundays," says Jeff Dagenhardt, who at the time played with his band the Unit and often snuck into the clubs on both the North and South sides to see Wolf and others. "This was before the freeway cut through it and ruined it. There was a party on Maxwell Street every Sunday. I would go to Chicago and talk to Hubert. The Wolf band was drop-dead gorgeous. The records, like with Hendrix, just don't do it justice. You came out of there so jacked up you couldn't stand yourself."

The band was very dynamic, with each band member playing at full tilt. But it was all controlled. "It was scary," Dagenhardt says. "They would destroy these places, they were all so good. I will never forget it. I know from Hubert, everything was worked out—all these snaky rhythms. They were not left to chance."

"One of the things that always intrigued me about Wolf's sound live was everybody in the band sort of going for it," says Bruce Iglauer, founder of Alligator Records. "So, you didn't have this feeling of, 'Okay, you are playing lead, you are playing rhythm, your job is to play chords.' It was much more like this loosely knitted cloth with big holes in it. It manages to be a piece of cloth, rather than falling apart. The fact that Wolf had so many busy and active but often not very chordally sophisticated piano players in the band made for part of that. So, you've got Hubert filling or playing partial chords or two or three notes of a chord and piano players doing the same thing, and somehow or another it makes this thing that is strong enough to support Wolf. With Hubert it was, 'I am playing some rhythm and some lead and I am commenting on what Wolf is singing. I am experimenting and doing all of these things simultaneously.'"

Charlie Musselwhite, another white bluesman, came to Chicago in 1962 after having run moonshine and worked as "a skinny teenager," he

says. Fed up with watching his friends drive into his hometown of
Memphis from the North in their new Buicks, flaunting their new
lifestyle and worldly possessions, Musselwhite hit the "Hillbilly Highway." He was working as a truck driver for an exterminator company
when the power of Chicago's blues scene dawned on him. "I had been
listening to all of their records and occasionally I would see Muddy and
Jimmy Reed playing in Memphis, but here I was like a kid in the candy
store," Musselwhite says. "Then it was like, 'Should I see Wolf tonight,
or Muddy, or Sonny Boy?' You had all of these people to pick from. It
was wonderful.

"I remember Wolf at Silvio's," Musselwhite continues. "Silvio's was
like Wolf's home club when he was not on the road. It was right at the
El stop going up Lake Avenue at Kedzie. You just got off the El and
walked off the train, walked down the stairs, and walked right in the
door. That is where I met Hubert. He was just the nicest guy in the
world from the moment we met. I never saw him with a bad attitude.
I always thought that if everybody in the world were like Hubert it
would be a lot nicer place.

"Man, Wolf had such a powerful band. Hubert's playing was just so
unlike anybody else. He attacked the guitar in such a great way. He had
his own sound and his own rhythm. It was even more so in person.
Often you'll hear a record by somebody and you go to hear them in person and it is kind of a letdown. But not with these guys. Wolf and
Hubert were even more electric in person than they were on record."

Though Musselwhite, Mike Bloomfield, and Paul Butterfield were
digging the blues and carving out their own piece of history, the popularity of the music was waning in the clubs and in American consciousness.
A new wave of R&B artists on Stax, Atlantic, and Motown was popular
and had displaced blues as the voice of young African-Americans. The
blues was old people's music, not current with the feeling of indignant,
defiant black pride that Rosa Parks, after refusing to sit in the back of a
city bus, instilled in the African-American community.

"When I came to Chicago, blues was adult music," Musselwhite
remembers. "Kids were not into blues—black or white. The artists at the
clubs were real knocked out that I was there and that I knew who they
were, and that I knew the names of the tunes. I had a job at a factory

then, and you'd sit around on your first break and talk about what you did over the weekend. I'd say, 'Well, I was hanging out over at Silvio's with Howlin' Wolf.' The black guys my age would say, 'Man, you got to get it together. That is the old folks' music. What is the matter with you?' They thought I was out of touch. 'You have to listen to the Supremes.'"

Hubert was not going to take this shift in musical preference sitting down. As if inspired by the soul and new R&B music surrounding him, he became more of a musical ranger—coming out, somewhat, from under Wolf's grip. In 1963's "Built for Comfort," a song in which Wolf warns listeners not to call him fat, we hear again how Hubert consumes the foreground. He babbles on and on, though he never roams too far from the chordal root of the song. He plays hide-and-seek with the droning horns, boogie-ragtimey piano, and thumping bass. Every time the basic chord is struck and reprised, Hubert seems to stop to let it shout out, then goes about his business of playing around with notes in key.

At the time, comparable musical explorations for African-American jazz musicians were taking on whole new contexts. Saxophonist Ornette Coleman had immersed himself in "free jazz" and the avant-garde with 1959's highly influential *The Shape of Jazz to Come.* This record, Coleman's 1960 *Free Jazz,* and John Coltrane's 1965 *Ascension* were musical landmarks in an unexplored realm in the history of mankind. Although Hubert's musical approach wasn't as structured or complex as Coleman's melodic systems (read: "harmolodics"), and there was only a hint of atonal abstract expressionism in his solos, he was an iconoclast in his own way.

When Hubert plays backed by a band, his riffs spill over measure upon measure. It's as if he is feeling his way around the beat—using the band as a human metronome. Still, he never fumbles in disseminating his minimalistic musical message. He doesn't have to play every note possible to nestle emotive visuals into your psyche (as in 1961's "I Ain't Superstitious" and 1963's "Hidden Charms"). From electrifying Delta one-chord vamps to sometimes dispensing with standard blues format altogether, Hubert's extemporaneous, 30-second, anything-goes solos seemingly changed directions as often as some jazzmen's hour-long, sweaty workouts in the smoky metropolitan clubs of the late '50s and early to mid-'60s. It bordered on the surreal.

The irony here is that Hubert *is* something of a surrealist (some might even dub him a "cerebralist"). His musical patterns seemed to have a mind of their own then. His blues was, and is, partly escapism—flights of fancy that use raw and true emotional value and depth as a springing point. Hubert's phrasing has become more voice-like (think iambic pentameter). Sometimes Hubert converses with other musicians; sometimes he is merely talking to himself. Sometimes he shrieks, yells, runs off at the mouth with a stop-start motion that yo-yos up and down like a jabbering lower jaw. If Hubert's very notes are speech, then the pulse of the music that surrounds them is the rhythm of life.

After recording with Jimmy Reed and Eddie Taylor, Hubert again toured with Muddy Waters for nearly six months during 1965 and 1966. One of the nastiest fights he had ever had with Wolf led to this second joining with Muddy. Hubert also found time to work with hotshot guitarist Magic Sam until he came back to the Wolf fold in 1966.

Chicago blues was already in the midst of transformation. Back in the late '50s, a raw yet vibrant form of electric blues had started emanating from clubs on the West Side and, to a lesser degree, the South Side. It reached a full-blown musical revolution of sorts in the mid-'60s with Magic Sam, Buddy Guy, Otis Rush, Freddie King, Eddy Clearwater, and others as the major proponents of the sound. In the case of southpaw Rush, his orgasmic screams of agony and ecstasy were matched only by those his guitar and amp could muster up. The "West Side Sound," as it was dubbed, was a stinging, minor key–oriented sound that energized and revamped the genre.

While the genre got a jolt from the West Siders, no one can deny that the blues was rejuvenated into a popular form of music again, thanks to the curious and adventurous whites. Some thought the music had been hijacked. "Some guys say that the blues was taken from us," says Bobby Rush, an R&B singer who emerged from Chicago's West Side to fuse folk and funk, and whose bands included such guitar greats as Freddie King, Luther Allison, and Earl Hooker. "There ain't nobody taking anything from us. You gave it away. You stopped doing it, you stopped appreciating it. I saw the white guys trying to learn how to play the blues as well as the black guys—and they learned it well."

That is the ultimate irony: whites rediscovering a form that they had played a big part in creating, both mentally and socially. As Koester notes, "Kids were coming around to see kids their own age. The folk thing was taken over by white kids. Dylan using Butterfield's [blues] band cracked the whole thing open." Still, by the 1960s, some clubs, particularly on Chicago's North Side, were against booking black blues acts. "There was a time when there was no blues on the North Side," says Koester.

That all changed once white musicians like Bloomfield and Butterfield were working regularly but saw that their heroes were not. As Mike Bloomfield, in a rare moment of humility, told *Rolling Stone* in an April 1968 interview, "The older cats have gotten a lot of work because the younger cats have talked about them, and said, 'Man, you think I'm good? You should hear cats like Little Walter…man, that cat can play harp.'" Musselwhite, who was rooming with Big Joe Williams before he was "rediscovered" on the North Side, points out, "The clubs on the North Side just had more money to pay, so this dried up the South Side and all the work switched over to the North Side for the blues."

Bloomfield and Musselwhite cut Jimmy Oden's "Goin' Down Slow" in December 1964 (Wolf had cut the song three years earlier and it became a live standard for him in later years). Bloomfield's seminal version of "Killing Floor" with his band the Electric Flag was a crushing performance rife with meaty horns, hand claps, screaming single-note, half-step bends, and funky rhythm guitar playing. In an April 1995 article, *Guitar Player* writer Andy Ellis broke down what it was about Bloomfield's scalding guitar playing on "Killing Floor" that created such musical tension. The approach? Very Hubert Sumlin:

"[Bloomfield would] typically follow a string of stuttered notes with a sustained, singing one…," Ellis wrote. "Bloomfield typically played on the leading edge of the beat, rarely laying back the way, say, Clapton did in the Bluesbreakers or Cream…. Michael gnaws on *C-major, C-sharp,* and *D* like a dog on a bone, creating plenty of minor/major/sus4 drama."

Whether Hubert was ever bothered by the fact that whites picked up on his style (and have made a fortune from it), he will never say. You know he could play rings around most people in the genre, though he rarely does—or wants to. "There's stuff I know, and I can educate 'em by playing," Hubert admits. "Someday maybe I'll pass on what I know to someone else. I am a proud person and I don't want nothing else, man. Music—that is all I want—that was all I ever wanted."

While the sharing of information was frequent among blacks and whites in the Chicago blues scene, Hubert recalls that sometimes the plan backfired. "When Butterfield wanted a different band, Sammy was out," Hubert says. "He came back to Wolf to ask for a job. Wolf said, 'No way, muthafucker. You turned your back on the Wolf.' Sammy said, 'But they wanted an all-white band.' Wolf said, 'I don't care what he wanted—if he wanted a black, white, or otherwise. We got a drummer.'" And Wolf told *Living Blues* magazine in 1970, "The one thing I feel bad about Paul [Butterfield], he kept the colored boys until he got straightened out like he wanted. From me—he took 'em away from me, you know? And he done put 'em down and got somebody else. That is the only thing I felt bad about him."

Chicago's rough South Side was being flooded by white kids who dug what was coming out of the blues clubs. "I would always tell my white friends that I would go, and they thought I was crazy or that I would get killed," says Jim O'Neal, co-founder of *Living Blues* magazine. "But I never got accosted or robbed or beaten or anything. Once in a while someone might get held up or something, but the blues clubs seemed pretty safe. The biggest problem we had was the white police. They would ask, 'What are you doing here? You don't belong here.' They were in one way trying to be protective and in another keeping the city segregated. Then there's the question that black people had: Why was I there? What was my motive? I remember one of the DJs who promoted a lot of shows and booked Wolf a lot, Pervis Spann on WVOM, who later said, 'We always thought you were from the FBI or CIA or IRS or something.'"

O'Neal clearly remembers the aura around Hubert every time he saw the Wolf band perform. "Most of the time [Hubert] was having a good time on the bandstand and really hittin' it. But then there were times when things would dissolve into chaos. It could be the most explosive, or dynamic, or funny, or totally chaotic. One time, I saw Wolf at Pepper's and he had just announced that the band wasn't playing the music right. He kicked them all off the stage. He sat down with the guitar. From what I can remember he spent the next ten minutes trying to tune the guitar… I wish I had gotten to hear him more, but I am glad that I saw Hubert with him. I love Hubert."

A recording of the Newport Folk Festival in July 1966 reveals Hubert and Wolf totally in sync. As Wolf cranks out a windy, seesaw harp run, Hubert, without missing a beat, plays those harp lines, note for note, in "Dust My Broom" (a song popularized and recorded by Robert Johnson as "I Believe I'll Dust My Broom" in 1936) and "How Many More Years." In "Down in the Bottom," Hubert's soft, almost sober strumming and picking belies the original. ("That's Wolf playing slide on the song originally," Hubert says. "He could play, man, but not a lot of people know that."). Hubert starts off slow, as if he expects his boss to take the lead, not him. And when Hubert does pick up, it seems it is with Wolf playing in tandem.

Conversely, this "Bizarro Wolf" naturally behaved independently of his boss. As Wolf chided a drunken Son House (who also appeared at the Newport Festival) for talking during Wolf's performance and pointed him out to the crowd, Hubert put his head down, lowered his eyes, and kept his mouth shut. While playing his harp, the wild-eyed Wolf sweated through his shirt and tie and shook his head back and forth, but Hubert coolly bobbed his head with his lips buttoned, flexed his fingers, and tucked his head down while playing counterpoint lines to Wolf's harp notes.

Hubert clearly was a genius at work. "The first time I talked to Hubert was at Joe's Place in Cambridge," says Dagenhardt. "That may have been around 1966 or 1967. That was the first time I had ever said anything to him, though we had seen each other a lot. He was standing at the bar, and I stood in awe at a distance and we started talking. I just remember him [murdering] the guitar. Like in the 'Shake for Me' solo, the rest of the band goes to beat 4 and he is already there. It is scary: I would try to figure it out, how he did it, and just sit in front of the stereo for hours."

The band was recorded in Cambridge, Massachusetts, in 1966 (*Live in Cambridge, 1966* was released in the early '90s as a low-grade-sound-quality CD on the New Rose label) and proved what a propulsive, undulating sea of musicality the crew was. Wolf's band members had to be ready to play their asses off on any given night, and on this night, they do. The playing is not only stellar—it's interstellar. The jams approach the same kind of collective, free-form arrangements typically found in jazz quartets and quintets. *Live in Cambridge, 1966* may have slipped under the commercial radar, but it shows Hubert's incredible energy and fire onstage. Amazingly, Hubert didn't know the record had been released until someone told him. "I don't even know how many I'm on out there," Hubert says. "But I'm out there."

In September 1966, *Time* magazine ran a story that compared the Chicago South Side blues scene to that of Memphis in the 1920s and New Orleans in the 1930s—when genres were fusing together, coalescing into one distinct style that combined jazz, Afro-Cuban rhythms, the music of the church, European folk, and the country-folk of the Delta. People across the nation (and in the Windy City) were finally starting to appreciate the blues, seeing it both as a treasured tradition steeped in history and a vital art form being kept alive by clubs like Silvio's, Theresa's, Turner's Blue Lounge, and many others.

While the Beatles and the Beach Boys were flipping out fans with their sonic explorations on *Sgt. Pepper's Lonely Hearts Club Band* and *Pet Sounds* respectively, and Pink Floyd and the Moody Blues were helping shape progressive rock with their respective *Piper at the Gates of Dawn* and *Days of Future Passed,* the Doors were breaking down blues barriers. This was largely due to the stoic poet persona of lead singer Jim Morrison, whose raspy rendition of the Wolf/Dixon "Back Door Man" on the band's 1967 self-titled debut further fueled the blues boom. (Morrison was arrested for obscenity while performing the song in December 1968 at the New Haven Arena in Connecticut.)

Many others followed suit, infusing popular music with the blues. Janis Joplin would soon make headlines and Johnny Winter (also from Texas) would take the rock world by storm, with influences ranging from Bessie Smith and Robert Johnson to Muddy Waters and Ray Charles.

Articles in *Rolling Stone* and *Time* proclaimed the rebirth of the blues as rockers rediscovered the blues art form. It was in 1968 that Jeff Beck covered "I Ain't Superstitious" and Cream did their version of "Sitting on Top of the World" (arguably one of their best blues covers). That year also saw the formation of one of America's hottest bands, the San Francisco Bay Area's Creedence Clearwater Revival. CCR injected a healthy dose of rock 'n' roll, soul, and blues into its rock. The band's lead singer and guitarist, John Fogerty, had expressed his love for Wolf songs like "Smokestack Lightnin'" and "Moaning at Midnight" from an early age, ever since he heard them on Oakland's KWBR radio station. Fogerty's soul-fried vocals were a combination of Little Richard's freak-out vibrato and Wolf's anguished yells. This is apparent in songs like "Tombstone Shadow," "Graveyard Train," "Proud Mary" (with a Wolf-like pronunciation of "burnin'" as "boinin'," as in Wolf's "Natchez Burnin'").

On the other side of the Atlantic, in swingin' London, Jimi Hendrix was gathering a buzz storm as a guitar phenom. The American Hendrix had, in fact, recorded a blazing version of "Killing Floor" for the British Broadcast Corporation (BBC) before the Jimi Hendrix Experience's own debut record, *Are You Experienced,* was finished. Recorded in March 1967, Hendrix's "Killing Floor" sent Sumlin's riffs through a psychedelic meat grinder. Hendrix's screaming notes billow like smoke clouds over burning, distorted ruins of a groove. One can even hear a faint influence of Sumlin and Buddy Guy (at least in spirit and style) in Hendrix's groovin' and visceral instrumental "Drivin' South." (These runs would in turn influence another guitarslinger, Stevie Ray Vaughan, who also saw intellect, power, and beauty in Guy's and Hubert's inimitable styles.)

Hubert remembers meeting Hendrix in Britain in the 1960s. "We played Liverpool—the Beatles' home—and in walks Jimi Hendrix. He just kept a-walkin', man. He went straight to the bandstand. He just act like he had been knowin' us for years, man. But I ain't never seen him before. He young at that time. He got up there and did a set with us." (It has been reported that Hendrix said Hubert was his favorite guitar player.)

By September 1967 Hubert was again in the studio, this time to record the full-length *The Super Super Blues Band.* A marketing tool used by Chess Records (actually released on its sub-label Checker) to generate more interest and sales for the waning blues genre, the record teamed the label's heaviest blues hitters: Bo Diddley, Muddy Waters, and Howlin' Wolf.

Nine months earlier, Marshall Chess, who had assumed creative decision-making for Chess Records, had teamed Wolf, Bo, and Muddy with Little Walter (about a year before his death in 1968). Now Marshall decided to bring three of the four together again, tack on a second "Super" to the band's name, and get a great backing band comprised of Hubert, Buddy Guy (on bass instead of guitar), pianist Otis Spann, drummer Clifton James, and Cookie Vee on vocals and tambourine. The ads for the record at that time read: "When Howlin' Wolf, Muddy Waters, and Bo Diddley got together to record this historic album, rehearsals weren't necessary. They've lived it, baby."

That is certainly true, and there are genuine moments of great blues here ("Goin' Down Slow," for one), but it is hard to think of this record as anything more than an entertaining romp. These hardened and grizzled bluesmen were ribbing each other, like something you'd hear in a rap-off to see who can spit the most fierce bars. Wolf, more often than not, tops Bo and Muddy. He barks, "…Muddy can't howl like me: I'm the King." And, "You don't know whatcha doin', Bo Diddley. Watch me howl."

However, the obvious attempt to contemporize the blues on this record—with its now-dated wah-wah guitar effects and horrific "girlie" screams painfully injected into some of the tracks—undercuts whatever integrity the jam had to begin with. And with the passing of time, ironically, this record works only as a novelty for fans who are already into Wolf, Muddy, and Bo.

One interesting note: Hubert's solo parts of "Spoonful" sounded very similar to Wolf's 1960 version. Though Hubert certainly had played the song live, here it was for all to hear—on record—with a jazzy slant. If Freddie King was on the original, then Hubert proved once again that he could play what he wants, when he wants. Further, his solo in "Sweet Little Angel," with its subtle, fade-away lines and spiraling repeated bars, has licks that are thought by some to be signature Eric Clapton riffs—riffs that are identifiable as Clapton's work, even as late as, say, 1989's *Journeyman* or 1994's *From the Cradle*.

A memorable performance in Wolf's career (and Hubert's) was the September 1969 inaugural Ann Arbor Blues Festival organized by students of the University of Michigan. On the bill were Howlin' Wolf, Muddy Waters, Son House, T-Bone Walker, Roosevelt Sykes, Arthur "Big Boy" Crudup, Junior Wells, Otis Rush, B.B. King, and many others. It was a special show for many reasons. For all intents and purposes, many were calling it the "Woodstock of the blues." It was the first major blues festival of its kind in the country and attracted nearly 20,000 attendees who plopped down on Fuller Flatlands, a grassy field owned by the University.

Like Woodstock before it, the three-day Ann Arbor Blues Festival was a place for young people to gather and appreciate music. But there was a greater emphasis on the music. "…Everyone had come to hear music—not to make the scene—and the enthusiastic response was a joy to behold," wrote Dan Morgenstern in *Down Beat* magazine in 1969.

The festival also had significance in the Wolf universe. "Muddy had a trailer, they had a big trailer for the bands and for the leaders," Hubert explains. "Everybody had their trailer. There was a big hole in the trailer, maybe the size of a Coke bottle. I believe it was Muddy's trailer. You could see through it. I heard all this here, 'Oh, Muddy.' 'Oh, Wolf.' I peeped through the goddarned hole and I said, 'What's goin' on?' These dudes hugged up, cryin', a bottle in each hand. I went off the stand and got Muddy's piano player, Otis Spann. We were supposed to be in our own trailer. I thought these dudes were putting on an act. It ain't an act. You know what: I'll never forget this. They was the same damn thing, man. They were some of the best musicians in the world and they come to realize…" Hubert's voice trails off.

"Years they was getting mad at each other," adds Detroit Junior, who joined Wolf's band in 1969. "Wolf would get mad at Muddy and add something to the story. Muddy get mad at Wolf and add something to the story. They had a thing going on. Wolf had a station wagon he had special built that said "Howlin' Wolf" on the side. Hubert take the wagon and gone down to Muddy's house and the old lady next door saw the wagon and thought Wolf had come down there to see his wife. That wasn't what it was. Before Wolf died, they made up. But for years it was going on this way."

On Saturday, the festival's second day, Wolf zoomed across the stage on a motorbike, hat turned sideways, ready for a bombastic, albeit bizarre, set. Col. Bruce Hampton, Ret. (of the Codetalkers and Aquarium Rescue Unit fame) was in attendance for this special show. "If I remember correctly," Hampton says, "Wolf knocked over all of Muddy's equipment. Muddy was coming on after Wolf. Wolf was crazy. He was literally howling at the moon for what had to be 20, maybe 30 minutes, uncontrollably. Then he started climbing all over the stage—up the side of it. He was just a madman. Big Bill Hill tried to get him to tone it down and get him off the stage, but nothing was working. He was wearing a backwards golf cap and riding a motorcycle or moped. It was something like what Andy Kaufman always wanted to do." Hubert adds, "I don't know what got into him. I did never know him to drink moonshine, but I'll be damned if it weren't."

Instead of the 45 minutes Wolf was allotted to play, the incorrigible frontman broke the time clock at nearly an hour and a half. Muddy went on next, and as memory serves Hubert, both Muddy and Wolf performed together after Muddy's set. "Pretty soon everyone, all the musicians, went to the bandstand together," Hubert recalls. "Both bands joined in. Whoopin' butt. That was the best band I had ever seen, I had ever been. The band sounded so good. You couldn't sound no better. They couldn't play no better."

Chicago looked different in 1969. For one thing, Leonard and Phil Chess had made the decision to sell Chess Records to General Recorded Tape (GRT) and inked the $6.5 million deal in January 1969. (GRT paid $4.7 million in cash and signed promissory notes for another $1.79 million.) And the pivotal Silvio's, which had burned down in April 1968 during the riots following the assassination of Dr. Martin Luther King, had reopened for business as the Riviera in November 1969. "They killed Martin Luther King in Memphis and they burned down Silvio's Lounge," remembers Jesse Sanders (aka Little Howlin' Wolf). "Chicago burned for eight days and eight nights."

Rising from the ashes, Silvio's regular Magic Sam (who had given a rousing performance with his trio at the Ann Arbor Blues Festival) was ready for the big time. He was one of Silvio's youngest and brightest stars, a soulful West Side singer and guitar player who bridged the gap between R&B, soul, and traditional Chicago blues. He was booked to tour Europe as part of the 1969 American Folk Blues Festival and was about to leave the Chicago scene—forever, unknowingly.

Hubert felt a kinship with Magic Sam, not only because he was a West Side guitar player but because he played electric guitar like Hubert: with the fingers of his right hand instead of a pick. And Sam was born on a farm not far from Grenada, Mississippi, some 20 miles from Hubert's birthplace in Greenwood. Sam and his family moved to Chicago in 1950, just a few years before Hubert would make his mark on the city's recording and nightclub scene with Wolf and then with Muddy.

"You know that Freddie King song 'Hide Away'? That's Magic Sam. That's where he got it from, man, Magic Sam," Hubert says. "Freddie, he heard something in what Sam was doin', you know what I mean? And he did his own thing with it. Sam come up with the music for 'All Your Love' [an Otis Rush tune] in my basement," Hubert continues. "We was only 16 blocks from each other. We could jog back and forth from one house to the other. I was teaching him, you understand? We'd be playing together."

(For the curious among us, Hubert demonstrates note for note on acoustic guitar how Otis Rush's "All Your Love" is played, in Homespun Video's *The Blues Guitar of Hubert Sumlin* hosted by Jimmy Vivino. Tucked inside the main riff of "All Your Love" are trill riffs reminiscent of "Lonely Avenue"—a fact acknowledged by Vivino, who is seated next to Hubert with his own acoustic. Hubert's left-hand fingers plough the highways of the third and fourth strings, bending the fourth string with his index finger at the fifth fret. Then his left hand reaches around the strings and he bends that string with his middle finger at the sixth fret. Next, the middle and ring fingers hammer on the third string at the sixth and seventh frets (recalling the classic vibrato riff), while his index finger is planted on the fourth string at the fifth fret. Hubert's right hand, meanwhile, is shaped like a spider crawling over the stings, presenting equally challenging runs. His thumb and forefinger lightly stroke, almost pinch, the third and fourth string at the soundhole. The bent tip of Hubert's thumb then catches the second string, and his ring finger and pinky strum the non-fretted fifth and sixth strings. In this way, the bottom- and top-end rhythms are maintained throughout the run.)

After returning home from the 1969 AFBF, Magic Sam suffered a fatal heart attack. Just as the younger Woodstock generation was rudely awakened by the tragic dénouement called Altamont in December 1969, so, too, the blues world was rocked when Sam died on December 1, 1969. He was 32. "Couldn't really believe it, you know," Hubert says. "He had an offer to go to Europe and he went. But when he came back, he died. He was gone. Just like that."

It's hard not to think of Magic Sam as the frontman Hubert might have become without Wolf. Watching Sam perform with his trio at the AFBF, his fingers diddling the strings on his Gibson Les Paul, one gets the feeling that Hubert, too, could have been this aggressive leader. But comparing Sam to Hubert is pointless. Wolf shaped Hubert, and in many ways gave him a legacy to uphold—one that Sam could never have, and never did have.

It was less than a year later, in September 1970, that Jimi Hendrix, another Wolf and Hubert disciple, died from an overdose of barbiturates. He was just 27 years old. Any instinctual brotherly and/or paternal feelings that Hubert felt for Sam and Jimi were now squelched, suddenly. Some of the most talented guitarists Hubert had helped influence were gone. "When he died, that was terrible," Hubert says. "So young."

En route to his next show, Hubert snaps his fingers and looks into the distance as the scenery changes by the second.

In another attempt to capitalize on the mainstreaming of the blues, Chess Records had a great idea: to pair blues great Muddy Waters with the Paul Butterfield Blues Band for *Fathers and Sons*. The other part of the plan was to team Howlin' Wolf with a variety of British rock royalty including Eric Clapton, Steve Winwood, Bill Wyman, and Charlie Watts for what would become *The London Howlin' Wolf Sessions*. These records followed in the footsteps of Muddy's *Electric Mud*—an attempt by Chess to fuse psychedelia and the blues—and Wolf's similar *Howlin' Wolf* on Cadet, which Wolf himself referred to as "dog shit."

THE LONDON HOWLIN' WOLF SESSIONS

featuring

Eric Clapton   Steve Winwood   Bill Wyman   Charlie Watts

Wolf told *Living Blues* in 1970 why he decided to do a psychedelic electric blues record in the first place: "[*Howlin' Wolf*] was Marshall Chess's idea, you know. I never did go for it and never did like it, 'cause that queer sound, that bow-wow, I just don't like it, I still don't like it. But the teenagers like it, you know. So, he's [Marshall Chess] out there, a young man out here with the young crowd, so I just made it for him, you know? Well, I been with him ever since he was a baby, you know?" Wolf was not the only one who hated wah-wah psychedelic effects. Hubert did, too. And still does. "They're nasty things," Hubert complained to the *Dallas Morning News*. "[Marshall Chess] bought us all wah-wahs and tried to get us to play them, but I hated them."

Still, 1968's *Howlin' Wolf* did open up new doors. Bands like Led Zeppelin found some meaning in the psychedelic electric blues records. *Howlin' Wolf* and *Electric Mud* reportedly were inspirations for the seminal "Black Dog" from Zeppelin's fourth album. Even today, there are fans of the bluesmen's foray into psychedelia. "I love the electric one,"

Jack White of the White Stripes says regarding Wolf's self-titled record. "Meg and I searched for that vinyl for a long time and then she finally found it first, at a vinyl store in Fargo, North Dakota, when we were on tour. No matter of pleading made her let me buy it. But I got my own soon after."

Regardless of Hubert's or Wolf's feelings about psychedelia and the blues, musicians still loved the band. Much in the way the Stones crusaded for Wolf for their appearance on *Shindig!*, Clapton championed Hubert for *The London Howlin' Wolf Sessions.* "Chess always hated me," Hubert says. "I don't know why. They didn't want me on those sessions. It was Eric [Clapton]. He said, 'That's it. Hubert comes or that's it.' He made the call."

When asked why Hubert wasn't initially invited to play on *The London Howlin' Wolf Sessions,* Marshall Chess explains that he had no say as to who was invited. "*The London Sessions* [as the record came to be known in inner circles] was at the tail end of my involvement with the label. However, I did go to those [recording] sessions. I can tell you that the artists treated Wolf like a god. They treated him with respect. I do remember that Wolf wasn't well during those sessions. He was sitting down a lot; he had just gotten over being really sick."

If Wolf was a god (albeit an ailing one with his share of medical problems including a heart condition), then Hubert was the Holy Ghost, fluttering about, sometimes heard, rarely seen. "If it weren't for Eric, I wouldn't have been there," Hubert declares. "They wanted all of those new artists, and they didn't want me."

Despite the power of Clapton (already known as God in the rock and blues-rock worlds) pushing for Hubert to be part of *The London Sessions,* Hubert is barely visible in the packaging of the album. You'll find one photo of a figure deep in the recesses of the background (Wolf is in the foreground) that appears to be Hubert, but it is too blurry to distinguish. Hubert was never even put on the wraparound cover of the original LP, which is an artist's rendering of Clapton, Winwood, Watts, Wyman, and Wolf sitting in the middle of Piccadilly Circus. "Not even a picture of me on there," Hubert points out, seemingly still rather snakebit by the whole thing. "Who'd know I was there? They got my name in this little line on there. That's okay," he reflects. "I know I was there."

Although he ended up right in the middle of the action on *The London Sessions,* Hubert narrowly missed not being there at all, save for Clapton's influence. Without question, Hubert was the most solid player of the bunch. How could he not be? He had performed these songs countless times and even had a hand in writing them. But, once again, Hubert was overshadowed by something. In this case, it was the celebrity power of the session.

Could Hubert have been more aggressive and carved himself a deeper place in history with these sessions? Perhaps. But in all fairness, Hubert wasn't really officially invited (at least not from the get-go) and he was caught between the compromised world of artistic music-making and the business of making music for commercial consumption. *The London Howlin' Wolf Sessions* was about making money, about exploiting the connection between popular white British rockers and the Chicago blues legend. Simple: if Hubert had wanted a bigger part in it, would anyone listen or even care?

What stings is that, in many ways, Hubert was the backbone of the guitar work on these sessions. "He was very good to have there," producer Norman Dayron told writer Bill Dahl for the liner notes of *The London Howlin' Wolf Sessions* (deluxe edition). "He was like a rock, because he would do exactly what you wanted. You never had to say anything to him more than once. You'd ask him to do something and he'd do it, and he would lock in the rhythm. Just the sweetest guy, willing to help out in any way he could. He was a great comfort to Wolf, to have his guitar man."

Hubert landed smack-dab in the middle of the notorious communication breakdown between the Brits and the American bluesman regarding the record's version of "The Red Rooster." Watts and Wyman, of course, had already recorded the Stones' version of the Wolf classic as "The Little Red Rooster," so it was Clapton who bore the brunt of Wolf's surliness about the song. In many ways, Hubert was a sympathetic comfort to Clapton while he struggled with the song.

The "false start and dialog" take of "The Red Rooster" makes it the most telling track and perhaps the most well-known feature of *The London Sessions.* The one-minute, 58-second track drips with the reverence Clapton and the boys have for the elder bluesman. Wolf begins to play his slide guitar in the opening, then stops and speaks: "Now, I'm just showin' you how to do it, you know? Now you and Hubert take it." Clapton seems perplexed by the timing and the feel, and attempts to coax Wolf to play acoustic guitar so he can better find his way through the song. Wolf seems reluctant to oblige. He sounds tired. "Oh, man, come on," Wolf says. It was as if he meant to say, "You supposed to be God, you figure it out!"

The irony is that Hubert, quiet and unobtrusive, had the guitar line down pat. Wolf knows this—or at least had gotten used to Hubert playing it—so he tells Clapton that the licks are easy to achieve: just count off to four and change. Clapton complains "I doubt that I can do it without you [Wolf] playing it." Finally, Wolf gives in and strums. "Listen! Let everybody get together then and we'll try to make it," Wolf orders. The very next track on the album is "The Red Rooster" in its entirety, picking up precisely where the "false start and dialog" track leaves off.

Clapton will never forget that moment of sheer humility when Wolf had to teach him to play the song correctly. "When that was happening, it was awful," Clapton said in the 1995 Martin Scorsese concert film *Nothing But the Blues.* "I wanted to just die, because [Wolf] kept grabbing my hand. He'd grab my wrist and shove it up and down the neck of the guitar. And he was angry. He was very angry."

While "The Red Rooster" conversational track and "The Red Rooster" musical track are the most infamous cuts on *The London Sessions,* they are not the best. "Rockin' Daddy" and "I Ain't Superstitious"—with "Richie" (aka Ringo Starr) on drums, displaying the same kind of fine hi-hat work and punchy kick patterns found on the Beatles' 1969 *Abbey Road*—are fresh and inspired; Wolf doesn't sound winded or pressed to get the lines out.

On the whole, the sessions were successful, partly due to Clapton's ability to funk up the tracks, as he had done for Robert Johnson's "Cross Road Blues" and Wolf's own "Smokestack Lightnin'." Perhaps Clapton's greatest gift as a guitar player was, and still is, his ability to revamp older blues songs to give them an immediacy and frenetic vibe. The strange thing is that Clapton and Hubert are often mirror images of each other. The interplay between the two is subtle—not mind-blowing, by any means—but still very conversational. For most of the record, Clapton is in the right channel and Hubert's in the left, but at points they sound identical—identical in their phrasing and tone. As *Guitar Player* noted in March 1998: "'Borrow, rework, borrow, rework.' This is the mantra of the blues gods…. Eric Clapton borrowed heavily from the greats—Hubert Sumlin and Freddie King, in particular—hot-rodded their lines, and then with Cream, used his supercharged blues to change the sound of rock guitar." Clapton, of course, playing "lead guitar" on *The London Sessions,* was the aggressor and was naturally recorded louder than Hubert in the mix. But a careful listen reveals Hubert's mellow noodling that sways like wheat stalks in the wind while Clapton ploughs the fertile, low ground.

While some purists like to sling arrows at this summit between the British blues revivalists and the American icon Wolf, *The London Howlin' Wolf Sessions* is not as lacking as some people may think. And the remastered deluxe edition, which includes bonus tracks from *London Revisited* (released by Chess in 1974 and comprised of leftover tracks from *The London Sessions* plus Muddy's London leftovers), is much more of a crawlin', scratchin', colorful mosaic of blues sounds than the original LP. And it did its job: it sold well and hit *Billboard*'s Top 100 Albums chart.

"My argument has always been that the purists are the same as fundamentalists," says Marshall Chess, nearing the end of his tenure as head of Chess Records but acting as chief consultant. "[Fundamentalists] want things that adhere to very strict rules. Like I always say, my job at Chess was to expand it, not to satisfy purists."

The legend of *The London Howlin' Wolf Sessions* doesn't end with the guys riding off into the sunset selling hundreds of thousands of copies. Rather, the epilogue of this tale has crossed over into myth. So many people have heard so many different versions of what happened that (like many of the stories that shroud Hubert) it has passed into myth, elevating Hubert to god-like status.

"When Hubert visited Eric Clapton in England he walked into a room Eric had filled with guitars," says Dan Beech, founder/owner of Blues Planet Records. "Eric said, 'You can have any guitar you want.' There was one guitar in the middle of the room. Clapton supposedly said, 'Hubert, no, any guitar but that one.' Eric eventually gave him the guitar."

Guitarist Steve Freund elaborates on the story: "They were doing *The London Sessions,* and at the end of the day they released the guys from the studio and Hubert started walking up the street and a car pulls over. It was a chauffeur-driven car, and inside is Clapton. Clapton says, 'Hubert, get in the car. C'mon. I'll take you up to my place.' Hubert got in and they went up to Clapton's mansion of some sort. Clapton had one room in this place that was completely devoted to guitars—they were hanging from the ceiling, from beams on wire holders, so they are all hanging in this room. There may have been dozens of them there. Maybe even one hundred. Clapton then tells Hubert, 'Go ahead, man. Take any guitar you want. It is my gift to you.' Hubert goes after this one guitar. To be honest, I'm not sure which guitar. But Clapton said, 'Oh, no, anything but that. Anything but that.'"

Some confusion still exists as to what guitar was actually given to Hubert. Was it a Stratocaster? Rickenbacker? Les Paul? Some have said that it was "Blackie"—Clapton's most famous guitar, which was by his side from 1970 to 1985. (The Guitar Center was the highest bidder when "Blackie" was auctioned off in July 2004 at Christie's in New York for nearly $1 million. All the money benefits Clapton's drug rehab facility, the Crossroad Centre, on Antigua in the Virgin Islands. Hubert auctioned off one of his guitars then as well—a Valco-Supro model 1540 Bermuda, circa 1963, with a handwritten inscription on the back of the headstock: "Pour Sambuca here.")

"The famous story of Hubert getting Clapton's guitar? I thought it was 'Brownie' that Hubert took from Clapton," chimes in Lloyd Petersen, whose Free Spirit Productions organizes the annual Mt. Baker Blues Festival in Deming, Washington (where Hubert has played in the past).

Here's what we can piece together from what Hubert told me. (At the outset I should say it's unclear whether this incident happened during the recording of *The London Sessions* or later in the 1970s when Hubert toured Europe; Mr. Clapton could not be reached for comment.) According to Hubert, after the sessions, a conversation broke out about guitars. Clapton took Hubert back to his home, to a large room full of guitars, all kinds. "Eric told me to 'take a look, Hubert—you can have any guitar in this room. Any one you want.' I said, 'How about that one?' I saw this little ole guitar poking out from under a piano—it was in this black case. He said, 'Ooooooh no. Not that. Pick another one.' I said, 'But, you just said any guitar I want. I want that one.' I took the guitar." Hubert could not recall the model or make of the guitar. "I never really did play the thing at all," Hubert says. "He gave the guitar to me and that's it. I kept it for a while and after that I gave it back."

Though Hubert did not record for Wolf on the Chess release *Message to the Young* (Chess as well as Hubert were beginning to branch out), he was far from being out of work. He recorded an LP titled *Hubert Sumlin and Friends: Kings of Chicago Blues, Vol. 2* for the French label Vogue on January 20, 1971 (released in the US two years later). Nearly half instrumental, the record features guitarist Jimmy Dawkins, bassist James Green, vocalist/guitarist Joe Carter, vocalist/harpist Billy Boy Arnold, drummer Fred Below, and saxophonist Eddie Shaw (who had played with Magic Sam and Otis Rush, and joined Wolf after leaving Muddy flat in 1966—another source of bad blood between the Chicago blues titans). Amid covers like "It Hurts Me, Too," Hubert pens such originals as "When Evelyn's Not Around," a musical reflection on his married life at that point.

"She was poisoning me," Hubert says. "I came to find out that she kept me from going to a lot of places. I woke up sometimes days later and realized what had happened." I ask Hubert what he really means by "she was poisoning me." He responds, "You know, I'd drink and she'd spend my money." So it comes as no surprise he should write such a grating, mischievous tune about his wife.

But Hubert is at his best when he draws from positive energy, and some of his most fiery, memorable work of that time period was recorded with Chicago piano legend Sunnyland Slim. Tracks from a 1971 session turned up on a 1998 disc released by Earwig Records called *She Got a Thing Goin' On*. Issued three years after Sunnyland's death in 1995, the record was recreated from LPs, 45s, and pieces of master tapes. It was all producer Michael Frank and edit/mastering engineer Blaise Barton could do to get these tracks on CD. While historically significant, this record's poor sound quality ensured that Hubert's good work can't and won't be fully appreciated here. The music is dampened, and Hubert's jagged guitar lines are diced and sliced by sound scratches and LP "pops." It's too bad: "Done You Wrong" with Eddie Taylor and Hubert on guitars and Sunnyland's glass-shattering voice is a subliminal track, fusing Chicago and boogie-woogie/ragtime blues styles. Harp man Mack Simmons paints in shades of colors, sometimes slightly darker or brighter than those used by Hubert, with nary a clash. The performances almost make you forget the degraded sound quality. Almost.

Despite not appearing on *Message to the Young,* Hubert's allegiance remained with Wolf. In Chicago in 1972, Wolf's band recorded its only live record, *Live and Cookin' at Alice's, Revisited.* It was Wolf's first full-length live release and it featured Hubert, Eddie Shaw, Sunnyland Slim, Fred Below, Dave Myers, and L.V. Williams on second guitar. Hubert is smokin' on this record, as is the entire band. *Live and Cookin' at Alice's, Revisited* shows that Hubert is a true anomaly. With all that has happened in blues (and rock) since the release of this record—with the arrival of players ranging from Stevie Ray Vaughan to modern rockers—you'd think Hubert's playing here would sound dated at best, or unimpressive at worst. It is neither; his zippy, zig-zagging lines represent boundless inventiveness. (Reports vary on the power play, though, within Wolf's band. Some sources claim that Shaw began the Wolf Gang in 1972 and stayed at the forefront of Wolf's band until Wolf's death in 1976; others point to Hubert as the man in charge.)

Hubert was still blowing away his admirers. "I was just amazed by his hands," explains Paul Rishell, acoustic country-blues guitarist who first jammed with Wolf and Hubert in 1972 at Joe's Place in Cambridge, Massachusetts. "There aren't a lot of guys who play the electric guitar with their hands. Most of them play with picks. I remember those nights that I would be watching them—when that band was playing and hitting on all eight. They were on all eight because Hubert was ready to go. He would noodle around in the beginning of the night. I remember stuff like his playing half a riff and then he would finger the rest of it, but he wouldn't play it, which I thought was really weird. He'd do this little riff—four little notes of a six-note riff—then he would finger the other three or six, but he wouldn't play them. I realized that he was just waiting. He was thinking up there. He'd play a little bit, stop, and put his hand up. I loved the fact that he had this relationship with the guitar that was so human."

Wolf and the band toured throughout the States and up to Canada, to the Colonial Tavern and the University of Waterloo, Ontario. Colin Linden, noted producer and guitar player, remembers one special swing the band took through the Great White North. "Eddie Shaw and Hubert were always so great to me," Linden says. "They treated me so fantastic. I'd see them at the Colonial Tavern in Toronto. Back then, the great blues guys were still doing six-nighters in clubs. They did matinees on Saturday. The Colonial was licensed as a restaurant as well, so kids my age could get in. I begged my mom to take me to the afternoon matinee of Howlin' Wolf."

Wolf had become a legend and moved on to myth, even in his lifetime. Jesse Sanders (Little Howlin' Wolf), Necktie Nate, Lee Solomon (Little Wolf) and James Yancy Jones (Tail Dragger) all made names for themselves as imitators of sorts, paying tribute to the Mighty Wolf. Wolf didn't mind being imitated—he embraced them all in his own way.

Jones started going to shows, watching Wolf, and learning. He wanted to play with Wolf and play his songs. After seeing Wolf and his band show after show, Jones was invited to play. "I'd sit in with the band," he says. "One night I had bad timing and Wolf got up on the mic and talked about it, and embarrassed me. Then I said, 'I don't know, man, teach me.' So, he sat down and started to teach me. That was how I got the name Tail Dragger, you know? I would always be late and my time was late."

It was often Hubert who would get these newfangled wolves up to speed. "I would go to Hubert's house; he was living up on Twenty-First Street when he and Evelyn were together," Jones explains. "I used to spend nights over there. The next day we would get up, ride, and talk and whatever. Me and Hubert. He would be out riding, explaining things to me."

"I went to Hubert and Evelyn's house, on the West Side on Seventy-Eighth Road," recalls Sanders, who married into the Wolf family. "I lived close and could walk to his house. When me and Hubert got together, he taught me. A lot of the stuff I know now on guitar, Hubert learned me how to play it. He's the one who learned me how to play 'Shake for Me,' 'Smokestack Lightnin',' 'Killing Floor,' 'Howlin' for My Darlin',' 'Somebody Walkin' in My Home.' Hubert taught me how to play it—not everybody could play it."

Those visits with Hubert were invaluable experience, especially for Jones, who became close with Hubert. "I really learned a lot with Hubert," Jones says. "It was beautiful playing with him. I mean, when it came to Howlin' Wolf songs, he was the man. He knew it inside out. He'd tell you when you were on, like, 'You got it now, partner. Keep it right there.' If I messed up, he'd tell me that, too. 'You messed up there, partner! You got to do it like this.' He was a great teacher, man." Jones may have been the perfect foil for Hubert, outside of Wolf himself, and they soon had regular gigs at David and Thelma's Lounge, the Rat Trap, the Blue Moon, and Joe's Lounge—all Chicago West Side clubs. "You know, years back, Hubert wasn't even centered on a mic," Jones notes. "He'd be scared of that mic. You couldn't get him to try to sing. All he do is play that guitar and smile at you. So, we made a good team."

In 1973, Wolf had a car accident that exacerbated his kidney problems (he was already on dialysis for failing kidneys). After playing the New Orleans Jazz and Heritage Festival and along the East Coast in the spring of 1973, Hubert joined Wolf in August for what would be, unknowingly, their last recording session together.

The result of that session was a full-length LP called *The Back Door Wolf.* It featured Hubert, but neither he nor the rest of the band were credited. (Hubert was later credited on subsequent CD prints.) It's a strong effort—a fitting swan song—with a great band though a somewhat derivative one: Hubert and Willie Harris on guitars, Eddie Shaw on sax, Detroit Junior on piano, S.P. Leary on drums, and James Green and Andrew MacMahon alternating bass duties.

Hubert plays riffs on the chest-thumping opener "Moving" that are nearly identical to his work on "Down in the Bottom." "Moving" references (and updates) the songs "Forty-Four," "Built for Comfort,"

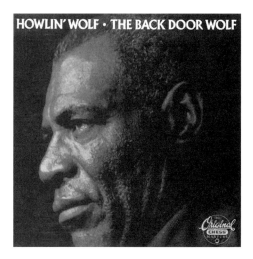

Hubert's final studio LP with Howlin' Wolf.

and "Back Door Man." Its finite ring gives the impression that Wolf is reintroducing himself and explaining his past works for a reason: he is leaving.

"Coon on the Moon" (credited to Eddie Shaw) has a sense of accomplishment mixed with hope and reminiscence. Wolf and Shaw imagine a world where African-Americans stamp the ridged soles of their space boots on the dusty surface of Earth's satellite (among other milestone achievements for their race).

"Watergate Blues" is an overt political statement that chides even as it seems to sympathize with former President Richard Nixon. Hubert scrambles and flirts with Detroit's harpsichord and even complements Wolf's voice after winding around the rhythm of the song. Hubert mysteriously and instinctually manages to land on the same beat as Wolf to close out his vocal in verse two. Perhaps the best song on the record, "Watergate Blues" is one in a line of biting political blues songs that features an equally biting guitar tone from Hubert (it also has a stop-action dynamic similar to Muddy's signature tune, "Mannish Boy"). The song showed how contemporary issues could work, and work well, within the framework of a revamped Delta-style song.

In some respects (though not all—check out the deceivingly titled "Speak Now Woman"), the progressive, determined atmosphere of the times had turned Wolf's music around 180 degrees. It was hardly "the blues" by some strict or even "white" definitions. *The Back Door Wolf* reveals how far Hubert's playing, Wolf's music, and African-American blues had come. In the Eisenhower era (1953–1960), Jim Crow (the slang term for legalized discrimination that separated blacks and whites on public transportation and in restaurants, restrooms, and other public places) had reached a new high (or low). The Civil Rights Act wouldn't be signed into law by then President Lyndon Johnson until 1964, and the country remained segregated both literally and figuratively. It is something that is painfully memorable to Hubert from his touring days with Wolf during the 1950s and 1960s.

"We couldn't stay in no hotels, because all the hotels we could have stayed in was white," Hubert recalls. "We had to live in a house, the places in the ghetto, where everybody could stay. We didn't have to pay that much. We did that for many years until things started getting right. Well, better." (Hubert would persevere against insurmountable odds and indescribable discrimination on the road. He told me about an incident when he had to stop in a honky-tonk on the side of the road because he needed to use the restroom. The owners refused. "Look, partner, I don't mean no harm. If I could, sir…" Hubert asked, pointing to the bathroom. "Just for one moment." Hubert's charm defused a situation in the honky-tonk and he was allowed to use the facilities.)

Though reverends, particularly in the Delta, were fuming at the injustices perpetrated on blacks in this country, and spoke their minds freely from the relative safety of their church pulpits, most bluesmen did not openly criticize the social conditions in which they were living. (Two exceptions were, of course, "Eisenhower Blues," J.B. Lenoir's sparse cry of hopelessness, and Big Bill Broonzy's "Black, Brown and White," recorded in 1949 but not released until 1956 because no American record label would touch it.) When some bluesmen did speak out, it was something of a minor defiant footnote, lost on a blissfully blind mainstream white America. Most singers simply found a way to disguise their derision of the American democratic system, or didn't sing of it at all.

"Trying to Forget You" is a variant of "Smokestack Lightnin'" (complete with Wolf yodel-howls and Hubert's twisting guitar lines rising, falling, rising, and falling again). "Can't Stay Here" is a revamped "Forty-Four" (including references to a few Charlie Patton tunes) with Hubert chugging along, sometimes playing on Leary's upbeat, or starting his guitar lines on the downstroke(s). The instrumental title song "The Back Door Wolf" is, strangely, quite settling despite its menacing title. Shaw glides through the number with the pomp of a rock 'n' roller's strut while Hubert flicks chunky chords just as he raises his riff sails to ensure that they gently flap in the song's mid-strength sonic winds. Songs like "You Turn Slick on Me" are far more low-down and feature Detroit Junior's harpsichord (perhaps a by-product of the influence younger white musicians had on the blues in the 1970s) and Hubert's quivering, metallic, biting tone.

Despite having a full-length record under his belt, Wolf continued to play the Chicago clubs and tour across the country. In June 1974, Wolf and the band landed a weeklong stint at a club called Richard's in Atlanta, Georgia. Wolf was the third major blues artist to come through there in the preceding three weeks; Muddy Waters and Willie Dixon had performed there just prior.

Wolf's health had badly deteriorated in just the last few years. Both saxophonist Eddie Shaw and Hubert would look after Wolf, drive him to his Veterans Administration hospitals. "I saw Wolf suffer," Hubert says. "He was sick, man. That old man was sick."

An upstart guitar player named Paul Cooper (who played with the likes of Sugar Blue and the Supremes) played host to Hubert and Wolf in Atlanta. "I feel fortunate that I had gotten to know Wolf for that week," says Cooper. "[Wolf] was on the kidney machine, dialysis treatment, which my mother had been doing as well. I knew about special food, I used to go out and get him no-salt food. It was great to be able to help him...but then Wolf went back on tour and didn't stay in Atlanta. If he was grumpy it was because he was sick, and to be touring when he was sick, well.... They lived in cheap motels and nobody cared for them but themselves. He didn't lack energy when he got onstage, though. It was a different energy—it was a passion.

"Hubert ended up staying at my apartment down there," Cooper continues. "He had been with the Wolf for so many years and they had a big argument, and Richard's told Hubert that if he wanted to have a go at it solo, he could use the house band. This was Hubert's first attempt to get his own band together. And I was his guitar player. It was a thrill for me to be in that band, being 21 or 22 years old at the time."

It seemed Hubert had taken Wolf's advice to break out on his own. "Wolf pulled me aside one day and said, 'Son, you got to play guitar on your own sometimes,'" Hubert reveals to me. "He was looking out for me, understand? He knew. He wanted me to have some longevity in this business."

The plan was to have a band backing Hubert through New York and then Europe. "I was supposed to be touring with Hubert," remembers Cooper. "Hubert was arranging his first tour. We were going to play Carnegie Hall and we were going to go over to Europe. And the contract came from the Europeans and they insisted that every musician had to be black. There were a couple of us white guys—reverse racism, in a sense. Hubert turned it down because of that. That is a beautiful part of his character. He stood by us. We were kids. He could have gotten any number of people to go along, but we were the band and we were playing together."

The tour never happened, and it was heartbreaking. But, of course, Hubert did eventually get back together with the Mighty Wolf. The reunion, however, would be briefer than either could have imagined.

Chapter 5
"Wolf Dead?...*You* Dead."

When saxophonist Eddie Shaw took control of Chicago's 1815 Club on West Roosevelt Road in June 1975, he solidified his place as "the next in line"—the heir to the Wolf throne.

The venue would become home to Wolf anytime he wanted to play—anytime he could play—and offered a gateway to Wolf's music for the many locals (including white kids) and out-of-towners who were jonesing for authentic Chicago blues. Over the years, Shaw had grown close to Wolf and it had always been rumored that Wolf had an investment interest in the 1815 Club but wished to keep it silent, for reasons that are unclear to this day.

Shaw's control of the club was a strange turn of events. Perhaps even stranger is that Hubert was so close to the Wolf, yet was passed over when it was determined who should own and/or operate the new club. But Hubert tells me his version of what happened: "Wolf paid a little over $100,000 for the club. Wolf got the club in Eddie Shaw's name. He didn't like people digging around in his past and asked me if I wanted anything to do with [the club]. I didn't. So, Eddie Shaw got the club."

As 1975 was drawing to a close, Wolf was in and out of the hospital. The band had just played a major show at the Chicago Amphitheater on November 7 with B.B. King, Albert King, Bobby "Blue" Bland, and others on the bill. The performance was part of a two-show, two-city package put together by DJ/promoter Pervis Spann (no relation to Otis

*Eddie Shaw at the
Speakeasy Club, Cambridge,
Massachusetts, in the late '70s.*

Spann). The Chicago performance stretched the very limits of Wolf's body, mind, and spirit. Backstage, he was exhausted.

"When we played the Amphitheatre in Chicago, Wolf was sick," Hubert confirms. "Wolf got sick, but we played the songs anyway. I think he might've fall out after two numbers, though. We were supposed to play that job—18,000 people—and then play the Paradise, in Memphis. But Wolf got sick and someone was going to call the fire department because Wolf was exhausted. B.B., Bobby, ain't nobody feel like playing after that."

Wolf didn't play Memphis the next day (as had been advertised), but he didn't go to the hospital that night, either. He couldn't stave off the inevitable, though, and by Thanksgiving he was admitted to the Veterans Administration hospital in Hines, Illinois. After being released in early December, he was readmitted later that month—the sign of an agonizing holiday season.

Wolf's condition in the hospital went from bad to worse. In the months and years prior, he had had two heart attacks and his kidneys had started to fail. Now his health rocked those closest to him. Imagine a seemingly unstoppable man the size of a giant being reduced to a shell of his former self. It was surreal. Things like this didn't happen. Not to *Wolf*.

Hubert himself couldn't accept it, but in the recesses of his mind he sensed the end was near. He called Gertrude Burnett, Wolf's mother, to try telling her about her son's precarious state of health. "I called and she said, 'What the fuck do you want?' I said, 'It's about your son…your son is in the hospital.' She said, 'I ain't got no son.' Oh, man, she was somethin'. I wouldn't tell Wolf nothing about that when I got to the hospital. I told 'im, I said, 'Your mother…'" Hubert's voice trails off. "Wolf said, 'My mother…she ain't gonna be at my funeral, is she?' He knew. I said, 'She'll be there.'"

While Wolf steadily declined in the hospital, professional obligation was calling Hubert. He had a pre-scheduled flight to Paris, France, where he and Wolf were supposed to gig as part of the Chicago Blues Festival tour. He wound up doing shows and cutting tracks for the French label Black and Blue—without the Mighty Wolf. It was December 1975 and the frigid Barclay Studios was an unlikely place for the blues to go down, but an impressive list of personnel was assembled there: Lonnie Brooks on guitar (he had toured and recorded with Jimmy Reed for Vee-Jay and recorded under the name "Guitar Junior," a name already assumed by another in Chicago), Willie Mabon on piano, Dave Myers on bass, Fred Below on drums, and, of course, Hubert Sumlin. These sessions would become Hubert's second solo record—and his second solo record released abroad.

If *Blues Anytime!* and *Hubert Sumlin and Friends: Kings of Chicago Blues, Vol. 2* were the warm-ups, then *My Guitar & Me* (originally titled *Groove* when released through Black and Blue) firmly planted him as a solo artist with his own ideas. Because Hubert's style of playing and singing is often understated (to say the least), his solo output has often been misinterpreted and is frustrating to reviewers who expect more from a Hubert Sumlin record. Often overlooked is Hubert's approach to lyric "writing." Unlike other fine bluesmen (Jody Williams admits he writes down lyrical ideas and prepares lines before recording or performing), Hubert riffs off the top of his head, paving a precarious psychological highway, challenging himself and the musicians around him with his off-center approach. Hubert's existential ramblin' and moanin' can sometimes make for a bumpy ride, but his poetic lyricism sometimes flows like water. While Hubert didn't go into these sessions "prepared" in the traditional sense, he was armed with something far better: he was attuned to the beat of his stuttering, sputtering, heavy heart.

Like any great artist pouring his heart out into the mic, Hubert reveals more of his psyche and interpersonal relations than he would if he were having a heart-to-heart talk with a friend. While the work may appear off-the-cuff (and often is), the sentiment is not, and the layers often take months, perhaps years, to decipher. He sings and speaks in riddles and lives the lines he sings. He's earned the right to the sad and stinging guitar acrobatics he casually flaunts.

The basis for the original title track ("Groove") was Hubert's experiences watching and listening to older Mississippi and Arkansas musicians messing with a multi-layered bassline groove on acoustic guitar. Throughout the song, Myers and Below push the rhythm by laying down an incessant groove, generating power for Hubert to abandon standard form and create a scatting, vocal–guitar sparring match.

"Easy, Hubert, Easy" seems to echo a Freddie King style (which would soon be captured beautifully by a boy from Austin named Stevie Ray Vaughan). Hubert plays four acoustic numbers on the record as well, the greatest of which, "Don't Forget," is in the Patton-Johnson motif: a simmering bassline roots the movement of the melody line. "I Wonder Why" is a quietly violent and scathing indictment of someone who has spent all of Hubert's hard-earned money.

Later in December, Hubert flip-flopped with Lonnie Brooks and played second guitar on Brooks's solo record *Sweet Home Chicago*. (The record is now issued on Evidence, but was recorded for the Black and Blue label in France during Brooks's break on the Chicago Blues Festival tour.) The title track, of course, has become a legendary standard among blues bands and was recorded by Robert Johnson in 1939 (based on an older Kokomo Arnold song). Once again, Below, Myers, Mabon, and Hubert were together, with the addition of Little Mac Simmons on harp.

Sweet Home Chicago proved Hubert and Lonnie made a great match. Brooks covers "Crosscut Saw," which floats in a more subdued vibe than the Albert King version, and Hubert provides the scratchy chatter underpinning the track (instead of King's Booker T. & The MGs and the Memphis Horns, Brooks is backed by Willie Mabon and Little Mac Simmons). "Things That I Used to Do" (originally co-written by Ray Charles and Guitar Slim) and "Two Guitars Shuffle" make for charged atmospheres.

Hubert cut yet more tracks while in Paris, for Luther "Snake" Johnson's *Lonesome in the Bedroom*—three months before Johnson died of cancer. Johnson, like Hubert, was a onetime member of the Muddy Waters band now considered a valuable sideman breaking out on his own, showcasing a solid band through originals and such covers as Muddy's "Honey Bee" and Jimmy Reed's "Hush, Hush."

Hubert was quite busy, forgetting the troubles—his sick friend and mentor—he had left behind in Chicago. Whatever slight respite Hubert got, it was soon cut short. "I was in Paris and I got this call, two-thirty in the morning," Hubert says. "I said, 'Hey, man, you better have a good reason for callin'.' It was Lillie Burnett, Wolf's wife. She says, 'Wolf has something to tell ya.' They called me, told me that he had something to tell me, and that maybe I wanted to come back home."

Hubert caught the next flight out of Paris and went to the V.A. hospital where his boss was being treated. "I go straight there and Wolf has his eyes taped," Hubert remembers. "It was about six-thirty in the morning. Somewhere along there. Well, it actually took me eight hours, so it was somewhere later in the morning. Anyway, when I get there, I knew something was wrong. I was his son. They said, 'He's resting.' My wife, she had met me at the hospital, she said, 'He squeezed my hand.' I said, 'Bitch! He didn't.' That man was already dead. He looked dead to me. We gets home and I raised the garage door and put the car in the garage. It looked like every phone was ringing. I picked up the phone and Lillie said, 'Your daddy's dead.'"

It was January 10, 1976, and Wolf, not yet 66 years of age, was gone.

When such a strong, polarizing figure is lost, denial tends to reign. Hubert tells me he is still befuddled about what had transpired in the hospital. He was even more perplexed by what Wolf may have wanted to tell him. "He passed and he didn't get a chance to tell me what it was that he had to tell me," Hubert laments. "I still don't know what it was that he wanted to say to me. I got an idea, though. I got an idea. I believe he wanted to tell me about things."

I ask Hubert if those "things" could be what to look out for in the business, or perhaps *who* to look out for. "Yeah, yeah," Hubert agrees. "You know what I mean? I couldn't get it out of Lillie and she wouldn't tell me anything. They weren't going to tell me anything."

Such a mammoth man with such mammoth talent, such a large presence in Hubert's life—the man who saved him from life on an Arkansas farm and raised him—was now gone. "I just couldn't believe it when Wolf died," Hubert says. "I didn't believe it. I just couldn't believe that that man was dead. I still don't."

A photo taken by Brian Smith in 1964 shows Hubert and Wolf backstage. Wolf is hunched over, cupping his harp in his huge hands, and Hubert, flashing that ear-to-ear grin that would be (and still is) his trademark, appears ready for action. His right hand is fingerpicking the strings at the bottom of the neck of his guitar. He is happy to be a part of Wolf's life and music. The two seem to be falling into one another,

Hubert and Wolf at the American Folk Blues Festival, 1964.

as if the very second after the flash popped they would embrace, and the great bear of a man would engulf Hubert in a hug and say to the cameraman, "This is my son!"

If you ripped this photo in half to create an individual shot of each man, you'd know something was missing—no matter how carefully you tore the picture to separate the two men. The bond between Hubert and the Wolf was that strong. It transcended physical laws.

Alone now with his guitar, Hubert had, indeed, been ripped in half. Now he was forced to go on without Wolf, searching for his missing half. Trouble is, once you've stood next to a mountain, once you've played with the Mount Everest of the Blues, once you've climbed uncharted heights into the musical stratosphere, what—if anything—is your next move?

Hubert was Wolf's son, and when Wolf died something inside Hubert died. Hubert was also Wolf's shadow—quiet and unassuming onstage, raucous when the rising tide of the Mighty Wolf's musical anger ebbed. At what point does a shadow know when to fade and evaporate into black? At what point does a shadow need to materialize to survive? Hubert had to grow into his own skin to find out.

Howlin' Wolf's funeral was held at the A.R. Leake Funeral Home on Cotton Grove on the South Side of Chicago. Hubert was listed as Wolf's "son" in the funeral program, along with Wolf's biological son, Floyd Frazier.

Although the father-and-son bond may have ended in a physical sense, Hubert tells me he still feels Wolf's presence and legacy every day. "I believe today these guys are somewhere jammin': Muddy, Wolf, Hound Dog Taylor, and the rest of 'em. Wolf is probably looking down on me, saying, 'I raised that little ole sonofagun. He think he shit.' I believe it. I betcha he proud. I believe."

The funeral was majestic. "I can remember Little Milton and Eddie Shaw and some other musicians were standing guard around the casket," says Jim O'Neal, co-founder of *Living Blues* magazine. "It was like soldiers with their fallen general. Music was playing, some of it from the record that Wolf hated so much—the electric Wolf album. But even at that, it was powerful, too. Then the preacher, he was young, he got up and he started to get into this fiery sermon. The sermons for these things were usually the same: that you have to make your peace and meet the Lord. Then it gets directed toward the people who are still here—you know, live your life right. But this preacher worked Wolf's lyrics and song titles into his sermon. It is still one of the most memorable events I have ever attended."

"They had it on a closed-circuit TV because there was so many people there—not everyone could see the old man," explains Jesse Sanders (aka Little Howlin' Wolf), who met his wife, Diane, Wolf's half-niece, at the funeral. "People from all over the world were there: France, Germany, Sweden, Spain, Australia, England, Switzerland, and all the States."

"The funeral had thousands of people," Hubert affirms. "Thousands. It looked like a ballpark. They couldn't get in. They couldn't even get into the ballroom, the main room of the funeral home, after the funeral. But Wolf's mother? She stayed home; she weren't at his funeral.

"It must have been $100,000 in expenses," Hubert continues. "Wolf didn't want it that way. He told his wife, I was there, he told his wife and he told us, 'Look, boys, don't bring me no flowers. I don't want nothing. I just want a hole in the ground.' Muddy died later, but Muddy was there, too. They played Wolf's music all the way through his funeral, like 'Shake for Me,' all the way through. When it was over, they all got together."

Howlin' Wolf was the second important Chicago bluesman to die in the past month. Theodore Roosevelt "Hound Dog" Taylor, a tireless worker and an 11-fingered slide guitarist, had died on December 17, 1975. (Jimmy Reed, a Chicago blues legend in his own right, would pass away eight months after Wolf, in August 1976.)

In many ways, having to face Wolf's death meant Hubert had to face his own mortality. After watching such a strong personality wither away, Hubert's spirit was punctured. The very meaning of his duty, his work, was lost. What did it mean to play guitar now that Wolf was gone? "I just couldn't go on without him," Hubert explains. "I'd put the guitar down for a while. I couldn't play it, you know?" Every time he picked up his guitar, he'd see Wolf's bespeckled face, with eyes lighting up like a rabid animal during a full moon. There was so much life inside Hubert's guitar, but he couldn't make it sing a word.

Between his heightened emotional state, mounting pressures to survive and reinvent himself as a musician, plus pressures to support the growing needs of his wife, Hubert ultimately just shut down. He became depressed every time he played, scratching the strings and going up and down them with no rhyme or reason—or much musicality. His motivation was gone. Hubert's mental state changed from day to day, hour to hour. Sensing the grief Hubert carried around with him, and how unstable he was during those first months after Wolf's death, some had speculated that Hubert was done. Finished. Perhaps Hubert felt that, too, and was beginning his deep separation from the world at large.

But he built up the emotional and mental armor to continue musically. He had to go on. He played around town with the likes of James Yancy Jones (Tail Dragger), Paul Cooper, drummer Willie Williams, bassist Queen Sylvia Embry, vocalist/harp man Big Leon Brooks, and Eddie Shaw's Wolf Gang when they came a-calling. "Wolf had wanted the band to continue after his death," explains drummer Chico Chism. "Wolf said, 'You keep this goin', boy, when I am gone. Daddy loves you.' I respected that, and him, immensely. He told me I put ten years to his life. That meant a lot to me."

The boys heeded Wolf's unifying calls and remained a unit with the Wolf Gang. The core band consisted of Chism, bassist Lafayette "Shorty" Gilbert (so nicknamed because a debilitating case of polio had stunted his growth), Shaw, and, of course, Hubert (there were also a number of pianists in the first few years).

Hubert forced himself to play. He needed the money, and he couldn't stay away from his first love—the guitar—for any length of time. Despite being spooked by Wolf's presence every time he'd pick up the instrument, Hubert was focused enough to channel the one (perhaps the only) positive, driving force in his life: creating music.

Today, playing air guitar in front of me, Hubert says, "Sometimes I'll be playing on the bandstand, and it's like Wolf, he is *not* dead, man. The man is *not* dead, you know what I'm talkin' 'bout? It's like he's right beside me. It's like he's guidin' me."

On a sweltering summer day in 1976, two New York street musicians made the decision to split the blues-stagnant Big Apple scene and venture to Chicago. Guitarists Steve Freund and Paul Cooper drove from New York to Chicago in Freund's parents' car and went straight to Eddie Shaw's 1815 Club.

"At about three o'clock, at the heat of the day, we knocked on the door and the door was locked," Freund explains. "All of a sudden the door opens and lo and behold it was the Wolf band. The whole band was there—Hubert, Eddie, Chico, Detroit, Shorty. They invited us back that night to their gig. We stayed about an hour and a half and we came back that night. And when we came back it was crowded, crowded with neighborhood people. Not many white people. They called me up to play and Hubert, I remember, still had his Les Paul Gold Top. He took it off his shoulders, and he put it over me. He treated me with a lot of respect. Here I was, a little nobody. He was that kind of person. He was remarkably gracious and he let Paul play a few numbers." (Freund later played with Hubert a number of times, from the late '70s through the late '80s.)

While Hubert and the Wolf Gang had plenty of admiring fans, plus aspiring musicians clamoring to learn a few licks and take the stage with the band, if truth be told the business of the blues in general was spiraling down and Hubert was caught in its maelstrom. It was the time of arena rock and million-selling bands who owed a great debt to Chicago and Texas blues styles. But there were not many kids (read: the white record-buying public) who cared (or even knew) how much the music they loved was rooted in African-American blues. Whatever traces of blues could be found in modern rock were slowly being smothered by increasingly processed and synthesized sounds of a dance music called disco.

Hubert, of course, did not escape unscathed. His indelible connection to his former boss was a blessing as well as an albatross. Yes, Wolf left him an incredible body of work, but he also left him a tremendous burden to keep it alive. And playing in a band that had the man's name in its title (yet another reminder that Hubert was Wolf's right-hand man) helped very little. "It was like we had to start all over," Hubert says. "We had to build a following all over again."

Hubert would get a lift, though, thanks to a budding nightclub entrepreneur in Austin, Texas. Seeing Bobby "Blue" Bland and James Brown perform at the National Guard Armory in Beaumont, Texas, had delivered Clifford Antone his calling in life. Then a clothing store owner in just his mid-twenties, Antone took a big chance and combined his love of the blues with his business acumen and opened Antone's nightclub on Austin's Sixth Street in July 1975.

The modus operandi of the club? Book the great Chicago bluesmen (and others)—preferably those still considered sidemen—and offer them good wages, warm crowds, and a gig for a week at a time. "We were just blues nuts and that was all there was to it," Antone says of his decision to open his nightclub. "We weren't like trying to be shrewd businessmen. We just loved blues, man. It is simple."

It was a far-fetched and risky idea to open a nightclub where country music reigned, plus Sixth Street was something of a commercial wasteland then. But once the 6,000-square-foot nightclub was erected, Antone's became the first sign that the area would be lifted out of obscurity and desolation.

Antone and his crew were going after the big fish: they tried to lure the mighty Howlin' Wolf to Austin in 1976. "Antone was supposed to book Wolf," Hubert says. "Wolf was the first five-thousand-dollar man, you know what I mean? He was supposed to come in for a week. But he got sick and, you know what happened." Antone adds, "We just couldn't get him down here. Later, after Wolf died, the guys from the Wolf Gang called me and said, 'Since you couldn't book Wolf, would you book the Wolf Gang?' All I wanted to know was if Hubert was in the band."

"We came in, Eddie Shaw & The Wolf Gang," Hubert recalls. "We listened to what Wolf said about 'Keep things going.' So, that is what we did. We played the place." Antone remembers, "That day [the Wolf Gang] got in, they were going to rehearse and they were just standing there. All I wanted to do was to meet Hubert. I said, 'Which one you-all is Hubert?' He had on these long socks and Bermuda shorts and they had all different colors on them. He raised his hand and said, 'I am.' I said, 'C'mon, man. Let's go.' He said, 'But we're rehearsing.' I said, 'That don't matter. Let's go.' He just got in my car and we left. We went to a barbecue my friend was having. We were best friends from the minute we met."

Just as this friendship was blossoming, the city of Austin was growing in leaps and bounds. Antone was part of a larger wave of activity that would place the city of Austin on the musical map. "I moved to Austin in 1968 and I am not exaggerating one bit: the cost of living was nothing," explains bassist Tommy Shannon, who played with Stevie Ray Vaughan as part of Double Trouble and with Johnny Winter in the early '70s. "You could play three nights a week and live comfortably in this town. It was just so cool here I couldn't even put it into words. There weren't as many clubs, but you could hear great music. Jimmie Vaughan, Stevie. The clubs were packed and it was all about good music. At the old Antone's, I played with Albert Collins, Albert King, Buddy Guy there. I played with so many there. Earl King, Koko Taylor. Clifford [Antone] brought in the blues club and there was some great music there."

In the late '70s Hubert and the Wolf Gang were a fixture of the Chicago scene, playing at such venues as the 1815 Club, Kingston Mines, and Buddy Mulligan's. The Wolf Gang was also on the road constantly, gigging in the upstate New York/New England corridor—places like Red Creek in Rochester, New York, and the Speakeasy Club in Cambridge, Massachusetts. In 1977 the Wolf Gang cut *Have Blues, Will Travel* for Simmons Records (produced by Little Mack Simmons). As always, Hubert added his own personal touch to the recording sessions, but he was falling deeper and deeper into a role that was no good for his career or his self-confidence: he was becoming Shaw's sideman, although he could have been much more than that. (In a sense, he was, though perhaps he had trouble admitting it to himself.)

"Eddie was the bandleader there and somehow the money didn't filter over to Hubert and Chico," explains friend and sometime guitar mate Curtis Obeda. "There is that famous shot on *Have Blues, Will Travel.* Hubert once pointed to it and said, 'Well, I'd like to point out that was Eddie with the camera and me under the bus.' I think that sums it up."

Hubert kept his mouth shut and joined the Wolf Gang in the studio again in 1978 to record for a series called *Living Chicago Blues* on

Bruce Iglauer's Alligator Records—a label established in 1971 for the sole purpose of recording Hound Dog Taylor and the Houserockers. "Eddie had rehearsed the band and the songs were real basic," remembers Iglauer. "We did a version of 'Sitting on Top of the World,' which everybody [in the band] knew. So it wasn't as though people were struggling in any way."

"Hubert is not a very predictable guitar player," Iglauer continues. "Hubert often seemed sort of a disorganized player. He'd reach for things, then decide not to do them, and then do something else. It seemed like there were a lot of things he was leaving out. It was definitely seat of the pants. I mean, with songs like 'Killing Floor,' there was already a very set way of approaching the recording. But in a lot of songs, it seemed that whatever happened to pop into his mind at the moment, he'd play."

The role of the bandleader often falls prey to a common misconception: most people think that the person out front is the leader. He takes care of paying the band, sets up the gig, makes sure every musician gets to the show on time, and so on. But with Wolf, and even with Muddy, this was not always the case. James Cotton was Muddy's bandleader for years, and Eddie Shaw became the bandleader for Wolf in the later years. But if Shaw was the bandleader in the sense that the musicians looked to him for scheduling, logistics, and payment, Hubert was the band's spiritual leader. Hubert might say, "You may know more about music, but I know more about Wolf and what Wolf wants."

For saxophonist Shaw, being the frontman was always a matter of survival. "...Wolf...taught me a lot about survival," Shaw told Dave Hoekstra of the *Chicago Sun-Times* in 1985. "Whether you're playing the back fields of Mississippi or a nice club in Chicago, you got to know what to do to compete and what to do to collect." Toward the end of Wolf's career, Shaw's sax would creep into the music, making the band sound more jazzy or even more rock 'n' roll. Either way, those original songs that had nary a horn were smattered and weighed down with the wind instrument's riffs. The top brass had taken over.

Others were critical of Shaw's seemingly overaggressive and callous behavior, thinking he had taken Wolf's words about survival a bit too literally. "At Wolf's funeral, Eddie was over there at the head of the casket and Hubert at the foot," says Jones. "He was over there telling people who wanted to view the body, 'Keep it movin'. Keep it movin'.' Like he some big shit."

The trouble with Shaw's Wolf Gang was that Wolf most likely didn't mean for one person to stand out in front while the others fell back. After all, it was the *Wolf* Gang. The band was meant to keep Wolf's legacy alive, and that was to be achieved as a team effort. Apparently, in this pack of wolves, some animals were more equal than others. What started out as camaraderie soon spoiled into mistrust and resentment. Regardless of how Hubert was treated, though, it can be argued that Hubert's guitar genius afforded him a certain amount of respect and creative space within the band that Shaw could never have.

After repeated attempts to interview Shaw via telephone I finally broke through the barriers, but he declined to speak with me. In an irritated manner he said, "I haven't talked to Hubert and I don't know *you*." Call it the "blues wall of silence": the unspoken rule that no bluesman shall speak badly about another bluesman—at least until he passes. Perhaps. Still, it is unsettling to think that Shaw believes he is the rightful heir to the Wolf throne. If anyone should have a right to the Wolf connection—especially in name—it should be Hubert.

Then again, Hubert was trying hard to break free of the stigma of being Wolf's guitar player. "After Wolf died," Hubert says, poking his finger into my chest, "they told me, 'Wolf dead? *You* dead.' It was like everyone went away, and no one wanted to hear about me or hire me. They saw us as being, you know, the same. I wasn't nothing without Wolf."

The mid- to late '70s were starting to have their way with Hubert: his marriage was crumbling; his former boss, friend, and mentor was gone; and his new boss would soon lose the very club that Wolf himself anointed as the place for the band to play. And when a day of reckoning came around, Hubert came up short.

In 1977, a large settlement was made to the Chester Burnett estate. Wolf and his wife, Lillie, had filed a suit against ARC Music and Chess Records in 1974 for unpaid royalties and for defrauding Wolf of copyrights and profits his music would make. The Wolf estate pocketed an undisclosed amount from the 1977 settlement and the suit went away. ARC still owns the publishing rights to the Wolf tunes, and MCA, which purchased the Chess/Argo/Checker/Cadet catalogs in 1985, announced it would pay royalties to artists (though it was under no legal obligation to do so).

Regardless of the merits of the case, Hubert never saw a penny of the settlement, though many people thought he should have, and still do. (In 1972, ARC and Led Zeppelin settled a copyright infringement involving Wolf's "Killing Floor" and Zep's "The Lemon Song." Hubert, naturally, did not see any money from this, either.) To see financial gain, Hubert would have had to file a separate lawsuit asserting that he was at least Wolf's co-author in some cases and that he should be rewarded royalties for writing credits. This has never happened.

As Marshall Chess notes, "I would love Howlin' Wolf, Willie Dixon, and Muddy Waters to sit in a room with Phil Chess and my father [Leonard Chess] and say these things like they owed the artists money. It wouldn't happen. I was young, I didn't know everything that happened back then. And Hubert sure as fuck doesn't know." When Hubert explains that he arranged a lot of Wolf's music (this coming from a man whose teeth are more easily extracted from his mouth than statements about his musical achievements), one has to wonder not about whether he made a writing contribution but about just how big that contribution was.

Hubert has let the whole sordid affair go. "They didn't owe me a penny," he relents. "But that's all right. I am living, you know? I am livin'. I think that is the best thing that ever happened to my ass, man. I thank God I'm still living."

Money posed a problem for Hubert, however. He and Evelyn were constantly fighting and the marriage was, for all intents and purposes, in name only. They were worlds apart. "My guitar comes first. Always did," Hubert admits. "That's it. It comes first. It's true, man. [My wives] knew what I was before we married. That is where I met 'em at, where I played. They knew what I was. Shit!"

Evelyn expected more from Hubert and demanded a certain lifestyle. "We were overseas sometimes, four or five times a year, and sometimes we were out for months," Hubert says. "Every time I come home, the house is new. I got a new house, every time I come home! I noticed that shit. I said, 'Oh, baby, look at this, you got this…' She said, 'I got to do this and I got to do that.' Goddammit! A brand-new carpet she tore up and she wanted more. She had new walls and wanted more. Every doggone thing. Everything new. Every year she did this, for four-teen fuckin' years, man. My money." Hubert thinks back to what Wolf told him about Evelyn: "Wolf gave me away, but he kept tellin' me, 'Please. The woman ain't no good. I'm tellin' you.' He said, 'You go and do what you want.' He has been right all of these years, I hoped he was wrong. I hoped he was wrong."

One explosive incident involving infidelity was the beginning of the end. "I come home one day," Hubert recalls, "and there's this young-ster… [Evelyn] wouldn't get the door, I was coming home from Europe, and I knock on the fuckin' door and I couldn't get in. I said, 'I am going to tear down the door if I have to.' I think, maybe I'll go through the win-dow and leave the door up. I said, 'Shit.' Then they see what I am doing and he's watching me, this youngster. [Evelyn] was crying. He opened the door and said, 'What are you looking for?' I said, 'I own this. Who are you?' He stuttered, 'She, she, she said she's alright.' I said, 'Lookithere, man.' I had my hand on Wolf's .38, man."

Some wondered why Hubert stayed with Evelyn at all. It wasn't like he didn't have other offers. His first "wife" (Bertha) from Arkansas had run into him one night as he was playing in Chicago. She was wonder-ing what he was up to. "Evelyn know her," Hubert says. "She came where I was playing at with Wolf and she tried to get back together with me and everything. She was matured. I told her that I was with some-body else."

Hubert turned away many women. Some of his former bandmates have no explanation for why he wouldn't leave Evelyn, except to say that it was witchcraft. "He acted like she had him fixed like a voodoo doll," says Detroit Junior. "She had him under a spell. There's more to the story. A whole lot of things happened before I joined Wolf. When I first joined the band, Wolf told me, 'Don't loan Hubert no money because his wife don't allow him to have none.' Wolf's wife would talk with Evelyn. Eve-lyn would tell Wolf's wife what she was doing and Wolf's wife would tell Wolf. Then Wolf would try to tell Hubert about what was goin' on."

"I can't say that [Evelyn] was all to blame that I could see. A lot of it was Hubert, too," Yancy Jones admits. "I was young and wild myself, so I know. She would get on Hubert about drinking, okay? That was the biggest problem. I don't think their marriage was bad. [Evelyn] had plenty of whiskey at home. She didn't mind him drinking at home, but she didn't want him drinking and driving. I guess she was looking out for him and I guess he didn't want to hear that. She'd also fuss with him about money.

"Hubert's a free-hearted person," Jones continues. "He would come from somewhere, out of town, and he would say, 'Hey, partner…' and he'd hand someone some money. 'What is this for, Hubert?' 'Just take it,' he'd say. He would just give it away, and she fussed about that. 'You start bringing the money home, Hubert,' she said. But Hubert didn't change. That was his way. He don't think about hisself."

Jones remembers that Hubert's generous nature was sometimes a fault, a hindrance to his own career. Jones was playing a show and invited Hubert to play, but Hubert declined. "Hubert say, 'Oh, partner, I can't go. Oh, partner, I can't go,'" Jones recalls, laughing. "I ask, 'Why not?' He won't come out and tell you what happened. 'What's wrong with you?' Then he'd tell you that he had to pawn his amplifier because he gave all his money away."

In one sense, the amalgam of Hubert's gentlemanly demeanor, humility, kindness, and graciousness was a great example of leadership to any number of up-and-comers. They respected and loved Hubert because of his heart and soul. "I remember we were playing one night and it was a real snowy night," Cooper says. "Well, as it turned out, Hubert made only a small amount of money. I felt strange handing him just a small amount, but I handed him the money anyway. He just bowed his head and said, 'Thank you.' He looked right at me when he said it. The money didn't mean anything to him."

"I was thrilled to meet Hubert, but completely surprised and moved that he immediately treated me like an old, special friend," notes Muddy Waters guitarist Bob Margolin, who first met Hubert in the late '70s. "When you hear Hubert say, 'I know *that's* right, partner!' and see that big smile, you'll be charmed, and dedicated to him for life."

In March 1978 Hubert and the Wolf Gang toured through Canada and one of the stops was at the El Macombo in Toronto, Ontario. Colin Linden, who had met Wolf when he was just 11 years old, was on hand to see Hubert. "He played a week at the El Macombo, downstairs, with the Wolf Gang, and they were staying at the Westminster Hotel. I remember going over to the Westminster Hotel and hanging out with Hubert one afternoon and he showing me, sitting down with me: 'This is how you play 'I Asked for Water.' This is how you play 'Smokestack Lightnin'.' Some of the songs, especially like the one-chord Wolf mantra songs, that kind of hypnotic thing that Wolf did so amazingly and uniquely...some of the signature licks that Hubert or Wolf came up with were similar. But it was a real testament to Wolf and Hubert's sense of composition. Hubert said, 'You don't play 'I Asked for Water' when you are doing 'Smokestack Lightnin'.' It is a real important thing. It instilled in me an idea that spoke of a certain depth. Not thinking of blues as generic. And Hubert took the time to show me these things."

No dosage of Hubert's charm could reverse his bandleader's bad luck, however. Eddie Shaw's 1815 Club started to go south. Call it bad business, call it a twist of fate, but Shaw let the club slip away from him. "They come out and locked the place up," Hubert recalls. "They ripped the gas meter and then next they turned the lights off and every goddarn thing. I said, 'Shit. Eddie got no club now.'"

The curtain was starting to close on Hubert's involvement with the Wolf Gang as well. He began playing with Cotton again, this time in James Cotton's Blues Band. A firebrand group that recorded for Buddah Records, they were perhaps the most explosive blues band of the 1970s. Matt "Guitar" Murphy (who'd go on to appear in the 1980 movie *The Blues Brothers* with comedians turned semi-pro musicians John Belushi and Dan Aykroyd) had just left the band, presenting Hubert with a great opportunity.

Ironically, Hubert had replaced Murphy (who was born in 1929 in Sunflower, Mississippi, and reportedly was a distant cousin of Hubert's) in Wolf's band nearly 25 years before. At that time, Hubert was a bit more malleable. But since then, he had spent years topping himself as Wolf's guitarist, being nothing but "Hubert." Now he had to fill in for Murphy—a different player with a different sensibility. Murphy's licks always had a self-propelled, driving feel. While Hubert had certainly proven he could play with the same brand of aggressiveness, raw power was not the only facet of his playing. Hubert was intentionally multi-dimensional, and taking a gig that tapped him to perform largely in one vein would be, in essence, a waste of his talent.

"I remember Cotton telling me that he had just hired Hubert," says Iglauer, who saw the band perform. "Cotton's band at that time was a rock-boogie band and Hubert's more spare guitar playing was not really what they needed. They needed someone who was driving a bass pattern and filling in full chords in between. That was more [Murphy's] style." It's true that despite Hubert's close friendship with Cotton, the musical bond just wasn't there. Hubert was—and still is—the musical embodiment of Muhammad Ali's mantra, "Float like a butterfly and sting like a bee." Cotton would have been better served by the musical equivalent of Mike Tyson's animalistic death charge.

Hubert was running out of options. His involvement with the Wolf Gang was all but over, and one incident in a Maine nightclub punctuated his entire experience with that band. "Eddie and me—we didn't see eye to eye," Hubert says. "We went to this place in Maine and they got this gambling room. [Eddie] went back there…we were not making but $35 at that time. Thirty-five dollars. Our asking price come down from $100, from when we were with Wolf. That was it for me. I said, 'Look, man. I'm cutting from you guys.' That was the last straw. 'You muthafuckers can go back to Chicago.' Eddie said, 'Hubert, oh, I figured you were going to do that. But will you learn my son? Just stay on a little while and learn him how to play those songs?' I said, 'Sure I will.' I stayed on and made sure Vaan knew the songs. He turned out to be a bad little guitar player. That's what happened. That was the best thing that happened to me in my life, since Wolf passed."

Vaan Shaw, having already experienced the Wolf (he'd sit and watch his dad with Hubert and Wolf on the bandstand), was primed for taking over for Hubert. "Back in the Howlin' Wolf days, [Vaan] would come in and play a little rhythm guitar behind Hubert," Shaw said in a 1985 *Chicago Sun-Times* interview. "He was about 13 at the time and Hubert showed him a lot of things. He taught him how to go into changes and how to play in unison."

The Wolf Gang was now a thing of the past. Perhaps the Mighty Wolf would be displeased, but there would be a lot of things he'd be unhappy with, had he lived. Besides, no one could possibly live up to the name Wolf, even the band members who played with him. It was too big a monster—the enormity of it. Hubert could no longer play a part.

Though guitar aces Magic Slim (Morris Holt) and Frank "Son" Seals offered Chicago blues new hope, the Windy City became a cold place in the late 1970s. Disco was big, and interest in traditional and Chicago blues waned. The rougher things got, the more weary and wayward Hubert seemed to become. Then it came to him: Austin. Hubert knew he could always go to Austin. In Austin, he had friends. Antone's club offered structure, safety, great music, and the chance to play unfettered and without prejudice. And musicians like Sunnyland Slim, Big Walter, and Jimmy Rogers—who were also hitting rough patches in Chicago—could always get a gig at Antone's.

Hubert and Stevie Ray Vaughan perform at Antone's ninth anniversary party, July 1984.

"After that first time Hubert played, the Wolf Gang never came again," Antone says. "But Hubert would just come on his own. He would do shows with Sunnyland and Big Walter and Eddie Taylor, Jimmy Rogers. That is how I started doing it: I'd just bring all those guys and let them play together." Hubert elaborates: "I stayed down there two fucking years, man. I had so much mail from Chicago, every club in the world say, 'Name your price.' Antone said, 'Fuck 'em. Wait a minute, I'll get [the price] up.' Every time they would give him a price, he'd jack that muthafucker up higher. That man kept jacking up the price on those muthafuckers, until it was $1,000 a night."

While Antone was working on shaping Hubert's career and culti-vating his prospects, the blues legend was exposed to Austin's crop of up-and-coming talents. "He got to meet all the young musicians in Austin: Kim [Wilson], Stevie [Vaughan], Angela [Strehli], Jimmie [Vaughan], and everybody," Antone says. "They all got to be friends. At that time I lived with Angela Strehli. Hubert lived with me and Angela in the 1970s. Sure, he would go off and do his thing with different peo-ple, but he was here a whole lot of that time."

"Just like their slogan says: 'Home of the blues,' Home of the fuckin' blues," Hubert declares. "They had every sonofagun down there. I remember picking Fats Domino up at the airport, when he retired. When he was supposedly retired. Piano, rings and jewelry, and nobody but him—his band was already there. He played at Antone's for weeks. B.B., Albert, Little Milton. Everybody was down there. They were somebody. John Lee Hooker, Muddy. He had these plaques up from everybody."

According to Antone, Hubert's time away from the Austin scene had hurt him immensely. Lesson No. 1 about Hubert: he lives a Zen-like, existential existence. When the Austin crowd wanted to help him, he'd willingly and willfully fall into Antone's eager arms, where he'd get the best of care. Lesson No. 2 about Hubert: when in Chicago, Hubert willingly gave himself to the vices of city life. "He'd come here, off the plane, and he would be in bad shape," explains Antone. "He couldn't hardly play guitar. We'd clean him up, make sure he'd eat at least twice a day. Around me he couldn't smoke or drink as much. I was on him all the time."

Antone, who was wild in his younger days (but had long since sworn off cigarettes and alcohol), provided much more for musicians than a stage on which to play. He made sure that Hubert got eyeglasses when he needed them, made sure Hubert had a roof over his head, and made sure he was eating right, all while monitoring his alcohol and nicotine intake. "Obviously Hubert was lost without the Wolf," says Fabulous Thunderbirds singer/harp man Kim Wilson. "Antone took care of him. Fed him. Made sure he was healthy. He did that with all of those guys. And Jimmy Reed and Eddie Taylor—he made sure that they went to the doctor as soon as they got there. When they got sick they would be gone from Austin. A lot of times they would be gone and die away from Austin, when they didn't have to. Hubert lived down [in Austin] a long time. They put him on a pedestal and made him feel special. That was really good for Hubert and he found himself. He started playing more than when they first came down there. When you are offering the guys who come in, like Hubert, Eddie Taylor, Luther Tucker, Jimmy Reed, and you are setting them up in apartments, then you are a caring guy. That is someone who really cares about these blues legends."

"That dude [Antone] helped a lot," Hubert agrees. "He still do. Shit, man."

With a renewed spirit, a new diet, and even a new wardrobe, Hubert became a fixture on the Austin scene. "Hubert wouldn't be playing there every day, he might be just hanging out," Wilson remembers. "Some of the stuff that would come out of his mouth was even better than his playing. He'd say stuff like, 'You *scowbugger.'* I don't know what it means and I can't even repeat some of the shit he said because it is impossible. You never knew what was going to come out of his ass." (skow-bugga \skow`-bug`ga\ *noun*\ circa 1940: an affectionate yet derogatory term to describe anyone who has gotten under the skin of another human being)

"He was a funny guy who always had a story," Shannon says. "He was telling us how one time he knocked himself in the head and was out for 30 minutes. We don't know how he did it, and I don't think he did either. That was just Hubert." Antone declares, "We loved Hubert. We looked at him as a national treasure. You got to give those guys credit, they created music that became rock 'n' roll and the psychedelic thing and they made the Eric Claptons and the Rolling Stoneses. Not that those guys weren't good, but you got to give the blues guys credit. That's the thing we tried to do: give them credit."

As the popularity of the club skyrocketed, more high-profile artists like Muddy Waters, John Lee Hooker, and Buddy Guy started coming down for days at a time. All of these legends soon made Antone's a true home of the blues. Some of the venue's bills were so crammed with great blues artists that the club's owner thinks it rivaled anything in Chicago at the time. "I would imagine that between 1975 and 1985, we had more important blues than any club in Chicago," Antone remarks. "I don't think anyone, even in Chicago, had as many important blues shows as we did. I don't think they could match up. You know, in 1975 there weren't many clubs in this country doing blues. There were a few. Nobody was doing it for five days in row. I'd bring Willie Dixon for five nights. Lafayette Leake and Carey Bell and Clifton James. Heavy stuff—five nights. Hubert would wind up playing with almost everybody here. He'd play with Koko Taylor in the old days, when she really had that old-fashioned blues band. Hubert played with everyone here. They all knew where they could find him."

In July 1979 Hubert joined pianist Willie Mabon and guitarist Eddie Taylor for a Chicago blues session that resulted in the aptly titled album *Chicago Blues Session!* Unlike a lot of other records on which Hubert is relegated to "sideman" status, Hubert breeds excitement here, pressed by Eddie Taylor—a close friend and former Jimmy Reed guitar ace who was also making trips down to Austin for gigs. (Hubert recorded with Taylor and Reed in 1964 for the Vivid label.) "Wolf was like a father to me," Hubert says. "We were father and son. Eddie Taylor was by Jimmy Reed the same way—they were very close. Same way, Otis Spann and Muddy." Taylor and Hubert hooking up made perfect sense.

Taylor was born in Benoit, Mississippi, in 1932 and as a youngster would hang outside the local Mississippi juke joints and listen to Charlie Patton and Robert Johnson. Aside from reportedly teaching Reed how to play and being his boyhood friend, Taylor (who had moved to

Chicago in 1949—six years after Reed) played guitar on many Reed classics, such as "Ain't That Lovin' You Baby," "Bright Lights, Big City," and "Big Boss Man" for Chess Records competitor Vee-Jay Records. "A bulk of credit for Reed's success must go to guitarist Eddie Taylor, his near-constant companion and creator of the rhythms that fueled Reed's blues," wrote Robert Santelli in *The Big Book of Blues.*

What do super-sidemen do when they have played with the likes of John Lee Hooker, Muddy Waters, Howlin' Wolf, and Elmore James? They team up and record, that's what. *Chicago Blues Session!* was the perfect barometer for Taylor and Hubert. Taylor could make the guitar whine and cry like Hubert could; they had similar sensibilities on the instrument.

Pianist Mabon, born in Hollywood, Tennessee, in 1925, had recorded for the Chess label Aristocrat from 1950 through the middle of the decade and was well known for his R&B hits "I Don't Know" and "I'm Mad" (both of which were re-recorded on *Chicago Blues Session!*). Hubert remembers one story about Mabon storming into the Chess recording studios, demanding money. "Willie Mabon," Hubert starts, then pauses before he continues. "He shot at Chess, Leonard, and missed him. I don't think he intended to kill 'im, but he was having a hard time—he thought he was owed some money, understand? They come up with some money for him, you know what I am saying? I saw all this shit, man."

But this was a new day and Mabon wasn't worried about being cheated, as they would be recording for German label L+R (Lippmann and Rau) Records. Europe had always had open arms for bluesmen, and *Chicago Blues Session!* delivers. Hubert truly speaks through his guitar and shouts for attention. There is great excitement here with Hubert in the left channel, Taylor in the right. And Mabon is in top form: his piano work weeps, sways, and rocks. Covers of "The Red Rooster" (titled "Little Red Rooster" here) and "Louise" are respectable and have a texture that is solely Mabon, not Mabon trying to be Wolf. (His voice on "Louise" is more Louis Armstrong than Chester Burnett.) While Hubert's solo on "Louise" isn't as frenzied as the original 1964 version (it's more of a shadowy, smoky mirror image), its bell- and horn-like tones, plus broken-meter phrasings topped with hammered notes and iced by riveting signature slides up the neck, are the peaks and valleys that define the rugged and ragged contours of the song.

In "It's a Shame," Hubert nearly crunches out the speaker when he takes the foreground. Even after he finishes his frontal assault, his vibrato can still be heard cryin' and creating a plume of sonic explosions in the distance. On "Moanin' Blues" (a tribute to Jimmy Reed, who died nearly three years earlier) and "Monday Woman" the two guitarists work in tandem. In fact, the playing is so locked in that the groove gives the illusion of one continuous, impossible guitar line. It is simply a relentless combination of alternating sugary and biting tones. Whatever holes Taylor's clean and clicking tones provide, Hubert plugs with sustained (and outside) notes that sound like tiny sirens. In effect, this record may be the closest Hubert has come, to date, to Wolf's heyday of the 1950s and 1960s. Just as the Wolf band would have all of its components firing up all the engines, so, too, this rockin' set is greater than the sum of its parts.

With *Chicago Blues Session!* completed, Hubert appeared on guitarist/singer-songwriter Iverson Minter's (Louisiana Red or "Red," as he likes to be called) *Reality Blues,* played on Wolf alumnus and Chicago piano great Sunnyland Slim's *Decoration Day,* and partnered with harp man Carey Bell for *Gamblin' Woman!* All three albums were released by Germany's L+R Records in 1980.

Red's *Reality Blues,* recorded in late January 1980 in Chicago and containing such powerful songs as "Jailhouse Blues," "You Can't Mistreat a Brother," and the title track, showcases stalwart bluesmen at the top of their games: Sunnyland, Bell, drummer Odie Payne, and the in-demand bassist Bob Stroger (who had provided the bottom end for such luminaries as Sunnyland, Otis Rush, and Jimmy Rogers). The music is at times animal-raw, at others quite sublime. On the whole, it feels spontaneous. "We didn't have to have no rehearsal for that record," recalls Red. "That is what I like about Chicago bands—they don't need or like to be over-prepared. We felt one another's feelings. We just went in there and did the work."

Perhaps more memorable than the music is the stunning LP cover that depicts the American flag with three holes cut into it. In two of these cutouts we see eyes peeking through and a mouth emerging from the gaping hole in the center. It's a strong, thought-provoking visual: the flag intentionally obscures an African-American male's facial features. It speaks volumes about what it meant to be black *and* American. (Red's personal experience with racism went farther than his fellow musicians' experiences: his father was killed by the Ku Klux Klan in 1941.) Frankly, this cover is the type of controversial political statement Hubert had steered clear of throughout his career, and Red remembers that *Reality Blues* sold better in Europe. "[That cover] hurt me in a way in the States, but it was really pretty big over here," explains Red, who has lived in Hannover, Germany, since the early '80s because, as he puts it, "I couldn't get no work in my own country."

Gamblin' Woman! is a down-home, mostly acoustic blues record that contains no overdubs and limited mics. The title track may well have been a referendum on Hubert's marriage to Evelyn. Over a slow acoustic groove plus poignant harp playing by Bell, Hubert sings, "She gamble in the morning, she gamble at night…. She threw all her money away, I don't know what she did with the rest. This little ole girl, she's a solid mess…. All day loooong she like to fight. I can't talk to her right….")

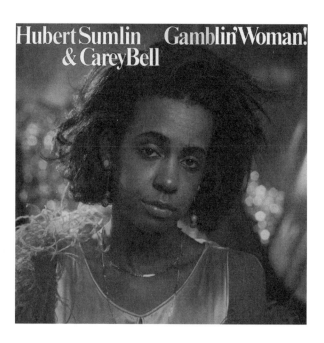

Hubert had built a strong, friendly relationship with Sunnyland Slim, and tracks that appear on Sunnyland's *Decoration Day* are a smoky mixture of Mississippi field hollers, deep and dark electric Chicago blues, ragtime/boogie-woogie/swing, and New Orleans jazz. With all due respect to second guitarist Jeff Swan, Hubert's ears and patience—his superior ability, wisdom, and experience that guide him to play the right notes—show a true master at work here.

In the spring of 1980 Hubert hit the road yet again (with Red, Taylor, Sunnyland, Bell, Stroger, Payne, and Mabon)—this time on a European tour during which he cut the seminal *American Folk Blues Festival '80,* again for L+R Records of Germany. (Hubert would tour Europe again with Red, Bell, Sunnyland, and others in 1981 as part of the American Folk Blues Festival.)

"I remember Hubert bought an expensive watch for Sunnyland when we was in Switzerland, in Geneva, on tour," notes Stroger. "We walked half the night to find Sunnyland that birthday present. We walked trying to find a watch and then we was walking around looking into the windows. When the stores opened up, he knew which watch he wanted for Sunnyland. I think that watch cost him seven hundred to eight hundred dollars. It always stuck with me, about how thoughtful he was of people, you know? Hubert is always thinking of other people. Every since I known him, that is the way he is. Same thing if he is on the bandstand. If another guitar player is on the bandstand with him, he'll think about him and he'll give the other guitar player all solos to make him happy."

But regardless of his musical ability and congeniality, Hubert's name was just a whisper in the wind as he had nearly faded off the radar in the US. Despite releasing three solo efforts (*Blues Anytime!*, *Hubert Sumlin and Friends: Kings of Chicago Blues, Vol. 2,* and *My Guitar and Me* or *Groove*), albeit on a European label, he had yet to make real inroads into higher-paying gigs. It was hard to break out of a cycle of anonymity. Some listeners point to his playing style as the reason he did not draw more attention. "Hubert may not have all that power like Buddy Guy—the blues that is more 'in your face'—but Hubert had and has that genius," explains Steve Arvey, a bassist who backed Hubert and also booked him. "It was hard to show what Hubert's guitar sound was.

It was hard to nail it down and tell people, 'This is what it is.' Guys that appreciated that style, like the Stevie Ray Vaughans and such, helped to raise his profile, but it was still hard. Hubert was not on Alligator. He was not on Delmark. There was no press package. No materials. Nothing for Hubert."

And locally, Hubert was not breaking through to every Chicago scene. Old story: "The North Side clubs in Chicago didn't care that much about Hubert at that time," explains Obeda, who moved to Chicago in the early '80s and began playing guitar with Hubert in places like Redmond's Lounge. "But the West Side—the West Side—Hubert still had friends there." At times, even Wolf alumni like Shaw would join in. Despite what had happened in the Wolf Gang, Eddie was always welcome. "It wasn't like Hubert and Chico hated his guts," Obeda says. "If somebody had asked about Eddie, Hubert and Chico would kind of look at each other and say, 'Oh, he has his own band now,' to deflect criticism. There wasn't any great animosity or anything, but they would simply say, 'We've moved on.'"

Hubert might have been free of the Wolf Gang and its many trappings (including being saddled with a band that bore the name of his former boss), but he was lost in a kind of Wolf wilderness—a forest of unforeseen dangers. Obeda remembers the crowds would constantly request nothing but Wolf tunes, over and over again. "We'd play 'Louise' for the church ladies who would come in. They'd request it all the time. There would be times that we would have to play it—literally—eight times a set," he laughs. And the pay wasn't the greatest, either. Obeda recalls payment of somewhere around $100 for a single night for the quartet of Chism, Hubert, himself, and Arvey. Still, Hubert was very loyal to the people he was playing with at the time. "Hubert would get calls from Eric Clapton to play Europe, but he would never go," Obeda notes. "I think if he went, he felt it was like letting us down."

Obeda also offers a window into Hubert's personality: "My dad and mother live in a suburb of St. Paul, Minnesota, called Roseville and we were staying there, we were practicing for a big East Coast tour—a tour that never happened, by the way. That's another story. Anyway, Hubert was washing his socks in the bathtub even though we had a washer and dryer. Somehow, I don't know how it happened, but maybe it was lint from the socks, but the bathtub stopped up. This was all at 6:00 a.m. People forget that Hubert is a country boy—he gets up early. This was before any of us were up. He walked down to the drugstore that was a quarter-mile away, got a whole can of Drāno and poured the entire thing down there, which you are not supposed to do. It gets hot and it solidifies. It was like cement. My dad actually had to pull the trap apart.

"If you want to hear a man apologize for six hours," Obeda continues, "Hubert is the king of that. I'll tell ya, he was flogging himself. Even my dad was saying, 'It is not a big deal.' It took me 45 minutes to get the pipe off and go to the hardware store to get a U-shaped pipe and we screwed it back on. Three hours later, we were back on. To this day, he sees my parents and puts his hand over his face. He still apologizes for that."

The blues boom, which would soon be called the blues revival, was just getting into full swing in Austin. As guitarist Jimmie Vaughan and his band the Fabulous Thunderbirds were starting to get national recognition, his younger brother, Stevie Ray Vaughan (formerly of the Nightcrawlers and the Cobras), was making his mark on the Texas town. Stevie Ray and Hubert would spend hours playing together, onstage and off. "Hubert is probably the heaviest, most original guitar player I've ever heard in my life. And that's the truth," Stevie Ray said in the Hubert Sumlin documentary *Living the Blues*. "…I ain't ever seen a grown man jump up and down, have so much fun, when he plays with his guitar. I love Hubert to death."

"Stevie's number one mentor was Albert King and that is where he got it [his sound]," claims Antone. "Outside of that, I'd say Hubert and Albert Collins were equal for second place. Hubert was right up there and so, of course, [Stevie Ray] was just ecstatic, as we all were, to meet Hubert. He got chances to play with Hubert. There was some real jamming happening with Hubert. Stevie gave him a suit and gave him a Rickenbacker guitar. They would play together every chance they got. We'd play to three-something in the morning, even though we'd have to quit selling liquor at two o'clock. Many nights, at the end of the evening, it would be just Stevie and Hubert sitting on chairs at the edge of the stage with their electric guitars and they would be playing something that wasn't even really a song. They'd just be sitting and playing together. No band. Stevie was just amazed with what Hubert could do. Stevie, like the rest of us, had known about him and marveled at those Howlin' Wolf songs. They spent a lot of time playing together."

"You wouldn't believe this, but Hubert is my dad," laughs Shannon, who recently reunited with Hubert at a Jimi Hendrix tribute concert in Seattle. "I love Hubert. Hubert would sit in with us, so we got to know him real well. Clifford Antone would book Hubert and when we'd go on the road, not always, but sometimes, we'd call him up to sit in with us. Stevie always said that he loved Hubert's playing with Wolf. Stevie wanted some attention drawn to Hubert and eventually got him playing more and more. Hubert just became happy again.

"I don't think Hubert is aware at all of the impact he has had on people," Shannon continues. "That is the way he grew up playing with Wolf. He had a good heart, and Stevie, he loved Hubert so much. His eyes filled with tears. It was a beautiful thing to see. Those are the cool things to see in the music business that people don't usually hear about. They only hear the surface stuff, but there is so much more."

Spearheaded by Vaughan, a new brand of blues was being molded, soon to be unleashed on the public. Instead of being based on the African-American work and gospel songs of the Delta that were the roots of electric blues, this fresh, stylized Texas blues (some might say blues-rock) was based on the great players of the past. The movement was led by whites—and politically correct or not, some critics simply think that whites can't truly capture the blues. "White people are like the fool who goes to the opera to listen to the symphony," says Delmark founder Bob Koester. "Blues is a folk music and it has become a performance music. The environment that produced blues has changed."

Even so, no one can deny that the 1980s were a time of renewal and maximum exposure for the blues, just as the 1960s had been. This was due, in large part, to white kids who dug the contemporary sounds of Bonnie Raitt, Stevie Ray Vaughan, and Robert Cray—who all fused rock, country, and R&B with the blues.

The 1980s were teeming with the blues: the Chicago Blues Festival came to life (as well as many other blues events across the country); Buddy Guy opened his now world-famous club, Legends; John Lee Hooker hit the comeback trail with his Grammy-winning *The Healer* (thanks, in part, to material and guest appearances by Raitt, Cray, George Thorogood, and Carlos Santana); B.B. King performed with rockers U2 on the band's *Rattle and Hum* (just a few years before opening his own club on Beale Street in Memphis); ZZ Hill released *Down Home* (destined to become a focal point of the blues boom); Iglauer's Alligator Records—following the success of Albert Collins's 1978 *Ice Pickin'*, among others—continued making waves with records by Clifton Chenier, Son Seals, Johnny Winter, and the team of Cray, Collins, and Johnny Copeland (*Showdown!*); and Bo Diddley appeared in a Nike commercial with then major-league(s) star athlete Bo Jackson.

Blues in the 1980s also meant big bucks. MCA bought Chess's back catalog (including the records released by subsidiaries Checker, Argo, and Cadet), paying more than $1 million to reissue material by Diddley, Chuck Berry, Howlin' Wolf, Muddy Waters, Sonny Boy Williamson, and Elmore James, among others. In a controversial move, Willie Dixon sued Led Zeppelin over Zep's "Whole Lotta Love"—some 16 years after the fact—for failure, Dixon believed, to credit him or pay him royalties for his 1962 song "You Need Love" (recorded by Muddy Waters).

Although there was money to be made in the 1980s blues world, Hubert was not a card-carrying member of the premium, mega-moola blues artist club. "At the time I met Hubert he was going through a nasty divorce," notes Obeda. "Hubert didn't have a band when we first met. In fact, Hubert didn't even have a guitar or amp when we first met. I'd bring my backup amp from my house. Hubert just left [Evelyn] everything. It was done on purpose—it was done with his full knowledge. Perhaps that was the best thing he could have done. He left everything behind—his guitars, everything." Hubert remembers it a bit differently: "The lady judge threw the book at me. Black, too, man. Threw the book at me. She said, 'I don't give a damn who you is. You don't deserve her.' She was saying not only that but 'I'm gonna show you that this is how you treat us.'"

According to those close to Hubert, the breakup was inevitable. "[Evelyn] wanted the glorified life," explains niece Charlene. "Wolf had gotten the glory and she was upset by that because that is what she always wanted. She really wanted more than what Uncle Hubert could give. That may have been what shot down the relationship." Sister Maggie adds, "She'd say Hubert 'wasn't nothin'.' Or 'Your playing is terrible.' She'd talk down to him."

Never one to be without a woman long, Hubert would have Sunnyland Slim to thank for introducing a new love—as well as some measure of stability—into his life. Sunnyland, who had played with Wolf in the 1930s, possessed a frame that rivaled Wolf's (standing at six-foot-five and weighing in at 200-plus pounds). He'd loom large in the 1980s and beyond for Hubert and his personal life. Helping those close to him (and some not so close) was a Sunnyland trademark. After all, Sunnyland has remarked, it was he who "got Muddy Waters off that truck"— referring to the delivery truck Waters used to drive in his early Chicago days—to accompany him on a recording session for Chess's Aristocrat Records in 1947, a session that led to Muddy's big break at Chess.

"Sunnyland loved helping people," says Stroger. "I think he could have been a lot bigger star if he wanted to, but that wasn't his thing. His thing was helping people. Sunny was also a hustler, and there wasn't enough money in music for Sunny, but his real thing was just doing for people because he loved to."

Hubert would play shows in Chicago and other cities with Sunnyland and his band, which included bassist Stroger, guitarist Freund, drummer Robert Covington, and saxophonist Sam Burckhardt. The band was tight—Sunnyland wouldn't have it any other way. "Sunnyland kind of kept us as a family," says Stroger. "He took us all under his wing and made men of us." Burckhardt, originally from Switzerland, had met Sunnyland in the mid-'70s and often played with Hubert. Above all, Burckhardt remembers Hubert's unpredictability. "Hubert might play songs that have more of a form and then other times he'll just sing," he notes. "One time, I was playing a gig with Hubert, Louis Myers, and Dave Myers. Bonnie Raitt was in the audience that night and Hubert was so inspired. He was playing great. By the time I catch on to where he was going, he is miles ahead. Hubert looks at me, 'Oh, baby, don't think anything of it. I am just too stupid to remember what I played.' It was so Hubert. He sees it from the other side because he can never play the same thing twice. He comes up with new stuff all the time. Hubert plays something no one has ever played before, even himself.'"

Sunnyland was living at 6714 South Halsted in Chicago and his band would show up regularly at his house, where his cousin, Willie Bea Reed, received visitors. A deeply religious woman, Bea was taking care of her ailing father and mother, Shelby and Rebecca Humble, on the third floor of Sunnyland's apartment house.

"Sunnyland owned this three-story brick building on Halsted that he bought," Hubert recalls. "I was with him—I was staying with him. We had this bottom floor where he had his Airway records. So, one day, all of a sudden, Willie Bea, his cousin, lives upstairs. She wasn't paying no rent. So, I get this bottom floor, painted it and decorated it, it was a basement studio. I get the whole goddamn thing done. But Sunnyland got tired of me staying at his goddamn muthafuckin' house—but here I am decorating the goddamn muthafuckin' place, you understand? Sunnyland said, 'But Hubert, my cousin likes you.' And she's lookin' good. I said, 'Oh, shit. Maybe he's right.' I went to church a couple of times to find out who she is."

Like many black Southern women (Bea was born in Lamberts, Mississippi, in 1917), Bea had grown up a churchgoing, God-fearing woman. She was a regular at Chicago's Cathedral of Love Missionary Baptist Church, which her deacon father had founded decades before. "She was very religious," Hubert says. "The church made millions of dollars. Her father, Willie Bea's father, owned the church. He owned every fuckin' thing." Hubert would often walk on eggshells around the deacon—being, after all, a bluesman.

"Bea was quiet, but there was a strength in that quietness," says Andy Cornett, band member of Henry Gray & The Cats and Gray's manager. "She was very, very religious and spiritual. She had a strong connection to Christianity. She was easygoing and a sweet, genuine person."

Sunnyland had a regular gig at B.L.U.E.S. on Halsted, where Hubert would sit in once in a while when he was in town, and Bea would come to see the band. "Bea was the sweetest person," remembers

Freund. "Bea would come down to see Sunnyland and we'd all be sitting around a table talking." "I'd see her at shows," Hubert says. "I knew who she was and, you know, we started talking."

But it would be several years before Hubert actually began to settle down with Bea. He was on the road constantly. He also had regular gigs in Chicago and in particular at the Delta Fish Market where he played with Eddie Taylor and occasionally with James Yancy Jones. "You had these two guitar greats on the same stage," says Arvey. "That was how it was in the 1980s—the Delta Fish Market, there were so many great guys around."

In May 1983, Hubert attended Muddy's funeral in Chicago. The third great Chicago blues giant had now joined the Mighty Wolf and Little Walter (as well as key bluesman Theodore Roosevelt "Hound Dog" Taylor). Hubert watched Buddy Guy and his old friend and Muddy cohort James Cotton jam at Guy's Checkerboard Lounge that evening after the funeral. It was a moving experience for many, and Hubert, for one, had to move on. "Muddy didn't have nothing—no kind of funeral—compared to Wolf," Hubert says flatly.

Howlin' Wolf and Muddy Waters were gone, but Hubert was very much alive—and he had plenty to live for. He was bouncing around from city to city. Antone was jetting Hubert back and forth between Chicago, Austin, and the world.

"We went all over and we flew out to San Francisco to see Luther Tucker, to see where he lived," explains Antone. "They had those big jets, with first class that had three different sections of seats: one on the left, one in the middle, and one on the right. We got on there and we fly first class and we would take this little tape player and fit it between us, between the seats, and play Howlin' Wolf on the jet. All the people would be looking at us. We wouldn't be playing it loud, but just enough so we could hear it. One time we had a limo waiting for us, and the limousine driver called the plane. The stewardess told us that the limo was going to be there. Well, it was in Hubert's name. So, all these people are looking funny at us because we're playing Howlin' Wolf. The stewardess was walking up and down the aisles—they were long aisles in those days—and she said, 'Paging Mr. Sumlin. Paging Mr. Sumlin.' She said, 'Mr. Sumlin, your limo wants you to know that it has arrived and is waiting for you.' All these people start looking at him like, 'Who is this guy?' It was so funny and so cool. They had been giving us all these dirty looks. I always do that to him: 'Paging Mr. Sumlin. Paging Mr. Sumlin.' It cracks him up," Antone smiles.

The laughter would end (at least for a while) in the summer of 1985 when Antone pled guilty to conspiracy to possess marijuana with intent to distribute and was ordered to serve a sentence in Big Spring prison. (Antone's sister, Susan, handled the club's business operations in his absence.) Though prosecutors charged that Antone was part of a small drug ring (law enforcement had reportedly been watching his moves for years), Antone's club has never come under the microscope. It is perhaps, even today, his one oasis.

"Let me tell you something: in the early days the money export of Austin was marijuana, okay?" explains Wilson. "It was grown there by the ton. Everybody came out on the weeknights because no one worked. The owner of the club—what could he do about that? And if you want to call marijuana growers criminal elements, fine. But I don't see it, other than that the drug itself is still illegal. But as far as being the patriarch of the money laundering going on in Austin," Wilson laughs, "that is the most ridiculous thing in the world! We were just there having a good time, you kidding me? It was the most family-oriented club in the first place, one of the few clubs that a woman could walk in there alone—one of the few clubs in that town—and know that she would never be hassled."

The year 1985 was a watershed for Hubert in another respect: in August, he and Willie Bea tied the knot in Chicago. "Oh, man, Bea. That was my wife," Hubert muses. "Out of all my sonofabitches, that was my wife. We had 16 years together."

Hubert has always been—and still is—quite the ladies' man. He comes across as unassuming, but that twinkle in his eye, that settling and easygoing presence, can make anyone instantly relaxed. Hubert can be disarming *and* charming. His spell over women is legendary—almost as legendary as his playing. But regardless of how many women willingly offered themselves to him, there was no way Hubert was going to leave Bea. She was the rock that Hubert needed, wanted—that stronghold at the water's edge he had been praying for as he was sliding downstream, desperately trying to hang on.

Bea was, indeed, a religious black Southern woman through and through. And she was inexplicably attracted to this bluesman. No matter how wild Hubert could get, he achieved a kind of grace through Bea. "Bea had a good sense of ethics and responsibility and honor, and she and Wolf's wife, Lillie Burnett, kind of kept those guys on their toes a lot," says Cornett. "It is like they balanced the bluesmen. You might even say they [Hubert and Wolf] owe their lives to them, that they were saved by their women."

Bea would feed Hubert properly, make sure he was dressed properly (much like Wolf had always demanded), and would eventually become his manager—dealing with promoters, reading contracts, fielding calls from reporters, and charting a touring schedule for him. In short, she handled the business end of "Hubert Sumlin, Inc." Bea was a sensible person who was suspicious of strangers, and she made sure no one ever took advantage of Hubert. "Baby," she'd say, "we'll eat bread and drink water before we do a dirty deed or work with someone we don't like."

With Bea's help, Hubert was ready to catapult to the next stratum of bluesman. But he needed a breakthrough record. He needed *any* record that the American public could get its hands on. When the opportunities to heighten his profile did not arise immediately, Hubert would get down on himself. "There were times when he was feeling lowdown and he was being overlooked and he was just a waste," Freund says. "I'd say, 'Hubert, there is nobody like you. You are the most individual musician I have ever heard.' That made him feel good. Truly, there is no way you could copy Hubert Sumlin's style. It is so individual and it is a dialect all his own. I have been there and witnessed up close his absolute sheer brilliance and creativity."

It would take a kid from Boston to help Hubert achieve his dream.

Chapter 6
A Dream in Blues

While Hubert was crisscrossing the country in the late '70s and early '80s—keeping Austin and Chicago as his base—Earl Horvath (aka Ronnie Earl) was co-leading a band called Sugar Ray & The Bluetones and would later join the band Roomful of Blues, replacing guitar wizard Duke Robillard. When Hubert got the chance to play with Ronnie Earl and Roomful, it was a fateful turn of events.

"Hubert was not happy and had left Eddie Shaw and was kind of floating around and we had a lot of wonderful blues players here [the Boston area]," Earl explains. "We had a club here called the Speakeasy in Cambridge, and Boston was filled with great blues players like David Maxwell, Roomful with Duke Robillard, and the Fabulous Thunderbirds, who were coming here a lot."

"In those days Eddie Shaw and the Wolf Gang would come through and play the Speakeasy," says Richard Rosenblatt, founder of Tone-Cool Records. "They were on the same tour schedule/route that my band, at the time, was on. I got to know Hubert when he'd come up there alone and he'd need a backing band. I'd be in it, playing harmonica."

The money wasn't great, but the atmosphere was simply priceless. On occasion, Hubert would spend a few days with Earl and the Sugar Ray band, who had managed to swing a flop rent-free. "Hubert was staying at my house and he had a room there," Earl says. "He were traveling in the van with us and going to gigs. I was so young and innocent. I had Wolf's rocking chair album [*Howlin' Wolf* on Chess, so called because of the rocking chair on the cover], but I was too young to take it all in and really understand how heavy this stuff was. Even now, at 51, I still can't really take it in how heavy it was. And we had Wolf's guitar player with us. We had Hubert."

"You could always count on the whole Boston scene—you know, Sugar Ray and whoever was not on the road—coming to see Hubert," bassist-turned-guitarist Steve Arvey says. "You could count on the best people coming to see him: Ronnie Earl, David Maxwell. We did Burlington, Vermont; we did Trenton and Stanhope, New Jersey. I will never forget there was a show with Hubert, Sugar Blue, Bob Margolin, and everybody thought Keith Richards would be in town, and who showed up? Carl Perkins. Even better."

"I had started playing with Hubert in the mid-'70s and we did stuff in the 1980s at a place called Nightstage in Cambridge," notes pianist David Maxwell, who sat in with Muddy and learned by watching such greats as Pinetop Perkins, Sunnyland Slim, and Otis Spann. "We also did just duo things—just the two of us. The synergy between Hubert and myself—it really amazes me every time we play together. Just the way we can feed each other lines. He responds well to the piano and the fact that I was fortunate enough that Otis Spann and Sunnyland Slim were still alive to help form my musical basis for the blues. They influenced my whole blues sound, particularly Spann. I know that Hubert responds to that well."

"Hubert really liked being with us," Earl smiles. "It was not like we treated him as if he was a rock star. We were poor. He and I were the same size and we were wearing suits and I would give him my suits."

When Earl crossed over to Roomful of Blues in 1980 he brought Hubert with him, and the guitar boss would sit in at a number of their gigs. Still, Hubert became restless: he needed more than just running from gig to gig. He wanted a place to hang his hat. "At that time, all I kept saying was, 'What I want more than anything else is to have an American solo record.' That is what I wanted," Hubert states emphatically.

Earl would record a slew of solo records for Black Top Records in the 1980s (*Smokin', Soul Searching, They Call Me Mr. Earl*) and talked to the label about signing Hubert to a deal. As Earl recalls, "'I have a deal and Hubert Sumlin doesn't?' I said. 'How can this be? How can he not have his own record out in America?' He knows all of these rock stars. Everybody loves him, but where are they? I felt like it was my duty, you know, to push for this record's release."

The label trusted Earl's vision, and under his guidance Hubert was soon engulfed by the region's best musicians. On tap were drummer extraordinaire John Rossi (dubbed "Father Time" because of his steady, in-the-pocket feel), piano ace and touring/studio vet Maxwell, harp man Jerry Portnoy (formerly with Muddy Waters), blues ace of bass Michael "Mudcat" Ward, and virtually the rest of the entire Roomful of Blues crew (Ron Levy on piano/keyboard, Greg Piccolo on tenor sax, Doug James on baritone sax, and Bob Enos on trumpet).

While the lineup was solid, Hammond Scott, Black Top Records owner and co-producer of this Hubert project, wanted something different. "Singing-wise, Hubert's most effective when he does down-home stuff," Scott told *Guitar Player* in 1987. "He gets sort of a Lightnin' Hopkins or Jimmy Reed type of sound by himself. But I didn't want to do the

Hubert's American Dream—his first U.S. solo release.

whole LP like that, so I brought in [Mighty Sam] McClain to sing songs that bring out the other side of Hubert's playing."

Sam McClain, having fallen from hitmaker in the 1960s with a cover of Patsy Cline's "Sweet Dreams" to living on the streets of New Orleans and selling his blood plasma just to survive the 1970s and early '80s, understood the significance of this project. It was an important building block in what would eventually become McClain's full-fledged comeback some five to six years later with the song "Give It Up to Love."

Titled *Blues Party,* the record would be a proving ground not only for McClain but for Hubert and Earl. Hubert, who was still very much in the throes of struggling with his own personal demons, wanted the record to be the best it could be. Earl, who was toying with leaving Roomful of Blues at this point, was battling depression on a daily basis.

The three musicians met on the first day of recording in September 1986, and by October the band and recording engineer Paul Arnold were in Newbury Sound studio in Boston. The plan was to do a couple of Wolf tunes, but no more. The record needed its own feel. After all, this was Sumlin solo, not a Wolf cover band.

On the surface the band seems like an odd configuration, like some sort of ragtag musical chain gang—as if Sumlin–Earl–McClain were shackled together and forced to live in uncomfortably tight quarters in payment for past sins. In reality, the combination is nothing short of explosive. The song "A Soul That's Been Abused" features McClain's powerful, quivering vocals that mix Aaron Neville and Bobby Bland, while Earl's plaintive, melodic opening guitar riff falls between Hubert and Mark Knopfler in terms of tone, texture, and sensibility (Earl cops a classic Hubert move by sliding his hand up the neck across one string). Horns punctuate and underscore Earl's riff as Hubert softly butters the track with his fluttering fade-in and fade-out runs.

Blues Party also contains one of Hubert's greatest solo songs: "Living the Blues." This tune is an autobiographical, chronological account of Hubert's life and career, from his field-plowing days in Mississippi, to his life in Arkansas (where his mother bought him his first guitar), his road work with James Cotton, and on up through his years with Wolf. A reworked "Down in the Bottom" is powered by a Texas shuffle that can only be described as boogie blues-rock. Very fitting. Hubert's time in Austin seems to have rubbed off. The entire record is pure feel. So much of it came together in one take. The sessions and final track mix were about mood in the studio, which seemed to switch and change directions more times than Hubert's guitar lines.

"One story is typical Hubert," Earl recalls. "We were listening back to 'Living the Blues' and there are horns on the track. So, we were trying to decide whether we wanted to keep the horns on the track, because we also had harmonica on there. So we are in the booth and I turn to Hubert and say, 'What do you think? Do you like the horns?' 'I love them. I think we should keep them. It sounds great.' Then we go outside the booth, where the horns are not playing, and I say, 'What do you think, Hubert: better with or without the horns?' 'No, I don't think we should have the horns.' The whole session was kind of like that."

"If you can set up a framework for him to work with, then right off the cuff he'll come up with something wild that sounds really great," Scott notes. "But if you go into a session expecting to lay everything on him—the tunes, the arrangements, and all of that—you're in trouble, because he won't do something the same way twice."

The kind of flying-by-the-seat-of-your-pants feel works for *Blues Party*. The irony is that it might be Hubert's most coherent record to date. *The Washington Post* described Hubert's playing as "downright spooky at times." And in September 2003, *Down Beat* magazine named *Blues Party* one of the Top 50 blues albums of all time.

Yet, for all of its assets, of which there are a considerable number, there are faults: namely, Hubert is not a true frontman on this record (although it is actually titled *Hubert Sumlin's Blues Party*). In and of itself, Hubert's hanging back is not a bad thing, though one might expect more from Sumlin solo. But again, this goes to the core of what Hubert Sumlin is: he is the juice that makes the engine run; his assets as a guitar player are the fragments of the overall mosaic. He is at once integral and large, yet infinitesimal. Expecting him to behave like a brash lead singer/lead guitarist is undeniably naïve.

Some were not happy with *Blues Party* and thought Hubert could do better in many ways. What seemed to sting Clifford Antone (even more than his 14-month prison sentence from late 1985 to early 1987) was the fact that Antone never released Hubert solo on his own label, Antone's Records. "That was a crucial turning point in Hubert's life," Antone says. "I never did put out any record on him. I'm the only one who knows how to handle Hubert and can record him the right way."

Even so, Hubert's 1980s recorded output, while a checkered lot to be sure, boasts solid efforts. Pound for pound, these are good records, but Hubert is constantly wrestling ghosts—ghosts of Wolf and ghosts of his own past. And contrary to what some might think, Hubert's records do have their own collective voice, but it seems muddled by the fact that he is, and will always be, for many, "Wolf's guitar player."

"It is a shame that Hubert can't transfer that energy, that warmth that he has when he tries to be the star," *Living Blues* magazine co-founder Jim O'Neal notes. "Sometimes it comes through. That onstage center-of-attention is not what he was ever about. There's an innocence to him, in a way. One time he started talking about Wolf, after Wolf had died, and went on and on about the circumstances of his death and started crying. It is still a big void in his life."

Earl, however, sees *Blues Party* as a major accomplishment. "It is one of the most important things that I got to do in my life. I feel good about it. His love and kindness touches me so deeply and makes me feel so good." It seems Hubert agreed with Earl. In a radio interview at the time of the record's release, he said, "I go home and I sleep so good. I am on the right track now."

A fascinating illustration by Bunny Matthews graces the cover of *Blues Party*. Hubert, Earl, and Sam are jamming in a bar, surrounded by long-haired bar babes. The backdrop—the walls of the joint—are going up in flames. But a graphic error sums up the Hubert phenomenon: the drawing shows Hubert holding a pick while he strums his guitar. He hadn't used a pick for over 20 years. In a sense, this album cover represents how Hubert's struggle for recognition, his very essence, was overlooked.

That aside, the record did help bump up Hubert's profile somewhat. A review of a June 1986 show at New York's Abilene Café (with drummer Bernard Purdie, guitarist John Liebman, tenor sax player David Newman, and pianist Teo Leyasmeyer) had *The New York Times* proclaiming: "With his raw tone and an extraordinary variety of attacks, [Sumlin] mixes singing blues phrases and slashes of sheer texture—plunking out low riffs, squeezing out delicate sighs in the upper register, making single notes moan, or suddenly swooping up or down for a metallic shriek."

Hubert was now reaping the benefits of a kind of blues renaissance. In a January 1987 essay (reprinted from a January 1977 *Guitar Player*), multi-talented musician Frank Zappa advised that anyone serious about learning how to play guitar solos ought to listen to Hubert. "Other examples of good guitar stuff…include…the work of Hubert Sumlin…on Howlin' Wolf's things," Zappa wrote.

Hubert continued to play gigs and slowly became recognized as a brilliant veteran player. (Only several years' distance from his Wolf stint could have afforded him this.) In June 1987 he hooked up with fellow Wolf alumnus Sunnyland Slim and Johnny Shines for the fourth annual Chicago Blues Festival. The following year, the nightclub B.L.U.E.S. would host a monthlong "Local Guitar Heroes" series in which Hubert, Buddy Guy, and Homesick James would appear.

Hubert had also made friends with a rising New York blues band called Little Mike & The Tornadoes. Little Mike Markowitz had assembled a seminal, hard-driving blues band that knew the history of the blues. Their collaboration with Hubert was a good one: Little Mike & The Tornadoes wanted to learn, and Hubert needed a steady, solid backing band. "After a while it just grew into a regular thing. We were his band," says Little Mike.

The band had to be rubbery and versatile to keep up with Hubert. As bassist Brad Vickers explains, "You never knew what you were in for with Hubert. When he was with us, anything could happen onstage. I've seen some amazing things and some, well, less than amazing things come from Hubert because he is so 'in the moment.' He is truly a creative genius because there is no preparation—it is all how he feels and what comes from that." (Vickers himself ensured a steady and simple bottom end by playing a three-stringed bass guitar.)

With Little Mike & The Tornadoes, Hubert found himself touring in and outside the country. Vickers usually roomed with Hubert and would hear fantastic stories about Wolf. Vickers got to know Hubert's tics, quirks, and kindness. "No matter what, Hubert would get up in the morning and he would put on his suit," Vickers reveals. "He would always be dressed, with a hat, too. He could get real quiet sometimes and you knew he was thinking something, but he would never let on what it was. Hubert is not the type of person who is going to badmouth anyone. In fact, it might take him years for any hostility, if you call it that, to surface at all. He might say, years after the fact, 'Remember so and so? Yeah, I don't like that guy.'"

Vickers and Little Mike remember a date in Canada in the winter of 1989 that served as a true bonding experience. "We were driving to a gig in Vancouver," Little Mike says. "It was an all-night drive, through a snowstorm. We kept our hopes up that we were going to be okay in the storm, and that we would make the gig. We just didn't know." Vickers adds, "We must have driven over 14 hours. You know? We weren't even late for the show. I don't know how we made it. It was almost as if we were transported on the spot. That's what it was like with Hubert: all of these outside elements fighting us, but we managed to pull through."

Another show, Vickers recalls, at the now-defunct Lone Star Roadhouse in New York, was a nearly surreal experience. "Someone passed me a note while we were playing. Once we stopped, I handed the note to Hubert and the note said that Stevie Ray Vaughan was outside and that he wanted to see Hubert. After the set, Hubert said he wanted me to come with him. I wasn't sure how I felt about that, but I went with him. Once we walked outside, we saw Vaughan, with five bodyguards, three limos, and there he was hanging out with his fiancée, smoking.

"[Vaughan] hugged Hubert and he was almost in tears, almost crying," Vickers continues. "He kept saying how much he loved Hubert and expressed how much he loved his guitar playing. He was a like a little kid looking up to his idol or something. You could just sense the love. He was so emotional about Hubert and his playing. It was quite a sight. I'll never forget it, as I'll never forget how Hubert behaved. Some people may not have asked me to join them, but Hubert did. I'll never forget that."

Vaughan's emotional outburst was spurred, at least partly, by the fact that Hubert had been going down to Austin less and less. Sure, he'd make regular visits to Vaughan's home base (even into the 1990s), but as Bea became more of a force in his life his desire to stay on the road for weeks and months at a time was lessening.

It was about this time that Vaughan was recording what would be his Grammy-winning album *In Step,* which broke the Top 40 on *Billboard*'s album charts and featured a cover of Wolf's "Love Me Darlin'." Given the impression Hubert had on Stevie Ray, and the invaluable precious time they had spent together in Austin playing at Antone's, some are left wondering why Vaughan never tapped Hubert to play with him on the record. "After they recorded [*In Step*] and before it came out, [Stevie] played it for me," Antone remembers. "We put it on the speakers in the club and it was good. But after listening to it, I asked, 'Why didn't you-all get Hubert on the record?' You know, I was just wishing that they had put Hubert on the record and had given him some kind of producing credit where he would have made a little bit of money off that record. I knew the contribution he had made to Stevie's growth as a musician."

Puzzling, too, was the track "Tell Me" from Vaughan's first record, *Texas Flood.* The first Wolf song Stevie Ray ever covered, "Tell Me" in its original Wolf version didn't have Hubert on guitar. While Hubert certainly appreciates kindnesses shown to him by many, there seems to be no getting around it: this is another example of a Hubert protégé missing an opportunity to help elevate Hubert's musical profile even further.

Perhaps we should consider Hubert's gentle temperament and the fact that celebrity doesn't seem to fascinate him in the least. Hubert doesn't care about fame. And today, slowed by his medical condition, Hubert often has to be talked into going to some very high-profile gigs. "One time Bea said, 'Hubeh, Eric Clapton is on the phone,'" recalls friend Curtis Obeda. "We were in his basement and we were having a few drinks, so, basically, Eric had to call back."

Little Mike would typically send out press kits full of material on Hubert to help land gigs wherever he could. When Hubert came through New York, he knew he had Little Mike & The Tornadoes at his disposal. The band was comprised of young musicians on their way up in the blues world, and they wanted to experience the party. Hubert was caught in the rush—and was battling the bottle—but he knew that this band, regardless of the atmosphere around them, offered him a solid base for his own musical explorations. Gigs like Little Mike & The Tornadoes kept Hubert grounded. And he liked to play with them. "They got the best band I done found in New York," Hubert declared in 1987.

The band, conversely, was getting an education every night onstage. Vickers and Little Mike never really knew what to expect. Just as Charlie Patton had "learned" Wolf, Hubert was taking these young New York blues players to school. But what sets Hubert apart from Patton, Wolf, and others—anyone who has ever held a 6-string—is his seemingly boundless creativity. His phrasing was either behind or ahead of, but rarely right on top of, the beat.

"Hubert would sometimes play something and it didn't sound as though he could correct it—it almost sounded wrong," admits Vickers. "But somehow he would make it work. That was the best education we could have had. We knew how lucky we were. Hubert could have been doing a lot more gigs, bigger and better gigs, especially in the earlier days of the band. But he stuck with us, playing smaller clubs in New York, which wasn't necessarily doing much for his name, but it meant a lot for us."

After years of playing with Hubert, Little Mike seized an opportunity to record for Blind Pig Records (a label that started in 1977 as an outgrowth of an Ann Arbor, Michigan, nightclub of the same name). "We had an 'in,'" he freely admits. "We wanted to record a record and we had Hubert. The company went for it."

The band went into Roxie Studios in New York to record Hubert's solo album *Heart & Soul*. The entire record has the vibrance of birth—it is a fresh, screaming life. Small wonder: it was recorded live with minimal overdubs, remembers mixing engineer Michael Freeman, a transplanted Brit now based in Chicago. "There was leakage from microphone to microphone [on the raw tracks] that we used fairly creatively," Freeman points out. "We used that to bring a lot of life into the tracks. There was a presence on them, a great performance. When you are mixing recordings in a genre like blues, especially from someone like Hubert, you want to find the essence of the performance and bring that out in the mix."

Freeman's talents and producer Jerry del Giudice's vision, coupled with Hubert's glassy, piercing, and alternately beeping/scratchy tones and the band's sparkling backup, yielded a powerful record. *Heart & Soul* bounces—partly due to drummer Pete de Coste's swingin' feel, plus James Cotton's horn-like harp that offers a conversational partner to Hubert's often jagged guitar runs.

*Backed by Little Mike and the Tornadoes, Hubert regained
some of his younger-day firepower.*

Cuts like the uptempo "Your Foxy Self" (another Cotton–Sumlin
conversation) and the blinding-fast version of Little Walter's 1952 hit
"Juke" (itself a nod to Snooky Pryor's 1948 "Boogie") are simply vicious.
The record also features Hubert's signature mid-tempo, funky instrumental "Chunky," recastings of "The Red Rooster" and "Sitting on Top
of the World" (Hubert lopping off words as he pleases in grand Wolf
style), "I Want You" (which certainly served as a blueprint for some of
Stevie Ray's stylings), and "Old Friends," a touching duet highlighting
the mighty, long friendship between Hubert and Cotton. "That was special," says Freeman. "I remember that Cotton and Hubert track as being
very emotional." (Little Mike claims it was his idea to reunite Cotton
with Hubert for *Heart & Soul.*)

But just as his solo career was getting into full swing, a show at
Hunter's in Wheaton, Maryland, seemed to bring Hubert back to
square one. "Some folks wanted to hear blues guitarist Hubert Sumlin
perform Robert Cray tunes at Hunter's in Wheaton Saturday night,"
wrote Mike Joyce for *The Washington Post* in January 1989, "while

others more familiar with Sumlin's career [wanted to hear Howlin' Wolf songs]." No matter how far Hubert had come, he was still dogged by his past connections, preconceived notions, and misconceptions. Hubert hoped to remedy that in May 1989, when he made his second recording for Black Top Records, *Healing Feeling*.

As evidenced by the album's cover, Hubert closed his eyes, held his breath, and flashed a face-contorting grin: this one he would approach in grand fashion. Hammond Scott and Ronnie Earl (having jettisoned Roomful of Blues in 1988) again were the production team and Earl tapped his new band, the Broadcasters, for backing duties.

Even more so than for Black Top's *Blues Party*, these sessions were spur-of-the-moment. Hubert was scheduled to perform at Black Top Records' Blues-a-Rama showcase at New Orleans hotspot Tipitina's the night before. The show spilled over into the early hours of the morning, and Hubert was supposed to record at noon. It was a harrowing experience for the producers, but Hubert was used to this kind of recording situation from his Chess Records days.

Highlights of *Healing Feeling* include "I Don't Want No Woman" (a song Magic Sam covered some 25 years earlier), the live "Come Back Little Girl" (from the prior evening's Blues-a-Rama, showcasing Hubert's unbridled, nasty brand of firepower), "Down the Dusty Road" (a punchy and playful solo electric guitar song), and "Just Like I Treat You" (a cover of the classic Wolf track). In the latter, Hubert's swooping, duck-and-cover complementing runs twist around the vocal lines, always stopping at precisely the same instant as the vocals. His fluid rhythms are simply amazing. When his guitar doesn't scream with orgasmic melodies, you can hear the clicking of the strings at a low volume. Hubert's patience is outwardly evident here. He pauses, revs up the strings, picks his spots, and waits for the right moment to strike them. "Blues for Henry" was written by Hubert and Earl, and dedicated to a friend of Earl's who died of cancer. "I had to write 'Blues for Henry.' I needed to come up with some songs," Earl explains. "Hubert wasn't writing that much at that moment. I needed a lead and Hubert took it from there."

Hubert and Earl open the record's title track with an exceptional call-and-response session over a wash of crash cymbals. Just as it was difficult to distinguish between Clapton's and Hubert's styles on *The*

London Sessions, here, too, Earl's and Hubert's approaches seem to meld into one. (They even played similar model and color Stratocasters.) But get past the opening and it is all Hubert. "Hubert has helped me more than I could ever help him," Earl says of this relationship.

On most if not all of *Healing Feeling,* Hubert takes command (although he sings on only two of the 11 songs). His guitar is mixed out front, and it simply is the centerpiece—a big difference from *Blues Party.* "Hubert was always very easy to work with," Earl notes. "He did a great version of the Wolf tune 'Just Like I Treat You' with Darrell [Nulish] singing. You know, '…some say you is, some say you ain't.…' I thought his playing was unbelievable on that tune. That was my favorite one on the record."

Hubert continued to muddle through in Chicago. Andy Cornett, Henry Gray's manager, remembers going with Gray from the Big Easy up to the Windy City to play with Hubert on June 8, 1989. (Gray was scheduled to play with Hubert at the sixth annual Chicago Blues Festival the next day.) "Hubert used to live on the South Side," says Cornett. "We drove up, touring the country in Hondas—a Honda wagon and a Civic or Acura. We said, 'South Side of Chicago. Somebody better stay and watch the car.' So we were about deciding who would stay and watch the car, when we hear this noise. We look up and it is Hubert standing at the door to his house with his cocked rifle. He said, 'Don't worry 'bout it; I got it covered. Come on.'

"We played a couple gigs with Hubert that night," continues Cornett. "We played B.L.U.E.S. on the North Side—that was the first time I played with Hubert. Duke Robillard had just given him a wireless transmitter and a guitar. At one point he took off from the club, and he was gone five to ten minutes. We could hear him and we knew he was playing, but we couldn't see him. Afterwards, we find out that he was lying down on cars, lying down in the street and everything—while he was playing. When he came back he had a big smile on his face."

Hubert may have been smiling, but something was terribly wrong. Despite finally getting his solo career off the ground in the US, Hubert's solo records were making little or no dent in the mainstream psyche (his Black Top material is currently out of print). And a superb film about his life made by Jim Kent, then head of the Massachusetts Institute of Technology film department, and bassist/filmmaker Sumner Burgwyn had not been released for national distribution (it still hasn't been). More importantly, Hubert was being pushed and pulled in many different directions, still playing in and banging around New York, Chicago, and, to some extent, Austin.

Then the decision that Bea and Hubert had talked about for months finally came to fruition: they were moving to Milwaukee. Having left Sunnyland's three-story building and rented their own place on the South Side, Bea and Hubert wanted to own their own real estate. Hubert reminisces, "We saw this plot of land—it was like a farm, almost. Every time we would go up to Milwaukee we'd pass this place and we knew we'd live there. So, that's what we did. We moved."

"They lived right in the heart of the core [of Chicago at the time]," says guitarist Jeff Dagenhardt, who would become a close friend when Hubert and Bea moved to Milwaukee. "Sam Lay lived only four blocks from him. When I would go visit Sam Lay, I'd call him from the Loop and say, 'I'm coming out to see ya.' Sam would meet me with guns. I'd pull up with my car and he'd unlock his car and he'd come out with a rifle in his hand and a gun in his waistband. He walked me into the apartment building. It is not even believable. The neighborhood kids would gang up on [Hubert] and take his guitars and stuff. Finally, they had had it with that neighborhood."

On the morning of June 9 (the day he was to play the Chicago Blues Festival), Hubert, Bea, and Bea's father (her mother had passed away in 1986) moved to a small bungalow house in a quiet northern Milwaukee suburb. Hubert said good-bye to Chicago, his home since the early '50s.

Some had questioned the rationale of the move, and even the foresight. But Bea, who was handling Hubert's interests as his manager, was a savvy businesswoman and sharper than some gave her credit for. She knew that the further away her husband was from his old life—a life fraught with ills, vices, and misdirection—the more stable he would become professionally and personally. Besides, Milwaukee—only 90 miles from Chicago—had history: Sunnyland had played up there. Wolf used to make trips up there. Even one of Hubert's idols, Charlie Patton, had recorded not far from Milwaukee, in nearby Grafton, Wisconsin, in 1929–1930. Milwaukee was a blues town built on the production of beer—the sudsy libation was so abundant it was literally spilling out into the street. Of course, the irony was that Hubert shouldn't be in a beer town, but with Bea's help he maintained a certain level of lucidity.

"I never met a woman of her character," remarks Dagenhardt. "I will never forget this. Some promoter was trying to hand her a line of baloney. She hung up the phone, and we are sitting in the front room watching TV with Hubert. We were watching wrestling, which he loves. Anyway, she hung up from this guy and she says, 'I never met a sleazeball that couldn't stand another greasing.' You knew she got the best of him. She wouldn't be fooled by anyone."

When Hubert got to the festival later on moving day, tens of thousands of fans watched him perform Wolf tunes with Sunnyland's band, James Cotton, and Pinetop Perkins, among others. But before the bands played, the crowd was treated to a special event. Hubert received the Howlin' Wolf Award, presented by Lillie Burnett (Wolf's widow) and Willie Dixon.

"We gave the award to Hubert because we wanted to honor him," says Barry Dolins, organizer of the annual Chicago Blues Festival. "The Wolf Award is still used today by the Blues Foundation to gain notoriety. Bea was there and Lillie Burnett [who liked the idea of having Wolf's name live on and donated the photo on the placard] was there. It really shows that behind every bluesman is a woman of some grace and charm. That is what you don't get in the common biographies. It is a privilege for me to be included in this family [the blues community] and looking at it as one big family."

In early 2004, Hubert makes the pilgrimage back to Chicago to open the Chicago Blues Festival on a rainy Thursday night in June—Howlin' Wolf's birthday. Wolf would have been 94 years old.

I can see that Chicago still feels like a second home to Hubert. The city's skyline comes into our line of vision as we drive on I-94 through the heart of downtown. "Sears Tower," he says, pointing to the black, obelisk-shaped tower. "Tallest building in the world. I've been up there. You look over to Michigan and all these different states. Oh, man. Miles up in the air. Ain't that somethin'? So many people got killed building this building, man."

It is a fitting analogy: so many lives sacrificed while building Chicago's world-famous Sears Tower; so many careers thrust into obscurity while making the blues an American art form and a Chicago attraction. How many unsung blues musicians have come and gone during the last 50 years? Too many to mention here. Still, the blues—with all the ridiculous talk of it being dead (how can a feeling be defunct?)—is alive and well, and the edifice that is now modern blues owes everything to carpenters like Hubert.

But this is not the same Chicago he came to as a young man in 1954; not the same Chicago he left in 1989. Silvio's is an empty lot. The 1815 Club is gone. What was once the Key Largo club (the infamous spot where Wolf fired his apprentice and gave Hubert his musical voice) is, of all things, part of a state trooper facility. "Things changed from when I first came here, was just changed, man," Hubert says. "Sonofagun. It just changed, that's all. Maybe it changed for the better."

The day is dreary with dank skies. We carefully navigate the slick roads and pelting rain. "You going downtown. Two exits to downtown," Hubert directs me. "We're goin' downtown. Hotel sitting right on Michigan. I was in Chicago over 30 years. Show you how old it is. The biggest fuckin' post office, you know what I am talkin' 'bout? All the way to the lake, all the way to the lake.

"I was here when they were building these expressways and everything," Hubert reminisces. "I took Highway 55 all the way down to Jackson, Mississippi. I done drove this sonofagun and we used to drive when this road was put up. We did it all with Wolf."

Though Hubert has often been known to bring the sunshine with him, not even his magic could clear the stormy skies this day. The rain seems to dampen and hush the spirits of the musicians that are gathering in the underground facilities of the festival venue as we approach.

Almost as soon as we arrive, word is spreading quickly that Ray Charles has died of liver cancer at age 73. Hubert is a bit shocked and speechless when the official announcement is made. He is a big fan, he is the same age, and he's been battling his own cancer in recent years. He had wanted to see Charles perform live, but his health and schedule never afforded him the opportunity. During an interview later in the day, Hubert is asked to talk about the death of Ray Charles, but he won't budge. He clams up.

Though some might argue that it was Charles's soulful blending of genres that helped usher traditional blues out of favor, he was nonetheless a musical pioneer, just like Wolf and Hubert. While Wolf and right-hand man Hubert, Muddy Waters, and the rest of the blues crew at Chess were forging a new musical path, Charles likewise was fusing gospel, soul, country, blues, and jazz to create new shades of R&B. And like many of the bluesmen, his brothers-in-arms, Charles felt the sting of prejudice from the religious black community that viewed his music as heretical.

Ray Charles's death is a great loss, and one more reminder that Hubert, though tired and often tested, is still going—one of the few authentic bluesmen able to testify to the blues. Hubert lowers his head and presses on.

Checking in at the festival stage for pre-show preparations, he finds singer/harp player David Johansen in rehearsal. His soaring harp notes echo through the canyon of the park, emanating from the edge of the Petrillo Music Shell's stage. Johansen's blowing is bold and magnificent, as towering as the skyline that casts its shadows on the park. The weather is crisp and a bit raw, but the rain has stopped and the open-air venue allows the notes to travel as some bystanders pause momentarily to watch the band, which includes Billy Hector on guitar and David Maxwell on piano, tighten up the arrangements and gauge each other's temperature.

Later, during the show, it's another story: the rain is relentless. The stage monitors, now covered with plastic, act as shields against the incessant watery bullets. Johansen howls against the storm, tempting the tide as it threatens to drench the band. His very words seem to create a dry force field around the stage. No campy Buster Poindexter personas or long dresses à la his New York Dolls band here.

The guys are digging in, reaching inside themselves, reaching down for more. Hector (who normally burns as a lead guitarist) holds down a steady foundation while Hubert, in a snazzy bright red sport jacket, tinted glasses, and a fedora on his familiarly lowered head, plucks away with his fingers, rocking in place in his chair center stage.

Johansen keeps goading Hubert to look up as he belts out the words into the mic, bending his body in half, prowling the stage in circles around Hubert. The master doesn't respond, but continues to look down, moving his head with every expressive guitar lick and stomping his feet. But there is an unspoken communication. Just as they had done on "Killing Floor" at the Salute to the Blues concert (which appears on *Lightning in a Bottle,* the soundtrack of Antoine Fuqua's concert film produced by visionary filmmaker Martin Scorsese), the vibe is there, and Johansen and Hubert have settled into each other's rhythm. It feels right—and the drenched crowd bounces and jumps in place like bobbing human pistons in an open-air juke joint.

The show is a hit—fans linger in the pouring rain even after the band's performance. (Despite the rain, the event drew nearly 700,000 people— the third largest in the festival's history, according to Chicago mayor's office estimates.) It's been a great night for Hubert, for a lot of reasons. Before the show, Harry Smith, the mayor of Greenwood, Mississippi, and his son Wesley (of the Blues Foundation in Memphis, Tennessee) had presented Hubert with the Heart of the Blues Award for his "lifetime contribution to the blues." A complete and utter surprise to Hubert, the award represented a sparkling achievement. He held it up high for the cameras' popping flash-bulbs: a proud moment. The blues community had finally recognized Hubert Sumlin, 73, as one of the pillars of electric blues guitar, an architect of the sound that made Chicago famous.

But it's the year 2004. It has taken Hubert all these years to be recognized in a city—in a genre—that he helped build. Why would such an artist, who had worked so hard to get noticed, just pick up and leave the town that birthed his career like Hubert left Chicago in 1989? Why would he start all over again in Milwaukee? And would this new city embrace him?

Chapter 7
Milwaukee:
Salvation...Retreat...Despair

In 1990 Little Mike finally inked a record deal of his own and invited Hubert, Ronnie Earl, Paul Butterfield, and Pinetop Perkins (whom he and the Tornadoes had backed on Perkins's *After Hours*) to perform on *Heart Attack*. It was something Little Mike & The Tornadoes had been working toward for years. Bill Dahl, writer for *Living Blues* magazine, penned these lines for the record's liner notes: "All these venerated blues giants knew instinctively that Little Mike & The Tornadoes are without a doubt the real thing. So batten down the hatches—there's a savage blues tornado headed right in your direction!"

Hubert is listed on four tracks, but it would take trained ears to figure out it's him on at least two of them. Hubert seems to fade into the background a bit. The song "Good Gal" is perhaps the only spot in which he stretches himself. But ultimately, Little Mike got what he wanted—a record deal—and Hubert was able to tour and play with a solid blues band. "The relationship was mutual," Hubert admits, with his eyes widened, arms crossed—no bullshit here. "They got somethin' they wanted and I got a good band to play with. And that's it."

The 1990s were the time of Hubert's reconstruction. The decade got off to a rocky start. Bea suffered a crushing blow with the death of her father in 1990 and became tied to the house. She couldn't—or wouldn't—go anywhere, not even to church.

Unlike in Chicago, where Bea and her father were faithful members of the Cathedral of Love Missionary Baptist Church, Bea never found a congregation in Milwaukee that she wanted to join. Not much interested in the nightlife that was Hubert's professional career, Bea was an intensely private person who read her Bible, quoted scripture, watched televangelists on a daily basis, and chose to stay as active as possible (from a distance) with her church in Chicago. "When [my mother] went to Milwaukee, she would talk with pastors from Chicago who would come up to see them," says daughter Ida Hicks. "Granddad was unable to go back and forth to the church that he was a faithful member of—that both my mother and my grandfather were faithful members of. They would keep in contact on a consistent basis and I think there was financial support when it could be done, as far as contributing to the church."

On August 25, 1990, one of Hubert's old musical partners, a student and a friend, left this earth forever. Stevie Ray Vaughan had played a concert at Alpine Valley Music Theatre in East Troy, Wisconsin, with Robert Cray, Eric Clapton, Jimmie Vaughan, Buddy Guy, and others. Flying out of Alpine Valley in treacherous weather conditions, Stevie Ray's helicopter crashed. It was a fatal crash sadly reminiscent of another midwestern rock music tragedy: the plane crash in Iowa that claimed the lives of Buddy Holly, the Big Bopper, and Ritchie Valens on February 3, 1959, subsequently dubbed "the day the music died."

"Stevie…they was coming outta Alpine Valley, just outside my house," Hubert remembers. "I fell asleep and dozed off in front of the TV and I woke up when there was a news flash on the TV about it. They said that a helicopter crashed." I ask Hubert about the rumors that he was supposed to be playing at the same show. "Nah. But he was tryin' to get me for some other stuff. I know he wanted me to open or something for him somewheres."

As if in spiritual sympathy, the heady concoction that was once the blues scene in Austin seemed to evaporate just at the time of Vaughan's death. "In 1990, something started happening and the population started growing," Vaughan bassist Tommy Shannon explains. "One day, I swear to God, I woke up, I got in my car and it hit me: Austin is dead. What it was is gone now. I would give anything to have something like that again."

Hubert's recording career, now hobbling after two records that received critical acclaim but not much else, needed a strong tonic.

Hubert decided to go back to the comforts of Europe—a land that had always embraced him and treated him like royalty. After nearly a month on the road with British guitarist/bassist Richard Studholme and drummer Steve Thorneycroft, Hubert signed a contract with JSP Records in London, England. Recorded at London's Triple X Studio, the session included Jack Hill on keyboards and was completed in one afternoon. It would become *Blues Guitar Boss*.

The liner notes boasted that this album would blow away any of Hubert's other efforts: "...Hubert Sumlin [is] a brilliant guitarist who has somehow managed to make some pretty damn awful albums under his own name since his days as Howlin' Wolf's guitarist...." The package is capped off with quotes from Clapton, Vaughan, and Jimmy Page. "I was always impressed with Hubert Sumlin...a great inspiration and influence on my work," Page said.

Given this forceful language, one might think that *Blues Guitar Boss* is chock-full of musical gems. The feel, however, is not very Hubert; it's more Jimmy Reed. It's not bad in and of itself, except for the fact that there really is no emotional punch or payoff to many of these songs— with, perhaps, the exceptions of "Sometimes I'm Right," "Spanish

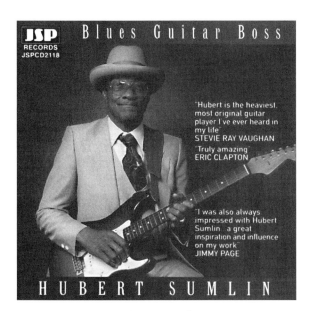

Everyone owes something to Hubert.

Greens," and "I Could Be You." In the latter, Hubert sounds as though he is talking to his ex-wife and explains that he will have to "put [her] down tonight" (that phrase could be open to many interpretations) because he found her with a man named John.

The record simply smacks of mostly working bluesmen who try to use Hubert's name to gain credibility. Hubert's paternal instinct sometimes gets the best of him and he helps the young ones learn to swim. The bottom line? *Blues Guitar Boss* seems slapped together and mediocre. A very un-Hubert record: his guitar playing does not dazzle, and his vocals (admittedly never his strongest point) are overly repetitive. Hubert has to get in "that zone" to create genius licks. Here he sounds tired, impatient, and unfocused. "With Hubert, when things are happening, it is a joy—the magic is there," pianist David Maxwell points out. "I think it has a lot to do with the musicians that he surrounds himself with."

Amidst such professional misfires, Hubert still had Bea to look after him. "When Hubert moved to Milwaukee, he had his teeth replaced," says guitarist and friend Curtis Obeda. "I remember he would sit down at the table and he would eat pork—I don't think he ate that much pork in his life, and Bea would get annoyed because the pork wasn't good for him."

Milwaukee gave Hubert a new feeling. Powered by Bea's love and strength, Hubert's home was a place where the guitar player could truly rest his head. Though Hubert and "Momma" Bea never had children of their own, they would "adopt" sons—virtual strangers who Bea felt were of good character. After a while, these strangers (Hubert called them "immigrants") became like family, and Bea and Hubert trusted and opened their house to them. "I was one of those adopted sons," Milwaukee guitarist Perry Weber says. "I spent some time with them. I was close with Bea and she would look out for people—people she trusted."

"I refer to her as Momma," says guitarist Jimmy D. Lane, birth son of guitar great Jimmy Rogers. "I missed two days of calling the house in Milwaukee, and Momma was on the phone. Something had better be wrong. If it wasn't, I'd catch holy hell. That's the way Momma was." Sax player Sam Burckhardt explains that Bea "was like a mother to me. She'd cook for me, and when Hubert and Bea still lived in Chicago she would do my laundry."

Now settled into his Milwaukee home, Hubert began to open up all the various boxes and trunks that held his personal belongings. One trunk was stuffed with memorabilia—photos and other mementos of the road, collected over the previous four decades. Hubert had the fantastic decorating idea to plaster all of his photos from the trunk onto the walls of his getaway room in the basement. It created quite a scene for first-time visitors.

"It was the history of the blues in this trunk," friend and fellow blues guitarist Jeff Dagenhardt remarks. "He had, willing to bet, no less than 5,000 pictures. It was Hubert with Albert King, Smokey Smothers, Jimmie Vaughan—everyone. The ceiling and walls in this little rec room in his basement was suddenly turned into a virtual blues museum." The basement was a place where Hubert could lose himself, entertain friends, and play guitar. It was a place where he could let it all hang out. "Hubert's dad was a bootlegger and he grew up drinking," Dagenhardt points out. "Once in a while he'd put a shine on. I might get lit with him. One day he started oiling everything in the house and nothing worked after that. He oiled the clock; he oiled things that didn't need to be oiled. He had this Marantz tape recorder that someone had given him and he oiled that. He oiled all the switches and went around with a regular oilcan like you would get from the hardware store. The next thing we know, the clocks didn't work, the tape recorder didn't work...."

Hubert has always been the quintessential bluesman. He is an amazing individual, but sometimes he needs an escape. It is tiring to be so constantly positive for the world. Because Hubert can't say no—he is afraid of hurting someone's feelings—and because he simply has not gotten the recognition he deserves, it all weighs on him. Hubert needs to get away, and if receding to his basement lair does the trick, so be it.

Besides, Hubert does much more than sit around in his basement room playing guitar. The guy just seems to be able to achieve anything he wants. Hubert has always been a kind of jack-of-all-trades around the house. He has a green thumb; he grows tomatoes and peppers in his backyard. Up until recently, he'd paint on a regular basis and do the plumbing when the pipes dripped. And he'd cook (he was, after all, the chief cook for the Wolf band on the road). At other times, Hubert has tried his hand at being a mechanic. "Hubert had this station wagon that someone gave him and he says that he pulled apart the engine piece by piece to try to figure out what was wrong with it," explains Chad Kassem, founder of APO Records. "When he finally got to what was wrong, he couldn't put it back together. So he had all the pieces of the car inside the station wagon," Kassem laughs.

Some car-related memories are not so funny. Hubert, who drove for both Wolf and Muddy at different points in their careers, had sworn off driving altogether because of one incident in which he could have been killed. "Why did I stop driving? I blacked out one day, son," Hubert admits to me. "Nothin' else to say. Just blacked out behind the wheel. I gave up driving. Then I went before the judge and I just said, 'I ain't drivin' no more. That's it. I'm taking myself out.' Before she could ever say anything, you know what I'm talkin' 'bout? Now people drive me. I don't drive anymore. I had it with driving. And you would have had it, too, if you went through it like I did—all those years driving Wolf and the band."

By April 1991 Hubert was in the studio again to record with guitarist John Primer and harmonica man Billy Branch, who had come off the critical success of 1990's *Harp Attack* with James Cotton, Carey Bell, and Junior Wells. Recorded at Chicago's Acme Studio by Paul Smith for the Austrian label Wolf Records, the album boasts some magical—and sometimes strained—musical moments. Hubert appears to be having a bit more fun in this session. In "First Song I Ever Did" he laughs mischievously after a solo acoustic guitar run in the middle of the piece. In "Real Far Away" Hubert opens up with a Hooker-esque subtle groove. The song explodes into a convergent, point-counterpoint guitar race between Hubert and Primer. There are other elements of sheer brutality and muscle here, such as Branch's strong vibrato harp playing in "You Can't Change Me" and "I've Been Gone."

At 60 years of age, Hubert was beginning to get his fire back. A June 1991 show at one of his favorite venues, New York's Abilene Café (later to become Chicago B.L.U.E.S.), was a "typical atypical"

*Hubert at the Burnley
National Blues Festival,
England, 1993.*

Hubert gig (Hubert's shows are always full of surprises). Here's how the story goes:

Hubert is accompanied by guitarist/harpist Jon Paris, drummer Charles Otis, bassist Mike Merritt, and pianist Teo Leyasmeyer on a small (some might say cramped) stage. Hubert is more than happy to allow Paris (whose talents as a slide and electric country-blues player have been vastly overlooked) to play his melodic solo runs, pointing at Paris and Otis as if to congratulate them after pulling off a tricky riff or beat, and also to coax the crowd into applause.

Sporting a white suit, dark-collared shirt, brown derby, and tinted glasses, Hubert mumbles more than sings, at times, over the rumble of Otis's beats. Still, even if Hubert were completely silent, you'd find yourself glued to him. His playing is rife with unexpected string bends, zigzag slides up the neck, and jerking motions of his arm as he saws across the strings, exploding from points where his 6-string is completely dormant.

After a few songs, Hubert takes off his guitar (a Les Paul Junior), signals to the sound engineer that he's "taking ten," and departs the stage, disappearing into the kitchen to grab some chow, leaving Paris to carry on. Now, Paris is an amazing guitar player and musician who has mastered harp, bass, and guitar. But that "Hubert-ness," which catches the audience and even the band off guard at times, has vanished. That wacky extemporaneousness, that absolute quirky insanity of abrupt endings, extended breaks, and vocal pauses (especially in "Sitting on Top of the World") has left the stage with Hubert. Like Wolf before him, Hubert proves again he is one of a kind.

Later, when he has returned to the stage and an annoying audience member keeps crying out for "Smokestack Lightnin'," Hubert finally obliges. But he lays down the number in a quieter, slow-burning groove, much closer to "I Asked for Water." It seems Hubert's penchant for pleasing everybody has limits. Where his kindness and gentleness end, his instinct to fuck with people takes over. One thing is for sure: with the grand wizard onstage, Hubert can't be pegged as a bored or tired player.

"It didn't happen at that show, but sometimes Hubert would use a pickup band and he wouldn't know the last name of the guys, just their first names," says Paris. "I'd use his line, 'Ladies and gentlemen…all the way from where he is from to be with you tonight…give it up for the guitar.'"

While Hubert does whatever the hell he feels like onstage, his attitude leads to frustration for anyone who expects him to play full tilt all the time—or even a majority of the time. No matter how much he pours into his guitar playing, no matter how much he bears onstage, he manages to hold back a part of himself. He won't perform like a circus animal doing tricks, not for anyone.

It was around this time that Hubert kick-started a string of recording dates that would extend through the rest of the decade. For Antone's Records, he cut "High Heel Sneakers" for Pinetop Perkins's 1992 *Pinetop's Boogie Woogie,* which "rises above most of Perkins's output," according to the *All Music Guide.* (The record features Rogers, Duke Robillard, Luther Tucker, Derek O'Brien, and Matt Murphy—Austin staples and residents.) Hubert also played on *Mighty Long Time* with boyhood buddy

James Cotton (also on Antone's label), recorded again with Little Mike & The Tornadoes (*Payday,* on Blind Pig), and in 1992 visited and toured South America. No one could suspect that his next solo record would be recorded on another continent, but in December 1993 Hubert traveled back to South America to cut *Made in Argentina 1993* for Blues Special Records, with Emilion Villanueva and his Kansas City Boys.

The record has its moments, but perhaps the greatest element attached to the project was that Hubert was once again being recognized internationally. (In all honesty, the record has the feel of an off-the-cuff proceeding.) "[Hubert would] play almost 50 songs in only one session, each song starting and ending in the most unusual and unexpected way; it was driving the band crazy," read *Made in Argentina 1993*'s liner notes. Again, Hubert flew by the seat of his pants and spontaneous music was made—amazing the band, who can follow only through their ears (and hearts) for the blues.

While in Argentina, Hubert played a live gig with drummer Tony Coleman, who has played with B.B. King, Buddy Guy, and his own Tony Coleman Band. Coleman was struck by Hubert's individuality. "Just listening to his guitar playing—that tone—his tone is Hubert,"

Hubert (right) with legendary blues piano man Willie "Pinetop" Perkins backstage at the Benson & Hedges Blues Festival, New York, 1988.

Coleman notes. "Now, it doesn't sound like B.B. King, Albert King, Muddy Waters, or Buddy Guy. It sounds like Hubert Sumlin. No one else sounds like him. That is the point. Today's guys are just copying people who were already copying others."

Hubert's next endeavor, with Jimmy Rogers, was a long time in the making. Bill Hickey, a close personal friend and a fantastic Chicago harp player, was working on his debut, *Bill's Blues*, for the Atomic Theory label. "He could play, man," Hubert says. "Hell of a harmonica player." As a teen, Hickey would play the Maxwell Street Market—the open-air marketplace where aspiring musicians had played and eventually worked their way into the clubs, long before Hickey ever thought about picking up a harp. While at the Market, Hickey played with one of his mentors, Big Walter Horton, a onetime backing band member for Rogers, Muddy Waters, Eddie Taylor, and even Howlin' Wolf.

Recorded at Prince's Paisley Park Studios in Chanhassen, Minnesota, over the Thanksgiving holiday in 1994, *Bill's Blues* certainly benefited from a burning backing band: Hubert, Burckhardt on sax, Lane on guitar, Bob Stroger on bass, Robert Covington on drums, Willie Murphy on guitar, and Charles Lewandowsky on keyboards. (One can only imagine the surreal experience that surely ensued—the harsh contrast of societal realms that no doubt snapped into focus—when His Purple Majesty, having legally changed his name the year before to a *symbol,* thus spawning the anti-moniker of sorts "The Artist Formerly Known As Prince," met this struggling, ragtag army of mostly blues veterans. Prince was living in extravagance—a right of any multimillion-selling artist—but Hubert and his friends were far from rivaling the rock star's lifestyle, even in their dreams.) *Bill's Blues* showed real promise. Hickey had a distinctive voice and his harp playing was simply scorching. The record may have been Hubert's greatest collection of guitar performances since *Healing Feeling.*

On "Feed Me," a song he had perfected onstage throughout his latter-day solo career, Hubert takes the mic and rattles off a laundry list of the food he likes to eat. If it wasn't so downright hilarious, it would be downright dirty. "…Pork chops and some butter beans/some sweet potatoes/you know what I mean/I can't understand why I can't eat right…. Can you understand me, sugar? You're gonna have to make love to me before I am stone...hungry." Hubert seems to have always had a fascination with food. "We were in Rockford, Illinois, after a gig, and the waitress is tired," Burckhardt relates. "Hubert starts reading items off the menu. We were scrunched up on the floor. Just the way he read it—'scramble-ed eggs'—it was hilarious and beautifully playful. It was also poking fun at himself without putting himself down. I think there is something I would like to say about Hubert: he is so unique.... When we did a gig together, I was always painfully aware that if we can get Hubert in a playing mode and having fun, then he is like nobody else."

Hickey had been one of Momma Bea's favorite adopted sons. Some have claimed that Bea was clairvoyant and had her radar up to ensure her kids were safe. She'd wake up sweating in the middle of the night because she had a bad dream involving one of her sons being in trouble. And though Hubert would deny it, clairvoyance has been an undercurrent throughout his life. He has never believed in legends such as the Robert Johnson or Peetie Wheatstraw "friend-of-the-devil" motifs, but he has a connection that goes beyond everyday life. Pianist Henry Gray thinks there may have been something extrasensory about the musical communication that he, Hubert, and Wolf had with one another. "We knew what he wanted. He didn't have to ask; we just gave him what he wanted," Gray explains. Even Hubert has to admit, "I gave him what he wanted before he could ask for it."

"Henry seems to be psychically sensitive. I wouldn't be surprised if Wolf was, too," notes Andy Cornett, Gray's manager. "Just the things he chose to sing and write about. I see it when Hubert and Henry and some of the other Wolf players are together. It's that reading between the lines when they are together—what they say and what they don't say." Perhaps all of this can be explained by Hubert's hypersensitivity to his surroundings. As a musician, he is attuned to certain people, moods, feelings, and nuances. His "powers" may also explain why he still feels a connection to Wolf today.

In March 1995, Sunnyland Slim died in Chicago. Hubert, Buddy Guy, Otis Rush, and a handful of others had become the last of the well-known, original Chicago bluesmen. It seemed that even in death, Sunnyland helped his former musician friends by elevating their status in the blues community.

Hubert was flooring people wherever he went. "We played Buddy Guy's Legends in Chicago, mid-'90s," explains Dagenhardt. "I was there with Hubert and Bob Stroger and Hubert calls off 'Hide Away' as the opener for the second set. Wouldn't you know it? He does this blistering note-for-note 'Hide Away'—with the 'Peter Gunn' break and all. I shit a brick. It is like I was looking at Freddie King, right? The band was curdled milk. You think: 'Okay, this guy is Wolf's guitar player,' but he has an immense vocabulary. The people were yelling and screaming."

Hubert is like Bruce Lee or Muhammad Ali in their prime. Misguided and lesser talents are always thinking they can beat the master, hoping for a chance meeting on the street to sucker-punch him and claim some cheesy, unearned victory. Hubert is the most congenial martial artist you'll ever meet, kind of like a human lethal weapon who doubles as a kindergarten teacher. Hubert will attack only when attacked. But when he agrees to spar, look out.

One scenario involving this very topic occurred in New York circa 1995, when Hubert was making a quick sweep along the East Coast. A friend of Hubert's was playing in Manhattan and invited him to the show. Once Hubert arrived at the venue, he was escorted backstage, where the guitar player begged him to play that evening. Hubert declined.

"No, partner, I just came to see you play. Go ahead and play."

"You mean you won't come onstage with me for just one song?" the guitarist asked.

Hubert shakes his head and rebuffs him. At show time, the guitar player takes the stage as Hubert chats backstage, listens to the music, and watches the younger player burn it up. Between sets, Hubert is again asked by the guitarist to perform with him onstage. Hubert demurs.

Finally, before the encore, the guitarist takes it upon himself to call Hubert onstage, and Hubert, not wanting to embarrass anyone, accepts the invitation. Partially annoyed, partially tired of being asked, and partially trying to prove a point, Hubert straps on his guitar and plugs himself into an amp. After tuning up momentarily, he raises the neck of the guitar, counts off to four, and blazes through a funky blues instrumental. He blows the lid off the joint, sending the guitarist cowering into the back corner of the stage. A devastating display.

"Maybe next time," Hubert grins, "he won't ask me."

In November 1996, Hubert played two shows a night for a week at Yoshi's, a Japanese restaurant and jazz club in Oakland, California, as part of the venue's Legends of Chicago Blues event. The plan was to bring together such heavyweights as Rogers, Detroit Junior (aka Emery Williams), Snooky Pryor, and Hubert. Hubert was definitely now securely in another echelon of musician. Said the *San Francisco Examiner*: "Sumlin is a distinctive guitar player and singer; he gets off some wicked guitar licks (not unlike the young Chuck Berry) and has a bag full of comments and vocal routines. He's humorous, sharp, and when he and [Jimmy D.] Lane get to dueting on guitars with [Freddie] Crawford's throbbing bass underneath, an excitement sweeps through the house."

Lane treasures his times with Hubert, then and now. Though he lives in Kansas now and doesn't see Hubert as often as he'd like, a special bond exists. "We were playing and something went on with the neck of my guitar," Lane remembers about one of his own gigs that Hubert attended in the 1990s. "I finished the night with it, but sometime later he looked at me and he said, 'Try this one.' I picked it up and it was nice. I was going to give it back to 'im, but then he said, 'Man, what are you doing? This is yours, go on.' I said, 'Huh? Hubert, this is yours. I can't accept this.' He said, 'You take that one.' I didn't want to take it, but he wouldn't take the guitar back. I still have it, to this day. That's an example of that cat's personality, man."

Having spent years playing on other people's records and cutting solo material that would have one or two Wolf tracks, Hubert decided to participate in the Telarc Records tribute to Howlin Wolf in 1997. The project involved Hubert, Henry Gray, Eddie Shaw, Sam Lay, Calvin "Fuzz" Jones, Colin Linden, and a host of other blues luminaries such as James Cotton, Cub Koda, Taj Mahal, Kenny Neal, and Lucinda Williams.

They all converged in a Maine studio to record some stunning versions of Wolf's best songs for *A Tribute to Howlin' Wolf*. Taj Mahal and Kenny Neal do fantastic impressions of the Wolf. Neal slides along on "The Red Rooster" while Hubert quietly holds down the fuzz-filled rhythm part. Hearing Hubert's playing juxtaposed to a slide player's, you have to believe that Hubert would never benefit from using a slide. He'd never have the same articulation he needs to create the understated staccato beats and knocking-and-pinning tones that are heard throughout these tunes (especially on "Just Like I Treat You"). "I never liked those things," Hubert says of bottleneck slides. "I can play it, but I hate the shit. I hate those muthafuckers who use it [in the blues]. I like it straight. Now, hillbilly and country-and-western guitar—I like listening to slide on that. They got their shit together."

The Wolf tribute sessions are brimming with excitement and are brighter, in some cases, than the originals, which seemed to simmer in slow-burning blues. And whatever differences the band members might have had among themselves in the past were put aside. Shaw even names the band members when he sings "Built for Comfort." "It was staggering how natural it all felt," says co-associate producer and guitarist/singer Linden. He got a chance to trade licks with Hubert on a number of the tracks: "Back Door Man," "Ooh Baby (Hold Me)," "Saddle My Pony," "Killing Floor" (a live staple for Hubert), "Baby How Long," and "Smokestack Lightnin'" (sung by Gray). "It is interesting that Hubert will say, 'When you hear Wolf you hear Hubert, and when you hear Hubert there's Wolf'," Linden remarks. "The two of them had that kind of chemistry. They have this huge contribution to Wolf's music. Hubert understood how heavy Wolf was."

While the band was getting to know one another, exchanging stories and niceties, Lay pulled out his home movies of Wolf and the band for evening entertainment after the recording sessions. "At the end of the second day of recording, Sam had all of these videotapes made from his home movies," Linden recalls. "I had never seen any of that footage and it blew me away. It was interesting when Sam showed all of these movies and was telling stories about all of these different people; I think it was a little too emotional for Hubert. He didn't come and watch them." Perhaps it was too emotionally difficult for Hubert. But he put his head down and worked harder—and arguably more coherently—on these sessions than on any other during the previous ten years. *A Tribute to Howlin' Wolf* seemed to kick off a recording spree.

In the past, no American record companies had been interested in recording Hubert solo. But now, in the late '90s, he had two deals: one from a small independent label, Blues Planet, and the other from Analogue Productions Originals (APO), known for their crisp audiophile-quality records. It was a true sign that Hubert's stature as a blues musician had unquestionably passed into the realm of living legend. Thanks to a younger generation of blues-lovers-turned-blues-industry-professionals (the same that had found Hubert through Eric Clapton, Jeff Beck, and the Rolling Stones), Hubert had perhaps finally been afforded the kind of reverence reserved for A-list blues veterans like B.B. King and Buddy Guy. Each record deal would set out to create *the* Sumlin solo effort. Unknowingly, the producers of those two records (what would become *Wake Up Call* on Blues Planet and *I Know You* on APO) would vie for shelf and cart space at local music stores and Web sites.

In October 1997, Hubert and a cast of legendary performers gathered at a Chicago recording studio for two days. Like so many of the

Big Bad Smitty and Hubert, Burnley Blues Festival, England, 1993.

records Hubert has made over the last two decades, *I Know You* was another reunion of sorts of Wolf players. Lay—Wolf's steady, handy drummer in the 1960s (he is the loudest in the mix, especially when his cowbell clanks)—lends his two cents (and four limbs) to the sessions. "I liked the cowbell—it was odd, it was different," Lay explains. "I was clicking away on the cowbell and they said, 'Wow, what kind of beat is that?' I said, 'I don't know, just trying to do something.'"

Lay had first joined Wolf's band after Hubert had called him at Wolf's request. Throughout his near seven-year tenure with Wolf, Sam and Hubert would grow close. It's a friendship that exists today. When he was living in Cleveland, Ohio, Lay used to see Hubert with Wolf and later with Muddy Waters. "When I came to Chicago he was back with Wolf. I got a call on a Wednesday night. Hubert called my house—actually it was an apartment building with a pay phone in the hall. A tap on the door and the telephone was for me. Wolf was playing at the Playhouse on Forty-Third and Lake Park. About half a block down from Muddy's house then. That was where he was staying. Wolf needed a drummer for that night. Could I do Wednesday night?"

The *I Know You* session also tapped Carey Bell, Muddy's and Willie Dixon's harpist throughout the early '70s, and Lane. "At APO Records, Chad Kassem [executive producer] and myself, we cut the majority of the stuff we do, live to two tracks—it is a pure analog recording," Lane notes. "So it is just like they did in the Chess studios. You set up the mics, you play. If something happens during the recording, we will scrap that one and start it over again."

Hubert cut *I Know You* plus Lane's *Legacy*, featuring Rogers, within a four-day span in October 1997 (Lane's famous father died two months after recording *Legacy*). Lane remembers the sessions as being very impromptu. "Hubert sings what comes to his mind," Lane says. "If you understand where he is going, you jump on it and you play. He had the confidence in me that I would understand this. He would start off a pattern and boom, I'd set it up for the band and translate it for them. It was pretty easy; I've listened to him all my life."

Lane had known Hubert since childhood. His father, of course, was very close to Hubert. "Pop went on the road with Wolf for a while and played some gigs together with Hubert and them. He was there when

Hubert was trying to save the day. As usual, Hubert wanted to try to make everything right. The vehicle overheated and Hubert was trying to help and opened the radiator cap and the car had to cool down. But the water shot out of there, all over Hubert. A hot stain. It scared them all to death and they didn't know if he was going to be okay. Hubert wound up being okay, and they always got along like brothers."

Its soft feel, crisp sound quality, and choice of material makes *I Know You* one of Hubert's most popular records. Hubert does whatever he wants, and when he wants to sound ferocious, he does. When he wants to cover Wolf songs, he does ("Howlin' for My Darlin'," "Mind Is Rambling"—featuring those classic Sam Lay cowbell patterns—"How Many More Years," and "Smokestack"). When he wants to whisper but retain a sense of polyrhythmic feel, he does it with ease.

"Don't Judge a Book by Its Cover" is a John Lee Hooker–like solo boogie that quietly bops along with the bass bumping while louder lead flourishes spike during the proceedings. The very depths of the swampy Delta can be heard, as can the motoring and buzz of trains and commerce in the city. Hubert's playing is busy, enjoyable, and nearly incomparable. This song is a variation on Hubert's signature song, "Groove," with that subtle, soupy mixture of swampy rhythmic meters he had soaked up as a youngster in the Mississippi Delta. That exposure seeped into his very soul and came out in this song. Other highlights of *I Know You* include Hubert performing a duet with Bell on "I'm Not Your Clown," "You My Best" (which mentions the preacher from Hubert's younger days who ate chicken with his family on a Sunday morning), and the slow blues of "I've Been Hurt." While some carping critics maintain that Hubert sounds unfocused on the CD (a condition many theorize was brought on by Hubert's alcohol intake at the time), nothing detracts from the simmering complexity of the music.

Just as recording for *I Know You* and *Legacy* wound down, New York record producers entertained visions of cutting the best Hubert record to date. For *Wake Up Call,* producers Jimmy Vivino and Jeff Alperin and executive producer Dan Beech wanted to put Hubert out in front of a competent, cohesive backing band that could let his talents shine.

Vivino, sometime guitar ace for television's *Late Night with Conan O'Brien,* has championed a number of players, such as legendary Chuck Berry "sideman" Johnnie Johnson. But playing with Hubert was to be a once-in-a-lifetime experience. Vivino and other *Conan O'Brien* alums, including Jimmy's brother Jerry, bassist Mike Merritt, and keyboardist Scott Healy, were chomping at the bit to play with the blues luminary. "I know that I am in some ways channeling players," Vivino admits. "What he can be, and all he can be, is Hubert Sumlin. And that is so great."

Hubert and Vivino hit it off so well that the younger player ended up giving Hubert a number of tokens of his appreciation. Vivino loaned Hubert a vintage 1953 Gibson Les Paul (which he plugged into a 1964 Fender Super Reverb) for the *Wake Up Call* sessions. When they ended, Vivino took that guitar back and presented Hubert with a 1955 Gibson Les Paul Gold Top. "I love Jimmy," Hubert says. "Jimmy gave me the diamond ring I got on. Not only that, he gave me six hats—four I ain't even wore yet. Jimmy means a lot to me. He gave me the guitar, Gibson guitar, just like the one I had [a Gold Top]."

"When I was talking to Hubert about doing *I Know You,* at the same time there was a guy up there in New York, Jimmy Vivino, who was going to do one," Lane recalls. "We didn't know they were doing one, and they didn't know we were. Consequently we had two records coming out back to back. It was no problem—the more music the better."

If Lane's *I Know You* was an audiophile's dream, then Vivino's *Wake Up Call* was a rip-roaring, nail-biting, "hope-we-got-that-one-on-tape" kind of session. "Hubert loved the record and I remember he said, 'Vivino felt my mind,'" Beech remarks.

Recorded in six hours at Sorcerer Sound in New York in 1997, the whirlwind recording session garnered ten power-packed guitar tracks. Hubert is in rare form here. You'd think that after recording in Chicago just a month prior he would be depleted, but the opposite is true. Hubert reconstituted himself in a big way, and sows a fertile land of sonic resources and possibilities. His phrasing and color is the stuff of legend—the type of playing to which any blues guitarist should be exposed, and might even kill or die to achieve. Hubert's stuttering, yelping, and

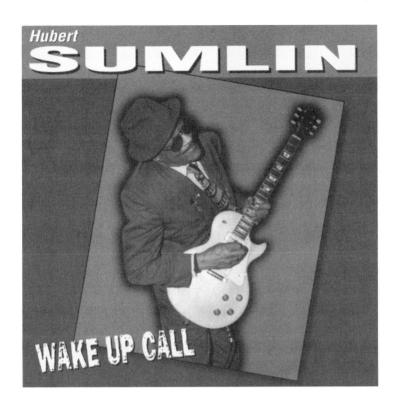

scratching sonic nosedives are so out of left field, even for this King of Spontaneity. Hubert also effectively uses silence, making things happen (or not happen), almost magically. Sounds just emanate.

The aptly titled *Wake Up Call* was a jolt, a bolt from out of the blue(s). Lightning in a bottle. It was a signal to Hubert that this was what the future held. It was also meant to inform the general public—largely unaware of Hubert—as to what it had been missing up to that point. Hubert's work on the record rivals even what he had done with the Wolf—one of the few times (if there had been any) that such a statement could be made.

"For all of those songs, Hubert was just making up words about his life—just singing," says Beech. "He was singing about everything, from his wife leaving him and all of this other stuff from his life. He'd make it all up on the spot. Hubert says that through it all he didn't even know we were recording half of the time." Hubert even commits to tape tales of his infamous cast of creepy characters. Every "sonofagun," "hippy-crit," "son of a two pair of britches," and "scuttabukka" (a variation on his "scowbugger") rears its ugly head. (He does, however, sing similar lines in "That's Why I Am Going to Leave You" on *I Know You.*) And Hubert's voice sounds appropriate in this mix (his voice is an aspect of his musical personality that critics have often called distracting and even harmful, but here it is just right).

Simply put, *Wake Up Call* is arguably Hubert's best solo effort ever released. Having said that, the rough mixes were even more representative of how ferocious Hubert was on those sessions. (He does, at times, tend to fall back into the flow on some songs instead of being the loudest component, as he should be.) Still, the album ranks as one of the guitar player's most daring, explosive, and passionate solo recordings.

In July 1998, after a Rolling Stones gig at the Stade de France in Paris, Hubert and a host of other Chicago bluesmen including Gray, Stroger, Little Smokey Smothers, Abb Locke, and Willie "Big Eyes" Smith jammed late into the night with Stones guitarists Ron Wood and Keith Richards, celebrating Mick Jagger's fifty-fifth birthday at the Plaza Anthene hotel in Paris.

This joining of Chicago blues legends and British rock royalty in the City of Lights evoked shades of recording *The London Howlin' Wolf Sessions* in the 1970s. Rumors abound about why Richards was not in attendance at those sessions, and upon investigating I never received a straight answer from any source. When I ask Hubert, he tells me, "I know Keith is upset about that. All of those young fellas was there, but he wasn't. He always says he wanted to be. I don't know why he wasn't." Then Hubert pauses and thinks about what he just said. "But he's sad about missing it."

Throughout 1999, Hubert continued to gig and record. He went into the studio to cut a song titled "Ain't That Somethin'?" with the Jim Liban Blues Combo (on Liban's *Blues for Shut-Ins* record). It was an unabashedly overt attempt to capitalize on the quirky elements of Hubert's music and personality. The lack of subtlety in the song makes it all the more funny. Vocalist/harpist Liban sings about staying healthy, about the truth of his life, and recent heartaches. All he can say is, "Ain't that somethin'?" Speaking with an emphatic "Ain't that somethin'?" or "Ain't this somethin'?," Hubert answers Liban's troubled, bluesy, creamy vocal. He also contributes guitar work to the track, weaving around the Latin beat and at other times sitting right on it.

The song brings out another musical side of Hubert, one that few people often see. It isn't hard to imagine Hubert, if given the right setting, coupling with a rapper. The possibilities would not only be hysterical but priceless. One can picture the dapper bluesman onstage, spouting off about lost love (or any subject that comes to mind) while a hot, young rapper spits bars and beefs up his performance with enough "Uhhhs" and "Ah-huhs" to make the MTV rotation. It's not so outlandish. B.B. King coupled with Heavy D for "Keep It Coming" on King's *Deuces Wild*. Rap seems to have seeped into everything these days, and for years now people have touted rap and hip-hop as the new blues. Hubert certainly has the street cred. The question is, can the same be said for the rappers with whom Hubert might partner?

Hubert truly feels what he sings—he lives or has lived it. One of the lines Liban sings in "Ain't That Somethin'?" is about Hubert's wife, who had almost died of a heart attack. "She bounced right back, man," Hubert declares. That attack was all too real for Hubert: Bea had major heart problems at the time. "Ain't That Somethin'?" was a good way to joke about serious issues and poke fun at his problems, but Hubert would soon realize that his life was no laughing matter.

Chapter 8
I Ain't Through Yet

The hospital bed call button is ringing, again. Hubert drops his guitar on the couch, rushes into the bedroom, and asks "Momma" Bea what she needs, what she wants.

This became a familiar scenario, Hubert tells me. Breathing easier on an oxygen machine but bedridden for months, Bea suffered with a heart condition in and out of the hospital for the better part of 1998 and 1999.

The force and focus that Hubert had brought to his music now had to be redirected: it was all for Bea. With the help of their adopted sons, Hubert completed every chore around the house and Bea got the best of care. "Everybody who was close to them rallied around," friend Jeff Dagenhardt confirms. "There are many people around here who were helping them out." Daughter Ida Hicks says, "I'd go up to Milwaukee and stay there for a week at a time if Hubert was on the road. I did that for nearly ten months."

Hubert was frightened. He was scared for Bea, and he was scared for himself. Though he hated to see Momma in this condition, at least when he wasn't on the road he could keep an eye on her himself. The last thing Hubert wanted was to be away from Bea for any length of time. Inevitably, though, Hubert would have to go on the road to earn money. It used to eat him up inside knowing that his wife, best friend, business manager, and rock was sick and in pain while he showed no outward signs of health problems and boarded planes, buses, and trains with ease.

Onstage or in hotel rooms, Hubert got no rest; his preoccupied mind rambled. Bea filled his every uncomfortable thought. Still, he had a hard time picking up the phone and calling her—not out of callousness, but fear. Fear that he'd hear her increasingly disintegrating voice calling for him to come home, or a caretaker telling him that something was wrong. What if something happened? He'd be miles away, sometimes across oceans, and he'd be powerless to help her. He was away when Wolf's spirit left this earth. *Goddammit, no one should be forced to go through that again.* Not again, and not with his beloved Bea. When prodded to call Milwaukee, Hubert would lower his head, get real quiet, and shake his head. "Oh, no. Oh, no. I can't call her. I can't call Momma."

Then, in late October 1999, as Hubert came back home to his Milwaukee suburb from the road, his worst fears were realized. Hubert found Bea collapsed. She was sprawled on the bathroom floor—a victim of an apparent heart attack. She was rushed to a nearby hospital, but it was too late. She was pronounced dead at 10:00 a.m. on October 26, 1999.

"She had congestive heart failure," explains Ida, now 68. "I had just left there that Sunday. Tuesday morning, the same day I had a breast biopsy, I got a call that something had happened to my mother. I knew what hospital she would always go to, so I called St. Michael's. I said that I understood that my mother had been brought there. They put me on hold and brought a doctor to the phone and I explained who I was again and I wanted to know what was going on with her. He said, 'I am sorry I have to tell you this…but she was pronounced dead this morning.'"

Hubert was devastated. Bea understood all of his faults, overlooked negative aspects of his personality, and healed him. She believed in Hubert more than he believed in himself. "I talked to him right after she passed," friend Jimmy D. Lane says. "He called me and said, 'Momma gone.' And we both cried."

For Hicks, there was some measure of closure. "I didn't know about Milwaukee at all when I was having my procedure. When a woman has a breast biopsy, they always give you a rose or a carnation when you leave the hospital. As I was driving in my car, the carnation just snapped. It broke. I go, 'Gee whiz, what is wrong with that carnation?' When I got in the house, I learned what had happened and thought, 'That was Mom… Mom letting me know she was okay.'"

But nothing could soothe Hubert's restless soul. He could hardly speak Bea's name. Even today there are times that Hubert gets emotional or stone-faced silent when Bea's name comes up. He still keeps her belongings around the house, and even locked up her costume jewelry (monetarily worthless, but sentimentally priceless) in a vault. As with Wolf's death, he hasn't fully grasped the concept of moving on. He can't.

Bea's wake was at Brookins Funeral Home on October 30, 1999, on the South Side of Chicago. Saxophonist Sam Burckhardt and keyboardist Allen Batts performed at the ceremony, and Burckhardt and harpist Bill Hickey were two of the six pallbearers. Bea was laid to rest at Washington Memory Gardens in Homewood, Illinois.

"I remember it [the cemetery] was outside of Rockford," says niece Charlene Higgs. "I was there when she was buried and I saw how distraught he was at the funeral. He was so pitiful to look at. I didn't think he was going to make it and come through. She was the one who helped him through hard times. But now she was gone. Who was going to help him?"

"Bea was really the one who made Hubert," bassist Bob Stroger notes. "She really did great things for him. I know he really misses her. She was about the only one I know who could get Hubert to do things. She could get him to do what he needed to do. Hubert could be stubborn, but she wouldn't allow that. He was a little wild back when we were touring together with Sunnyland. I used to keep his money for 'im and this way he'd have money when he came home."

"I don't know if he ever found anybody who he respected and loved as much as Wolf," friend Andy Cornett says. "And with Bea dying, sometimes I feel as though he is kind of waiting for that connection again. That is kind of missing in his life, you know?" Hubert's current manager, Toni Ann Mamary, recalls, "For months after, Hubert wouldn't touch anything in the house that belonged to her. There was a Bible on the kitchen table that I tried to move one day and he got really mad: 'Leave that. Don't touch that! What are you doing?'"

"Hubert took it very hard," Hicks confirms. "He stayed away from the house. He wanted me to stay at the house at the time. I would go there and stay a week at a time. Come back, stay in Rockford maybe a week, and go back up there."

Depressed, Hubert hid inside his music. In February 2000, he made the trek to Los Angeles for the Grammy Awards ceremony. His record *Legends* with piano great Pinetop Perkins (who had played with Muddy Waters and the Legendary Blues Band) was up for an award. As usual, Hubert—regardless of his own mental or physical situation—spread his kindness. "We hung out for the pre-party and that whole night," says Susan Tedeschi, who was up for Best New Artist. "Hubert made it bearable. It was nice to hang out with someone who was real."

"The whole experience was so…it was just the opposite of what I believe music is about," says Tedeschi's husband, Derek Trucks, of the Allman Brothers Band. "It was completely bumming me out. Halfway through it, we ran into Pinetop and Hubert and it made the whole trip worthwhile. Hubert and I had the same vest on, and he was so funny. He said, 'Man, we are handsome.' I told Susan, 'That saved it for me.' Meeting Hubert made the whole trip worthwhile."

Far from the pomp and circumstance of the Grammy Awards, later that year Hubert found himself in a small New York studio with avant-blues guitarist Elliott Sharp and his band, Terraplane, for Sharp's socially conscious *Blues for Next*. It is amazing how far-reaching Hubert's style has been. Guitarists from nearly every genre cite him as an influence. Sharp was an admitted science geek as a teen, and that has had a big influence on his compositional approach to writing music. Having the unpredictable Hubert as a fly in the ointment was appealing to Sharp, so he asked the veteran to cut the tracks "Rollin' & Tumblin'" and "S-Boogie" alone in the studio (the band was overdubbed on top of Hubert's tracks). Sharp's avant-garde approach worked well with Hubert's sense of time and spontaneous creations, blending a combustible brew of blues in another dimension. "I loved it, the tracks really breathed," Sharp says. "Those tracks, for me, are the highlights of the record. We eventually got an offer to bring Hubert to Paris for a week—which we did."

In September, Hubert visited the burgeoning Howlin' Wolf Museum in West Point, Mississippi, and played at the Howlin' Wolf Memorial Blues Festival for Wolf's ninetieth birthday celebration with Eddie Shaw,

Shorty Gilbert, Henry Gray, and Sam Lay. Aside from being born in West Point, Wolf had often returned to the area to fish and hunt. In the center of town stands a bronze statue of him—patterned after the famous photo of a lanky Chester Burnett (lanky for Wolf) in a grocery store playing an electric guitar. The instrument looks like a child's toy instrument in Wolf's huge hands.

"When we flew Hubert down for the festival, he didn't want to fly into Columbus on a small plane, so we sent a limo into Memphis," recalls Richard Ramsey, program director of West Point's Howlin' Wolf Blues Society. "Wolf considered Hubert his son, and he would bring him down to West Point. Sometimes it would be with the band, and sometimes it would be just Wolf. I remember Hubert coming down with him. And Hubert remembered coming into my dad's store—Ramsey's Tire and Appliance—because it was the easiest place for Wolf and the guys to get a hunting and fishing license. So, I said, 'You remember Miss Annie Eggerson' [formerly Annie Stevenson, who married Wolf's cousin Levy Eggerson]? Hubert says, 'Yeah. Oh, lord! I slept on

Hubert at the Bury Blues Festival, England, 2000.

her front porch and she cooked chicken. Wolf could eat two whole chickens and two whole pans of biscuits.' Then when he arrived at the Howlin' Wolf statue here...he squalled like a baby in my arms at that statue. That was pretty heavy."

"Every time we would tour the South, we would always stop [in West Point] and spend the night and people would put the whole band up," Hubert says. "These are the people who raised me. And I ain't never seen another statue like that in my life. It is like the W.C. Handy Park statue [in Memphis]. It is beautiful to be remembered."

Just around the corner was new hope for Hubert's career. He would soon embark on a recording project so wide in scope, its effects are still felt today.

The initial concept was to have Hubert cover a number of songs popularized (but not necessarily written) by Muddy Waters—a bit of a curveball, since most people expect Hubert to dig into Howlin' Wolf's vast catalog. This surprise element attracted certain interested parties. "Remember when they would have records like the Beatles vs. the Four Seasons?" quizzes Arnie Goodman, whose Viceroy Music (later Mystic Entertainment) was involved with the project.

"We felt that since Hubert played with Muddy for a period of his life that it was a logical choice," says Rob Fraboni, producer of such artists as Eric Clapton, The Band, and the Rolling Stones and the man who would head up the new project. "Besides, where are you going to find good new blues songs to record? We felt it didn't make sense to do Wolf songs. We thought we should get great material and that will set us off on the right foot."

The project soon morphed into a rather explosive one: Fraboni wanted to bring in two very high-profile rockers who were influenced by Hubert. "European labels would give Hubert a record deal and have him make a record and he would sing," Fraboni explains. "Hubert is not really a singer, you know? He is a guitar player. So, if we are going to do this record, he should really play guitar. And then we could get some different people to sing. Just get some cool voices. However, there are two high-profile guests we have to get: one is Eric Clapton, who came on board immediately after hearing what we were doing.

"I knew of Wolf, but I had not zoned in on Hubert at that point," Fraboni continues. "The first time I went to [Eric's] house in England he played me a track, 'Ooh Baby,' the flip of 'Tell Me What I've Done,' on the jukebox. It has this killer solo—well, the whole thing is killer. I'll never forget it and it means a lot to me. Eric said, 'Listen to this. Listen to the guitar playing. It doesn't get any better than this.' Then when I met Keith [Richards] he also started talking to me about Hubert and he said that Hubert was 'the architect of the blues guitar.' That is what he called him. He is right in a lot of ways, if you think about that. I mean, all of the licks that he came up with…."

The second major name that Fraboni wanted to bring on board was, in fact, none other than Rolling Stone Keith Richards. "I met Hubert once when I was with Keith at a Stones show," Fraboni explains. "It was probably in 1985. I just met him, he came there with his wife [Bea], and came and said hello to Keith and hung out in the dressing room for 20 minutes before the show. Then Arnie [Goodman] said to me that he wanted to do a record with Hubert. I met with Hubert at that time. Then, it was funny, we met with Keith before we started the record."

It was settled: Clapton and Richards were in, and soon a stellar cast of musicians was invited to participate: guitarist Bob Margolin, harpist/guitarist Paul Oscher, pianist David Maxwell, harpist James Cotton, vocalist David Johansen, drummer Levon Helm, drummer/vocalist George Receli, vocalist/bassist Nathaniel Peterson, bassist Michael "Mudcat" Ward, and others. The project was then given a name: *About Them Shoes* (more on that in a moment).

"I believe I am going to kick some ass on this one," Hubert told Fraboni in a recorded interview during the making of the record. "They are all coming to my rescue. You never know who will be thinking about you [in this business]."

Margolin was the bandleader for the principal recording sessions, which took place in March 2000 at the Showplace in Dover, New Jersey. As the leader, it was up to Margolin to get things moving, and moving smoothly. (He would later try a similar star-power concept with his 2003 Telarc release *All Star Blues Jam,* which features Hubert on two tracks, recorded on a hard-disk recorder at Margolin's North Carolina home). "If someone didn't lead it, we would have just hung out and jammed," Margolin says. "After setting up the first day, we listened to Muddy songs that I brought in and chose some."

About the album's title: admittedly, it's an odd one. The liner notes reveal the origin of *About Them Shoes*, but when I ask Hubert about the record's title, he gives me an entirely different response. "We just got the idea for the album when we were sitting in the studio trying to figure out what to name the record," Hubert recalls. "Then Levon spoke: 'What about *Them Shoes?*' I said, '*What* fuckin' shoes?' Then I said, 'Wait! That's a name!' And everybody agreed.

"I got to thinking about the name," Hubert continues. "Those shoes—that makes you think of anybody who you gets into this business and love the way they are doing it. It's about *walking in those shoes* and making people happy—doing it every day. Once you are in *those shoes*, you have found your place. Other people say, 'Muddy walked in these shoes,' and 'Wolf walked in these shoes.'"

Hubert had broken in plenty a pair of those with Wolf and Muddy. He shared their time, music, headspace, and very living quarters. "The shoes fit," so to speak. However, there has always been speculation as to whether Hubert actually played on some of the classic Muddy tracks. But after hearing the originals again (in an effort to choose a suitable group of songs for *About Them Shoes*), Margolin was convinced that Hubert was on at least one track that is not normally credited to him. "Hubert apparently *did* play on the original of 'Don't Go No Farther,'" Margolin points out. "I didn't realize. So it was an amusing surprise when I suggested that song and Hubert smiled and said, 'That's me.' It certainly is."

Hubert may not be credited with playing on some Muddy Waters records (as the liner notes to two Muddy anthologies state), but that is easily explained. Liner notes can often be wrong, as Hubert himself has said many times. Whether Chess Records should have taken more care to document the proceedings is a matter of question. They were in the record-making and record-selling business. As Marshall Chess admits, "We were not interested in making great art."

One thing is for sure, though: Muddy was always fond of Hubert's playing. According to Margolin, "We had run into Hubert with Eddie

Shaw & The Wolf Gang, not long after Wolf died, when they opened for Muddy at a club in western Massachusetts. Muddy mentioned that Hubert had played with him for a while. It seemed that Hubert and Muddy were good friends and that Muddy enjoyed Hubert's playing."

Excitement brewed for days before Clapton arrived in the studio for *About Them Shoes.* "I remember having this big black trunk in my hallway that had big white block letters that read 'Eric Clapton,'" says recording engineer Ben Elliott. "I couldn't believe Clapton was coming to New Jersey." Maxwell remembers, "Eric came in, polite, and there was the usual snapping of the photos with him."

Clapton's first song was "I'm Ready," written by Willie Dixon for Muddy in 1954. The song is a boisterous, ridiculously overt display of braggadocio that can't be taken seriously. (It's a subtle aspect of these tunes that is sometimes lost on later generations.) The singer is begging for someone to pick a fight with him. Sure, there are tough elements to the song, and Clapton fires up his Strat to conquer them, but his somewhat lighthearted approach captures the satirical elements perfectly. How else could a singer, straight-faced, play off the hyperbole of lines like "I'm drinkin' TNT/I'm smokin' dynamite/I hope some screwball start a fight."

"I'm Ready" is a great leadoff song. Hubert takes the first solo (after Clapton yells "Hubert!"), Oscher follows with a river of melodic fury, then Clapton rips a contrasting mellow/screaming solo. "Instead of doing it in *E*, he did it in *E-flat*," Maxwell points out. "That was interesting. I guess he wanted to sing it that way. I think with a chromatic harp it would be *E-flat*. With the chromatic harp you can get a *D-minor* sound, but with the button pushed you can get an *E-flat minor* sound. That's how Paul Oscher did it. That was fun."

The ambience of the track makes it one of the best-sounding songs on *About Them Shoes.* Fraboni explains why: "The room at the Showplace is probably 30 feet by 21 feet, and 12 feet high. It is a pretty good-sized room. When Eric was singing he was standing right in the middle of the room—with no baffles or anything. The musicians weren't in isolation booths at all. The record has an old ambient sound like an old Chess record. Those records were all made with half a dozen mics at the max." After ripping through "I'm Ready," Clapton and Fraboni decided to do "Long Distance Call." "We did his two songs live in the studio in two and a half hours," Fraboni says.

Indeed, many of these tracks sound straight out of a lost, late-night Chess Records session, especially "Come Home Baby" featuring Oscher and "Long Distance Call" featuring Clapton. They have the feel of a band that unwound on a smoky Chicago nightclub stage, loaded up the car, and landed in the studio at 4:00 a.m.

A number of the players were intimate with Muddy's material—Maxwell, Oscher, and Margolin in particular. They provided a solid base for Hubert to play what he wanted. "That was a fun rhythm section, Mudcat on bass," says Helm, who played with Muddy as part of The Band's *The Last Waltz* production. "We just tried to support Hubert's fills and flavoring. We all got around Hubert and made up the rhythm section. George [Receli] is a better session player than I am, that's the truth. He don't have more fun than I do, but he is better at it. We are both from down yonder, so we have the heavy-on-the-backbeat approach to it. That's what makes it rock."

If Clapton's two tracks were the most accessible, then "Still a Fool," Keith Richards's first track, might be the most passionate. It is one of the most gritty and sizzling vocal performances Richards has ever delivered. "Keith's track is incredible," Fraboni says. "He is singing live and just nailed it." Hubert's unpredictable lines and the piercing feedback and sustain actually punctuate Richards's lead vocal. Receli shakes a tambourine and stomps four on the floor with his kick drum. The interplay between Hubert and Richards works very well. These are two grizzled, been-there-done-that guitar players getting the chance to perform front and center. Aptly, they don't overdo it, but feed off each other, allowing a small sonic flame to burn and create a kind of subtle tension between the two. This is true blues—what *About Them Shoes* was all about.

Richards (whose world-famous band took their name from a Muddy song) was the last person to record on the formal session, even though he had done some studio work with Hubert at his Connecticut home before the recording process for *About Them Shoes* began in earnest at the Showplace. "Two weeks, I did tracks at his house," Hubert says. "I said, 'Man, you got to play some fuckin' blues, man. Can you play the blues?' He said, 'Goddammit, I can play the fuckin' blues.' I said, 'Well,

Hubert with photo of Keith Richards, 2002.

you know, I am just sayin'.' Keith said, 'Ain't nobody but me and him.' He was right. Keith, he can play the blues, man. He can play the blues!"

Fraboni tells of an earlier encounter: "I brought Hubert up to Keith's house and he met Keith's mom; she happened to be over there from England that day. She got so excited. She was hugging him and squeezing him and jumping up and down. Eighty years old and she couldn't believe she was meeting him. Keith and Hubert, of course, had met, but always on the road. He would come and visit Keith when the Stones came to town. But he had never been to his house."

When Richards finally made it to the Showplace to officially cut tracks for *About Them Shoes,* somehow word got out. "Clapton did his tracks and he was gone," Maxwell says. "When Keith came, it was more of a party. People were just hanging out. People were out there at the studio to see Keith."

It became a circus, with people trying to get into the studio, people standing outside in the parking lot to catch a glimpse of a rock icon or perhaps hear him cutting a track or two. At one point someone called the cops. "They almost got all of us busted in one of those little towns down in New Jersey," Helm says. "We all got rousted by the cops and got our room searched. It was a hell of a mess. I'm still trying to figure out why we didn't use my studio up here in Woodstock. I've got the best damn studio in New York. The cops don't roust people out of bed up here and search the goddamned rooms."

There are several great renditions on *About Them Shoes*. On the original "Don't Go No Farther," Hubert's restrained noodling is in sharp contrast to Muddy's rough yelps. The 2000 version is like Muddy resurrected: vocalist Nathaniel Peterson is spot-on for the Hoochie Coochie Man, while Hubert's tinny tone acts as a laser beam cutting through the haze of distorted guitar and amplified harp.

David Johansen came in for two tracks: "Walkin' Thru the Park" and "The Same Thing." "Walkin' Thru the Park" (on 1969's *Fathers and Sons*) featured Lay's idiosyncratic cowbell pattern, here replaced by maracas and ride cymbal. Oscher takes the high road, providing what would normally be the lead guitarist's role. Hubert holds down the fort. Johansen normally performs with his requisite rough Wolf vocals, but tackling Muddy's creamier and, in some ways, deeper voice seems nearly impossible. He manages, though, to catch a bit of Muddy in what he is doing. "David is great at taking on a character like a Wolf or Muddy," Fraboni notes. "He is the master at that."

Unlike Johansen, Hubert is not a chameleon and never has been. Although Johansen can easily morph himself into different personas to fit a given musical setting, in Hubert there exists only one distinct personality. Hubert's guitar tone and attack have always said "Hubert Sumlin." These aspects of his playing are his musical fingerprints.

Throughout the sessions Hubert used his pinkish/red-faced guitar that's much like a Stratocaster and the 1955 Gibson Les Paul Gold Top that Jimmy Vivino gave him. Hubert plugged into his 30-watt HS M12C Louis Electric amp. "I brought Keith to meet Les Paul one night, and when we went to that show, Louis [Rosano, founder of Louis Electric Amplifier Company] happened to be there to see Les," Fraboni explains. "He came up to me and he gave me the amp to give to Keith. So [Keith] took the amp, and this was right before I did the initial sessions for Hubert's record. I called Louis and we used only his amps. Hubert's was a funky little amp—we were trying to emulate the amps Hubert had back in the day."

"Years ago Hubert was into Sears Silvertones," says Rosano. "In the old gear, the speaker coils, what winds around the magnet, were made out of paper and some of the ones today are made out of plastic. Plastic can dissipate heat better and they are more reliable, but they don't have the tone. That's what we focus on and what Hubert wants."

Perhaps it has to do with the equipment, Hubert's playing, or just the fact that all of the musicians involved were "in a zone," but *About Them Shoes* sounds so cohesive, so together, that no one would have guessed at the outset how the entire process would unfold. Despite the intensity of the music, at presstime of this book the record had yet to be released for a variety of reasons. At first, it seemed that everyone had the best of intentions in coming out and supporting Hubert. But after a while, it looked as if the project was about everything *but* Hubert.

Where to start?

Fraboni's label, Domino, was bought by Arnie Goodman and became Viceroy Music. Then Viceroy was bought by Mystic Entertainment. "During the Internet craze, Mystic came in and made an offer of

Hubert at the Citadel Arts Centre, St. Helens, England, 2000.

ridiculously big money for Viceroy," Goodman says. Not long after that buyout, and during the making of *About Them Shoes,* Mystic went bankrupt. "My check and Hubert's check bounced the day we were in the studio with Clapton, funny enough," Fraboni notes. "And so, that's the first thing that threw everything into limbo."

Goodman tells me that he did eventually write personal checks to Hubert and Fraboni, but for nine months the record sat in a state of inertia, and the recording and production fees hadn't been paid in full. An initial investor, Greg Russell, had relinquished the project. Jordan Birnbaum, a former Juno.com executive, bought the then-incomplete recordings from Russell, shouldering the bulk of the costs and signing on to see *About Them Shoes* through to fruition. Birnbaum would continue to fund the record, down to the artwork. He explains: "Where we ran into problems was A, getting all of our clearances taken care of, and B, finding a distributor and someone who would have the money to market the project, because I would pretty much tap myself out by the time this recording was over. It was definitely going to need another [business] player to take the finished product and market it."

"The thing is," Fraboni adds, "Keith's deal is that if he does the vocals on any tracks, he owns the track. So that was kind of…that made it a little unsmooth. Then the problem was that neither Keith nor Mick [Jagger] could put out something on a record where they sing lead during what is a 'Stones year,' meaning when the Stones are active. That was part of the holdup."

Still more problems occurred. "At that time, Rob Fraboni and I were trying to start a new business," Birnbaum says. "The business became unfeasible and it turned out that we were not really right to work together. So, as that separation happened, the record got pulled into that energy."

For a time there was a question about where the *About Them Shoes* tracks were physically (they were finally located) and who actually owned them. As far as he is concerned, Birnbaum is confident he has the paperwork in place to ensure that he is still the owner of the tracks.

"All those guys, man, coming out for me—it'll come out," Hubert sums up. "I know it will." Hubert lowers his head, checks his shoes, and nods. I wonder if he really believes his own words.

Months after the 9/11 terrorist attacks, after work was halted on Richards's tracks for *About Them Shoes* (precisely because of those attacks), Hubert was experiencing problems breathing. He couldn't shake a nagging, hacking cough. He began to complain of chest pains, and the thought of heart failure—the same thing his wife died of— terrified him.

Toni, Hubert's personal manager for over five years, wasn't taking any chances, and had Hubert see a few doctors to find out what was wrong, if anything. The prognosis wasn't good. It was lung cancer. The disease was the amalgam of years on the road—years of smoking and inhaling secondhand smoke in blues joints.

"He was really matter-of-fact about life and death at that time," Dagenhardt remembers. "He would always say, 'Well, you gotta go, you gotta go.' We would discuss Wolf and Muddy and it was almost his way of saying, 'It is a fact of life and let's talk about something else.' He thought it was curtains, you know?"

It seemed Bea's death had consumed Hubert's own life. And a number of other family members had been diagnosed with cancer. Hubert's spirit seemed ravaged. "It was right after Bea had passed, and it was just like a cluster surrounding him," Dagenhardt says. "Then he found out about himself. It was grim."

Toni and Hubert didn't like the answers, or options, they were being fed by the doctors. "One doctor wrote him off," Toni points out. "He said, 'You might as well let him continue to do the things he's doing.' I was like…," Toni gasps. "That was it for that doctor."

On the advice of Levon Helm, who has spent the better part of the past decade battling throat cancer (the disease has decimated his once powerful singing voice), Toni took Hubert to Memorial Sloan-Kettering Cancer Center for another opinion. "I got in the hospital, New York cancer hospital, where Levon Helm was operated on for cancer," Hubert says. "I got in the door and I had to walk about a block from the car to the hospital, and it felt like I was having a heart attack. I'm thinking, 'If this is the way I got to go, take me now.' It was hurtin' that bad. I knows that when I got in the door, I could not breathe. I was just making it in the door. Then, I don't know, man, everything just got well. Then it stopped hurtin' when I got inside. At least I thought it was all better."

It was only a momentary lapse in the pain. Something far more serious was happening. "I turned around, but they forced me to see a doctor," Hubert says. "It wasn't the heart, it was the lung. The left lung. I come out and I had a hole in my lung as big as a silver dollar, in the middle of my left lung—that is what the doctor told me. They told me, 'Mr. Sumlin, there is nothing wrong with your other lung.'" Hubert had to accept the prognosis. There was no doubt: he had cancer of his left lung. "The doctor told me, 'We have to take the whole lung.' You know what? I told him, 'God bless.' That is what I told 'em."

The blues world was stunned and held its breath. "When these Huberts, Buddys, and B.B.s are gone, I mean, who do we have left?" asks up-and-comer Renee Austin, a W.C. Handy Award nominee. "The masters are slowly dwindling in numbers," Col. Bruce Hampton says. "He is the last of a lineage that goes back to the Delta. There is no replacing Hubert Sumlin."

On November 7, 2002, Hubert Sumlin entered New York's Memorial Sloan-Kettering Cancer Center to undergo pneumonectomy (the complete surgical removal of a lung). "They operated on me and went over me, they scanned my brain and everything I got in the world," Hubert declares. "They did everything to see if I had prostate [cancer], did I have this or that? They went down my throat with a camera…oh. I didn't feel nothin'. I woke up the next morning, I am hungry like a sonofagun. I was ready to go to work. I was ready to get back on the road."

"Hubert had surgery on a Friday, and I visited him on a Sunday and he was up walking around, two days after the surgery," explains New York bluesman Jon Paris. "It was incredible. Hubert was so excited about getting phone calls from Elvis Costello and Eric Clapton and all of these major stars trying to find out how he was. He was so 'up.' If I had gone through that, I don't know how I would have done it."

Hubert recovered for a few days in the hospital, and then spent a few weeks at Toni's home in suburban New Jersey. "Now, I don't have to have chemo, I don't have to do nothin'," Hubert says. "Just every three months I have to [go in for a check-up]. I could have had cancer

all over me. Oh, lord! Yes, I am lucky, that is what I am talking about."
Hubert may very well be lucky: the consequences could have been a lot
worse. The cancer did not spread through his body and he has made a
miraculous recovery. "The man must have angels watching over him,"
Toni says. "He is blessed."

Within a few months, Hubert was playing on *Late Night with
Conan O'Brien* with his pal Jimmy Vivino, and crisscrossing the country for benefit concerts in his honor. "I felt like I had been born again.
The doctor told me, 'Mr. Sumlin, it may take you a year, maybe it won't.
May take you longer to get back to 90 percent. But you are going to get
back.' That made me feel good. I am taking my medicine and everything. I started thinking, 'I got a second chance here. And I am going to
make the best of it.'"

Hubert wasn't out of the woods yet. His healthcare coverage
didn't cover all of his medical bills. To help lighten his financial burden,
three benefits were organized: one in New York, one in Asbury Park,
New Jersey, and another in Memphis. The New York concert at B.B.
King's Blues Club & Grill on January 22, 2003, brought the highest
financial returns. Organized primarily by Toni with Bob Putignano, DJ
for WFUV-FM radio (Fairleigh Dickinson University in Teaneck, New
Jersey) and the director of the New York Jazz and Blues Society, the
show boasted some heavyweight names: Jimmy Vivino, Vernon Reid,
Marc Ribot, David Maxwell, Levon Helm, Elliott Sharp, Michael Hill,
David Johansen, Greg Piccolo, and others.

Earlier in the afternoon, guitarist Michael Hill had played on Putignano's radio program with Hubert. "For me it is an honor to play with
Hubert Sumlin," Hill says. "He is a master of the form. It reminds me
of when I played rhythm guitar with B.B. King. With B.B., he opens his
mouth and the spirit is there. Hubert Sumlin is like that. He plays with
the same kind of feeling and passion. It is palpable, and so that was a
creative experience for me. In fact, I wound up improvising a song
about Hubert Sumlin on [the radio] show, and then we played it at the
benefit. It was Hubert Sumlin, Elliott Sharp, Marc Ribot, and myself
for a guitar quartet.

"'Strumming with Hubert Sumlin' is the name of it," Hill continues.
"The lyrics go: 'Are we getting ready?/Gettin' ready?/Gettin' set?/Hubert

has been under the knife but he is not finished yet/The man was rid-
ing shotgun when the Wolf was on the prowl/the Wolf has the voice/
Hubert made the guitar howl/So, we're picking and strumming, with
Hubert Sumlin.'"

Despite the celebrity of the players and the spiritually uplifting
mood of the event, benefit organizers were worried that the biting January cold would keep the crowds away. It didn't. People showed up and
opened their wallets for Hubert. The benefit raised nearly $12,000.
"There was a boatload of CDs," Putignano says. "We went to all the
labels [for CD donations]. We had signed CDs, posters, pictures of
Hubert. Dick Waterman even gave us a print. All of the raffles were just
shy of $2,000."

The benefits at B.B. King's Blues Club & Grill in Memphis and the
Stone Pony in Asbury Park were similar star-studded affairs, and proved
how much one blues guitarist means to the music community. "Hubert
played—but we tried to get him *not* to play," says Tom Cucchiara,
organizer of the Pony Up for Hubert event in Asbury Park. "He wanted
to play. We waited until that evening to bring him up."

Today Hubert continues to record and travel. He cut three tracks in
2003 with Elliott Sharp's Terraplane (a politically charged record titled
Do the Don't, a play on the song "Do the Do") on which he used one of
Sharp's semi-acoustic electric Gibsons. These tracks prove once again
that Hubert can sound the same no matter what tool he uses—slippery
and indescribable. He defies steady metric pulse and electronic drumming ("In the Drift") and flirts with chaos and restraint ("Oil Blues").
Which one he courts is a matter of mood and taste at the moment.

Unlike Sharp's *Blues for Next,* for *Do the Don't* Hubert went into
Sharp's home studio after a rhythm track was laid down. "Hubert just
came over to my place and placed his solos over tracks. It is amazing
how quickly he gets it," Sharp says. "For a song like 'Oil Blues,' I plugged
Hubert into a Fender Vibrolux Reverb reissue, which is an amp that will
give you clean gain. You crack the volume to two and it is the perfect
blues tone. Then, I took a DI [direct input] off of him and ran that

through a compressor and recorded it right into Pro Tools. I like a punchy guitar tone, and having the DI allows me to have that. I had a condenser mic on Hubert's amp and then I had a duplicate of the DI run through a plug-in. I found out that Hubert plays with such incredible tone, I really didn't have to do much at all [in Pro Tools]. He was playing a Silvertone, an ES-335 knockoff, really, and it sounded great. I've always believed that tone is in the fingers." (Hubert fans take note: an unreleased Sumlin solo record is in Sharp's can. It features guests such as S.P. Leary and Calvin "Fuzz" Jones, and Hubert and David Maxwell do a duet version of "Forty-Four.")

Meanwhile, more and more musicians and music fans were getting the blues. Hubert began to appear everywhere: on public television's *Martin Scorsese Presents The Blues*, in a DVD about the life of Howlin' Wolf, in a Wolf biography, and on a new record with Eric Bibb and James Cotton. With this higher profile came more work. Recently he's been through Australia, Canada, Europe, the West Coast—you name it. Hubert pushes on.

"After he had a few good jobs and the prognosis was good, he snapped back real well," Dagenhardt says. "I had him visit my doctor here in Milwaukee as well as the Sloan-Kettering, and the guy couldn't believe that he had lost a lung. He couldn't believe that the guy had bounced back with such a vengeance. He has this heavy-duty fuse. He has a cast-iron constitution."

Hubert, of course, is not the only musician who deals with a medical condition on a daily basis. B.B. King, for instance, who still tours internationally and plays over 250 dates a year, has been living with diabetes since 1990. "It can be hard on a musician who has diabetes to constantly prick your fingers [to take blood glucose levels] like that," King says. "It hurts to play. But I have been living with it for a long time. I have been in 89 countries around the globe. In fact, we just came back from Brazil, where we sold out."

Hubert is working through his medical condition and fending off temptation as much as possible. As his colleagues attest, he is still very much out and about: "He was wearing the patch when he was in Scandinavia," Maxwell notes about a recent tour through the Nordic countries. "Hubert was playing strongly, really coming out with amazing lines. He is a man of the moment. He'll play the classic Wolf tunes, but the way he embellishes and responds to what is around him is extraordinary. He comes up with slides and nuances and licks, stuff I have never heard before."

"Bryon Bay is Australia's premier roots music event, a five-day extravaganza with huge crowds and plenty of big name acts," says Aussie guitarist/songwriter Fiona Boyes. "The expectations of a big crowd coupled with the band's growing confidence in playing with Hubert all coalesced into a very satisfying show. While the festival had an impressive array of headlining talent—James Brown, Solomon Burke, Dr. John, Mavis Staples, Robben Ford, Burning Spear, Steve Earl, Taj Mahal— many people said that we were the best, bluesiest thing they heard." Hubert elaborates: "Twenty-five hours on a plane, man. But it was great. Got a chance to play with everyone in the world. They got everybody in the world there, man. James Brown, Dr. John...."

"I got the invitation to go to Seattle to play at the Hendrix tribute concert in February," Jimmy D. Lane says. "It was Hubert, Tommy Shannon, and Chris Layton, along with Mike Macready from Pearl Jam. All of us were onstage doing 'Killing Floor.' We had a Wang Dang Doodle, man. We were playing and laughing on stage and having a good time." Shannon adds, "I remember we were onstage and I looked over and he was sitting on a chair and he had this big ole grin on his face. My heart—I just had a good feeling coming over me. He played real quiet, for one thing. Hubert was sitting on a stool and he and Buddy Guy played together so well. There are no words for some things. It was fun hearing every note. It was such a groove. The two of them together, it blended so well and all I had to do was kind of jump in the river and let it guide me."

"There is something about his groove," explains Allman Brothers Band member Derek Trucks, who also fronts his own band. "His appearance in March of this year [2004] was the highlight of [ABB's] run at the Beacon Theatre for me. We played a three-hour show with the Allman Brothers and he got up there and he just locked into this groove for about 15 seconds. It just seemed so authentic. It was amazing. It makes you think, 'What am I doing up here?' I hear him do that and it is so in his blood. He is just one of those magical players."

"Eric came into my dressing room and we laid down the set list," Robert Cray recalls of a show-ending blues jam at Eric Clapton's Cross-roads Guitar Festival in June 2004. "Everybody kept loose. It was fun and we did 'Killing Floor' with Hubert. Amazing. We let 'er rip off the top."

"When I saw him at the Wheeling, West Virginia, festival six months ago, he was like a little boy," Col. Bruce Hampton says. "You'd never know that he had but one lung. He didn't care. He jumped up and down a lot, and got up on his chair and started jumping up and down—out of breath. It was actually inspiring."

Hubert may be pressing on, performing such minor miracles before musicians' eyes, but his lung surgery and the cumulative effect of years on the road have taken their toll. He is on daily blood pressure medication and sometimes can't catch his breath. He has to hook himself up to his oxygen machine—a relic left behind by Bea. He has tried to stay away from cigarettes and alcohol since his operation, switching to the nicotine patch for his cravings. His friends worry about him.

"Last time we worked together," Stroger says, "I think me and Willie Smith broke out on his butt on it, you know? Hubert don't know that

Jimmie Vaughan, David Johansen, and Hubert
at the Crossroads Festival, 2004.

everybody loves him and we all worry about him. I used to smoke like a choo-choo train, but that is something that you want to do yourself. You have to want to stop. I know I gave it up cold turkey. Willie Smith gave it up cold turkey. He knows I'm gonna get on his ass about that anytime I see him."

Hubert played his autographed Les Paul at the Crossroads Guitar Festival in 2004. The axe was signed by many of the stars present at the "Year of the Blues" tribute at Radio City Music Hall in 2003.

Henry Gray can sympathize with Hubert's dilemma. "I admit that I had a problem," says Gray, who claims he hasn't had a drop in years. "I've told him to stop. A lot of people have. He's drinking and wants to drink, ain't none o' my business. But I know we's always tight, always were—Wolf, Hubert, and myself." Andy Cornett adds, "All of those guys used to smoke and drink. Henry played with Sonny Boy Williamson II, and Sonny would go through a fifth or two a night. He'd buy everybody a bottle of whatever he wanted. Then he'd take his bottle out, take the top off, take his dick out, and rub it on the top of his bottle. Then he say, 'Okay, you ain't taking my shit.' Literally marking his territory."

Hubert and Toni say that Hubert's drink intake is minimal these days. They do, however, have to monitor his smokes. "I can't bear to look at him when he is very sick," Toni says. "I am not over the first bout with lung cancer. To me it feels like yesterday."

"I'm still here," Hubert says. "I ain't through yet. Everyone else is gone, but I'm still here."

An iconoclast electric blues player, Hubert won't break with tradition in one sense. Like most bluesmen, he doesn't sit around and let life pass him by. He works. He travels. Bluesmen play because they love to play—because they have to.

In 2004, Hubert got some great news: a letter from the Keith Richards camp to Hubert's lawyer, Robert Baldori, granted the go-ahead to release Richards's lead vocal contribution to *About Them Shoes*, "Still a Fool." So as this book went to print, the 13 tracks on *About Them Shoes* were: "I'm Ready" (Dixon), "Still a Fool" (McKinley Morganfield, aka Muddy Waters), "She's into Something" (Wright), "Iodine in My Coffee" (Morganfield), "Look What You've Done" (Morganfield), "Come Home Baby" (Morganfield), "Evil" (Morganfield), "Long Distance Call" (Morganfield), "The Same Thing" (Dixon), "Don't Go No Farther" (Dixon), "I Love the Life I Live" (Dixon) (with Recile on vocals, Richards on guitar and background vocals), "Walkin' Thru the Park" (Morganfield) (with Johansen on vocals), and "Little Girl, This Is the End" (Sumlin) (an acoustic number with Richards and Hubert on acoustic guitars, Hubert on vocals).

And more great news: I've learned that Tone-Cool Records/Artemis Records has finalized a deal with the Sumlin camp to release *About Them Shoes* in early 2005—even though it's a "Stones year."

Coda:
Healing Feeling

I was scheduled to travel again with Hubert to visit his brother A.D. Smith in Elaine, Arkansas, and his sister Maggie Watkins in Memphis. But Hubert complained of feeling ill and the trip was postponed indefinitely. Two weeks later Hubert had a heart attack, landing in critical but stable condition in a Milwaukee hospital. He had just returned from the ninth annual Mount Baker Blues Festival in Washington State where, via cell phone, he had told me the show went well and that he was feeling fine. "Yeah, I'm okay, son," he said in his everything's-gonna-be-alright tone.

It seems that while enjoying himself at a casino in Milwaukee, Hubert had blacked out and needed to be revived. He refused to go to the hospital, choosing instead to go home and rest. While at home, Hubert blacked out again and was rushed to the hospital. Bleeding internally, he regained consciousness and was given a transfusion of six units of blood. Doctors believed that the internal bleeding caused the blackouts and put a massive strain on his heart, which later caused the heart attack.

Hubert returned to the road in the fall of 2004. His first performance was September 18 with the Nighthawks at the Taste of the Blue Ridge Blues & Jazz Festival in Roanoke, Virginia. According to Hubert's manager, Toni Ann Mamary, Hubert was "jumping up and down like a little boy" at the show.

The cause of Hubert's internal bleeding remains a mystery. At presstime he was residing in New Jersey and making regular visits to doctors in New York City.

When Hubert opens the front door of his home in Glendale, Wisconsin, near Milwaukee, he's got soft plastic oxygen tubes jutting out of his nostrils. "Don't be worried, son," Hubert says, as he extends his arm and invites me in.

As I step into his dimly lit home and walk through the entranceway, I am struck by a placard that reads "Faith Hope and Love." Wrestling collectibles and memorabilia abound. The top of his TV/entertainment center boasts a Ray Charles performing doll (press a red button and Ray sings and sways his head). Mirrored tiles cover the walls, encircling the entire living room. It's a quiet, cool refuge from the oppressive Milwaukee heat.

Hubert takes a seat in front of the TV, plastic cords spiraling around his bare feet and extending to an oxygen machine inside his bedroom, right around the corner. Just as Wolf was relegated to taking pills for his heart and seeking dialysis treatment at V.A. hospitals across the country, Hubert must put himself through a daily regimen of pills for his blood pressure, tests for cancer every three months, and frequent oxygen inhalation sessions.

The sun is trying desperately to burn its way through the faded, lacy curtains of the living room, but the room holds its gloom. The darkness and heaviness of the atmosphere evokes an ancient religious ritual marking the passing of a spirit—it chills you to the bone.

You are comforted, though, by Hubert's many blues awards—displayed on the walls like a court of arms. It gives the room life and bestows a regal quality to his home. Hubert has impressed everyone in the blues community, as evidenced from his plaques: the New York Blues and Jazz Society, Fox Valley Blues Society, an award commemorating Hubert Sumlin Day in Milwaukee (July 9, 1997) ordained by Mayor John O. Norquist, a lifetime achievement award from the Jersey Shore Jazz & Blues Society, and the Wisconsin Area Music Industry award. Autographed photos of George Thorogood and Susan Tedeschi are in plain view.

Atop Hubert's computer rests his cherished Howlin' Wolf Award. "That was the same weekend we moved to Milwaukee," remembers Hubert as he points to the Wolf Award. "Yes, sir. You see. This is a nice neighborhood. Very nice neighborhood."

Hubert and Bea came to Milwaukee to start a new life together. And Bea's presence is still here—her warmth, her hope and strength are still here. Look no further than the hanging needlepoint crosses and religious items. Although you won't find too many photos of Bea, there are other signs that she has touched Hubert's life. Pictures of loving "adopted" children clutter the area. One black-and-white shot of a smiling, younger Hubert standing with a Les Paul in front of an unknown amp, a line of liquor at his feet, is signed "Your sons, Red and Alex."

Hubert's house is not what it used to be, though. Sadly, Hubert's basement blues museum no longer exists in its entirety. Due to water damage, some of the pictures have been destroyed. What's left on the walls is dried tape and the stained, faded remnants of where many of the pictures hung.

Howlin' Wolf may have been larger than Hubert in life—even in death—but Hubert has outlived them all. Wolf, Muddy, Hound Dog Taylor, Magic Sam, Eddie Taylor, Jimmy Rogers—friends one and all, all gone. But sitting at the edge of his cushioned chair Hubert seems deflated now, as if he has accepted the apparent permanence of his poor health. Hubert can be the most positive person in the world, but it hasn't been easy the last few months. He loses his breath climbing stairs, walking city streets, and even playing onstage some nights.

"I don't know how much longer I'll be here," he says.

It's a startling confession. He points to various fixtures and things on the walls: "I've been trying to pack up all of this stuff around here. I don't think I'll be here much longer. The other lung may go soon, too."

Friends who have known Hubert for decades have heard him say things like this before—always in his most dire moments. "Some of the doctors had written him off before he went to Sloan-Kettering," guitarist Curtis Obeda explains. "That was before he knew he had hope. The last time we played before the surgery, Hubert was making out like I was never going to see him again."

Still, Hubert makes it clear that he's going to do whatever he wants. In a weird way, you almost respect it. There's honor in his soldiering on, even if it is sometimes painful to see. But it doesn't stop people from constantly trying to look out for him. Toni was brought to tears during Hubert's recent bout with cancer. "I can't go through that ordeal again," she says. "It was a terrible time and I can't go back there again." She admits that worrying about Hubert has escalated her own smoking habits.

When it seems Hubert's spirits are at their lowest, though, he manages to bounce back. He smiles, with that curved mouth, squinted eyes: it's so devilishly playful and childlike. When he speaks, his inflection, tone, the side-to-side head motions, curled lips, and gleaming cheeks you want to pinch all serve as a funny visual aid to whatever tale he spins. He can make even the surliest among us bust a gut with laughter.

"When I get onstage, I'll be alright, son," Hubert assures me, referring to the show he must play tomorrow. I'll drive him to the airport soon. "All I need is my music and my guitar. It's like that record of mine, *Healing Feeling*. It's a true healing feeling. Everything is okay when I play guitar."

Hubert can be a lot of things to a lot of people: an overgrown child bursting with joy, a barrel of laughs, a frustrating and stubborn man who won't let you in, a loyal friend, a pillar of strength, an absolute genius, and the sweetest guy in the world. Still, even the sweetest guy in the world has his moments. "People don't know…they don't know," Hubert says, shaking his head. "They don't know about me. There's always someone wanting something from me, no matter what it is. Interviews, radio shows. Always something."

There is a bit of anger in his divine countenance. It's true: people *don't* know that about Hubert. He can be tough when he wants to be. He can be intimidating when he wants to be. When Hubert looks into your eyes and pokes you with his index finger, he looks inside you, as if to say, "I know about you. I know you."

When you look into his soul-piercing blue-gray eyes, it's like you have witnessed something cosmic. His eyes resemble lunar eclipses: the outer rims are blue and much lighter than the centers, which are deep, dark pools of intensity. You believe in the impossibility of the Hubert Sumlin magic—that he can know things about you that you've never spoken. To anyone. Just as he does onstage, Hubert picks up on vibes around him.

"I don't even think Hubert fully realizes what he has, himself," suggests Bob Putignano, director of the New York Jazz and Blues Society. "I think it is just this extrasensory perception that he has about people. He has the ability to feel moods. There might be something on my mind and he'll feel this weight. It's incredible, actually. I think that is what makes him a good musician. He can sense things." That kind of magnetism attracts crowds—musicians, admirers, fans, and all kinds. Hubert is a generous spirit. "The way Hubert makes people around him feel good is a gift and a blessing," confirms Muddy Waters guitarist Bob Margolin.

Even when he appears cranky and out of breath, Hubert is loquacious to passersby in taverns and clubs, even talking and walking with enthusiastic fans before shows and between sets, discussing blues, Wolf, and his own incredible guitar playing. What other legendary bluesman would make himself so available to his fans?

Hubert and Buddy Guy at Hendrix Tribute concert, 2004. Hubert often refuses to take up the challenge of a guitar duel. He has nothing to prove.

"Ever since I had the operation, people have been saying that I bring sunshine," Hubert reveals. "They say it rains so much before I arrive somewhere, and once I'm there the sun comes out. I remember that every time I was doing a blues festival [in Mississippi]. It rained at the first Howlin' Wolf festival. So much mud on the ground, for two days, before I got there. But when I got there, beautiful weather. And it stayed that way until I left there. I'm just sayin'."

People sense Hubert's goodness, or, at the very least, his willingness to please. Unfortunately, he is like a broken faucet—he can't fix the kindness he gushes. He just lets the bathtub fill up until he is almost drowning in other people's interests. And now that his state of health needs constant attention—a state that not everyone seems to respect—he won't (or can't) change.

This makes for a constant tussle between outside forces that want something from Hubert and people like Toni who are trying to *protect* him from those forces. If Hubert's camp is leery of outsiders, they have good reason. There have been too many hotel room crashers and rabid fans who've camped out in tents in his backyard.

While Hubert's mettle has been tested in instances involving so-called friends, business associates, and acquaintances, he sees a bittersweet, wicked humor in the circus that is sometimes unleashed around him. "You see what kind of stuff I'm in, don't ya?" Hubert asks me with a sly laugh. "You ever seen such muthafuckers fighting over people, man? That is the way it is. I just want to go somewhere and get out of their way, you know what I'm talkin' 'bout? Let them sonofaguns wonder. Boy, that would be something."

And his globe-trotting doesn't help matters. He has become very visible in the past few years, and now people expect to see him and spend time with him when he's on the road. At this stage of his life, Hubert should be the Robert Jr. Lockwood of Milwaukee, with a weekly gig at the corner nightclub (that pays a sizable fee), playing two sets (the second ending before midnight), and getting to bed by 12:30 a.m.

One would have to think that Hubert would at least be secure working in Milwaukee and cherry-picking occasional touring dates that wouldn't take him far from home or put much stress on his ailing body. But Milwaukee is a strange town. Besides paying some lip service to

Hubert, and throwing a party for his sixty-seventh birthday in 1998 at the Ambassador Hotel, not a lot is done for him here.

"There was a place on the East Side called the Nomad that I had played quite a bit," guitarist Jeff Dagenhardt says. "The promoter there would have Hubert come and play, but he is not there anymore. That is the section of town that was a hippie enclave that turned into big business. I was trying to get [a regular gig for Hubert], but with his illness, and his sister's death, a lot of things were curtained, starting with when Bea passed. We just never got it going."

"It is amazing that Hubert has not been embraced by the community more completely," notes Hugh Southard, president of Hubert's booking agency, Blue Mountain Artists, LLC. "Just in the last year and a half he has played with the Rolling Stones at Madison Square Garden, and Aerosmith, Santana, Eric Clapton, Derek Trucks, the Allman Brothers, Hot Tuna—endless musicians just want the opportunity to share the stage with Hubert."

The trouble is, to make the higher-paying wages—even just to get a job—Hubert has to leave Milwaukee. And his popularity has a reciprocal relationship with his health: the more recognition he gets, the more he wants to work. The more he is asked to work outside Milwaukee, the weaker he gets. "I've seen him onstage in 90-degree weather when he has no business being up there," explains Minneapolis-based blues writer Richard Benson. "It was too hot for me; I could imagine what it must have been for him."

Here in Hubert's air-conditioned home I learn that Hubert likes things in moderation. "I can't stand too much of nothin'…" Hubert breaks off. "That is too cold for me," he says, signaling me to turn off the air conditioner. "I'm sittin' here cold as a muthafucker."

I comply and Hubert continues: "I can't stand too much of nothing. On the bandstand, these muthafuckers sweating like a muthafucker. I'm on the bandstand in a suit. I'm cold. I know what makes them hot: booze. But these muthafuckers don't know how hot it can get. I used to do it, you know?"

Hubert doesn't do nearly half as many of the things he used to do, or half as much, including drink. Even so, some shows seem to push him to the limit. I witnessed a concert in 2004 at B.B. King's Blues Club & Grill in New York that stretched Hubert to the extreme:

A searing, silver spotlight streaks through the darkened club. The clanking of glasses, chatter, and impatience resonate through the crowd. The show, delayed a few minutes, has been built up to be a blockbuster.

Hubert waltzes across the stage where a chair awaits him, picks up his guitar, fiddles with it a bit, fusses with his guitar strap, and then takes off the guitar. He rests it on its cradle and slowly sinks into the chair, then takes off his jacket.

Jimmy Vivino, the bandleader and second guitar this night, yells out to the crowd, "Uh-oh, there goes the jacket. Some serious music is going down tonight."

Hubert's crack band this evening is Vivino, singer David Johansen, bassist Mike Merritt, drummer Levon Helm, and pianist David Maxwell. They'll plow through a crushing set of Howlin' Wolf music.

Hubert plugs his pinkish-red, Strat-like guitar into his Louis HS tube amp and appears ready to go. The band is on. Johansen is doing his best Wolf, Vivino calls the tunes, and Helm isn't missing a beat— his shuffling is performed with ease, at times playing only his snare to create a rhythmic rustling of pure groove elation.

Vivino, ever the consummate bandleader, goads Hubert into ripping the most expressive, extemporaneous solo he can. For the most part, the constant prodding seems to work. The smile on Hubert's face says it all. He is simply dabbling in the art of deep blues magic from his throne, lit up like an excitable boy, nodding his head, twisting his face sideways, pulling off a difficult run. Hubert's enticing musical turns conjure up visions of the guitarist as a young man—Wolf's wunderkind—that flash before my eyes. It's as if he has transported us all back in time to the heyday of Chicago blues. With each successive guitar line, Hubert takes more chances, ripping improv solos—the notes and runs spiral around the music. He breaks apart riffs where most people don't or won't (or can't), clumping together notes and balancing the time, nearly breaking with the tune's grounded meter. It all works, somehow, even though it sounds and looks as if it will all fall apart at any minute. Hubert is the solder, the glue, spiritually and musically holding together the timing and sense of rhythm and melody propelled by the band.

You'd swear that his musical excursions would land him flat on the floor. But with his guitar cocked at a 45-degree angle from his body and a grimace of joy, anguish, and pain contorting the left side of his face, he is surprisingly routed for takeoff and landing without incident.

Before long, the band is joined by such stalwart artists as John Sebastian, Jon Paris, and the crazy dancin', growlin', overall-wearin' Eric Mingus—the howlin', scattin' vocalist son of the jazz iconoclast Charles Mingus (an association he does not exploit), who Hubert affectionately calls "My Mingus."

The atmosphere is charged with electricity. Something is brewing. Something beyond the performers' or audience members' control. Then Hubert slumps further into his chair. From time to time Johansen asks Hubert if he's okay. Hubert doesn't look at Johansen, nor does he seem to indicate how he feels. He remains unresponsive as he fiddles with his guitar. He often stops playing altogether and rests his guitar on his lap, upright, as if waiting for his mental and physical batteries to recharge.

The band continues, even as Hubert sinks further into his chair. Some people in the crowd seem uncomfortable, shifting in their seats.

*Hubert at B.B. King's with
Eric Mingus looking on, 2004.*

A look of genuine concern comes over bassist Merritt's face as his eyes follow Hubert with each successive slump. Merritt seems nearly ready to let go of his bass and prop up the elder statesman, but he manages to pay as much attention to his bass notes as he does to Hubert's slumped position in the chair. Johansen, clearly distracted, keeps looking back at Hubert. When he is not singing, the erstwhile Buster Poindexter walks over to Hubert to check on his condition.

Just a few weeks earlier, Hubert had appeared healthy and robust for a production of *The Downtown Messiah* at the Bottom Line (one of the final musical productions at the legendary Greenwich Village venue before it went bust). But now this crowd at B.B.'s senses Hubert's discomfort every time he leans forward, and gasps with him nearly every time he takes a breath. Hubert thrusts himself flush against the back of his chair and cups the back of his neck with his hand, supporting his upper body. Vivino calls out "Forty-Four" and Maxwell begins the piano overture he learned through years of absorbing the stylings of Otis Spann. Vivino picks Jody Williams's classic bottom-end rhythm guitar line. Then, as if on cue, Hubert gets up from his chair, moves across the stage, and descends the stairs off the side.

"I was exhausted," Hubert tells me after the show, his head bowed, as if he is reliving the experience. "The wind just got out of me."

A gaping hole is left in the band onstage—if not musically, then spiritually. These are high-caliber players, but the blues is about feeling. With Hubert's radiance gone, they're not feeling it. It's as if the band has been sucker-punched. But moments later Hubert re-emerges to applause, many people jumping to their feet. He shuffles slowly across the stage to his chair.

It's clear to all of us that Hubert is a trouper. He plays even when he is out of breath, as if telling the fates to back off. He seems better equipped to handle the inevitable with a guitar in his hands. The band whips through a few more numbers until Hubert pushes himself up from his chair and hands his guitar off to anyone around. Maxwell is the closest person and the piano vet jumps from behind his keyboard to grab the guitar. Within a moment Hubert disappears once again backstage.

The show is over and the house lights come on. A small crowd of fans slowly sways toward the backstage area. A cluster of white,

predominantly middle-class, winter-coat-clad fans, some carrying guitar cases, wait impatiently on the public side of the black velvet curtain
that separates the club's tables from the dressing rooms. The milling
and murmuring is starting to gain momentum. People are impatient and
they want to see Hubert.

The crowd is fully aware that Hubert is one of the few living people on this earth who can intimately attest to the behavior of one of the
twentieth century's greatest blues musicians, one of the most unique
and powerful voices ever recorded: Howlin' Wolf. The crowd is also
aware that Hubert shares the same historic province as Wolf and
Muddy Waters, having grown up in Mississippi and Arkansas and eventually landing in Chicago. It all makes Hubert the real deal.

Slipping into manager mode, Toni tells the crowd that Hubert can't
come out from backstage. "He needs to rest," she declares, not speaking to anyone in particular. "C'mon, he has one lung." It was a wonder
the show went on at all. But like Howlin' Wolf, who virtually collapsed
at a show in Chicago in November 1975 (two months before his death),
Hubert is going to play to his dying day.

"Hubert was backstage and I was starting to worry about him a little bit," Helm reveals. "All of a sudden he was back in the dressing room
and he didn't feel well. God love 'im, Jimmy V. sensed it and saw it, felt
it, and just kind of delayed the start time by about ten minutes, which
gave Hubert some extra time, and we put a chair out there so Hubert
wouldn't have to stand up." Maxwell adds, " I don't think Hubert was
feeling that great, and I don't think he likes to be coerced. He'll do what
he can. He was sitting back there and I was glad I was on his side. We
were playing off each other at times."

Toni apologizes for Hubert not making an appearance and the crowd
starts to thin, but not everyone leaves. One unidentified middle-aged
couple won't take "no" for an answer. The female, who appears to be
drunk, tries to peek behind the curtain to get a glimpse of Hubert, or
something—anything—backstage. She nearly climbs the wall, pushing
aside the velvet ropes, and begins to pull back the curtain in a half-dazed,
half-crazed effort to achieve temporary VIP status. A large bouncer gets
right up in her face: "Don't come through here," he commands. "Don't
touch my ropes." Toni peeks from behind the curtain to see what all the

commotion is about. The female agitator ignores the bouncer's warnings and the man-mountain again says, "Don't touch my ropes."

"Are you threatening me?" asks the woman.

Toni comes back out in front of the crowd and recognizes an acquaintance and apologizes for not being able to get him backstage. She looks harried. "I don't know what to do. It's crazy. The man has one lung."

The unidentified drunken woman again tries to get backstage, and this time the bouncer will have no part of it. He could snap her in two like a twig, but instead he whips out his walkie-talkie and calls for backup security. That seems to shoo her away, but most of the remaining crowd won't leave. Toni makes another appearance, says hi to one or two more people, and then is sucked behind the curtain—into what the crowd sees as the great beyond, the exclusiveness of backstage.

Instead of giving in to the temptation to please the impatient crowd this night, Hubert listens to his manager (and himself) and does not emerge from the crowd to sign autographs or say hello to the well-intentioned, though clamoring, fans. But despite being out of breath, despite recovering from a near-fatal illness, Hubert knows he has let his fans down. And he hurts because of it. Dagenhardt, a close friend for over 30 years, underscores the predicament Hubert finds himself in night after night when he is on tour: "It ain't easy bein' Hubert Sumlin."

For Hubert, every show is a work of art in the truest sense: he doesn't do things half-assed. Hubert will make things up before and during a show, sometimes to the surprise of his bandmates. He is one of the rare musicians who can (and often does) go wherever inside the music he wants, dispensing with formula—and still making it work.

"Some musicians can fake their way through a gig, you know?" Vivino explains, "and have it sound okay. But Hubert is totally heart with his hands. That is what makes him a real blues player. Not like someone who can dissect it, you know?"

Hubert has always been heart and soul, a human being whose strengths, weaknesses, and passions are directed by the moment.

Regardless of the dark periods in his life, Hubert somehow lets his light, his gift, shine for the world. Because it shines so brightly, there are those who wish to bottle him up. "Everybody always wants a piece of me," he says. "Everybody is always looking for something."

Hubert doesn't like to be prodded for information or shellacked with praise. He is likable and loquacious in people's company, but constant hounding weighs on him. He gets defensive and shuts down. In fact, there were times when Hubert would simply say to me, "I don't feel like talking." To have forced the issue would have been pointless. Better to let Hubert speak when he wants.

As Hubert and I sit in his home now and talk about his life, Wolf, and everything but the weather, he becomes more animated. "Just talking with people, it makes me feel better," he says. "I start to feel better in their company, you know what I mean?" His mind wanders to his brother, who also has been diagnosed with cancer. "My brother, he lives near Hughes [in Elaine, Arkansas]. I know sometime he think about me and how he never played or got out and he say, 'But you…' I say, 'You have a family.' That's all right. He own all the goddamn thing, the plantation down there. He did okay."

Willie "Pinetop" Perkins, Hubert, and Eddie Shaw in 2002.

The fact is, no matter how much power Hubert extracts from people to heal himself, the only real cure or antidote is music. Of course, the music he happens to play is the blues—and fittingly so. Nonetheless, that blues speaks to him and gives him joys in ways that no one can understand or fully grasp. No thing, person, idea, or conversation could ever seduce him the way a 6-string can. Music is the one constant in this journeyman's life. Hubert will undoubtedly continue to catch planes, hop from small club to small club in tiny towns, from country to country, to earn what he needs to live.

As we drive down the sun-blinded road to the airport for his flight to tomorrow's gig, Hubert prefers to doze in the passenger's seat. Tilting down his black derby, he settles in and says, "I'm not gonna say much. I don't feel like talkin'." He settles deeper into his seat, closes his eyes, mumbles a few words, and off to dreamland he sails.

When we arrive at the airport, Hubert darts out of the car, only to find himself breathless yet again. We walk to the automatic doors of the airline terminal, and he suddenly stops. He slowly lowers himself and

Hubert backstage at Hendrix Tribute concert, 2004.

grabs the closest available seat: the platform of the baggage roller. He breathes heavily and I ask if he is okay. He pants, "Yeah," though it is obvious that it's a strain on him just to take in the air. Hubert can't speak and we sit in silence for a few moments while his batteries recharge.

A moment or so later he gets up and I ask if he wants me to go in with him, to do anything for him, to get help or carry his bag. He waves me off, nearly beseeching me to leave him be: "Nah, please, son." It's a difficult thing to witness: no one likes to see another person in pain or in need of help. I watch as he saunters through the automatic doors, looks both ways, and finds the right direction to his plane's gate.

Then it hits me. My mind flashes back to when I arrived at his home and saw the oxygen tubes coming out of his nose and he said, "People don't know." Perhaps more than anything else, Hubert just wants to be left alone. But there is always one more show, one more interview, one more person coming over and disturbing his quiet time, one more autograph to sign, one more track to cut for a business associate, one more person tugging on his shirt sleeve asking him to recite another Howlin' Wolf story. In every way, people demand a little piece of him and his greatness.

Hubert is the Holy Grail of blues musicians. People seek him out, need to touch him in some way, draw his power without really understanding it. They think by getting closer to Hubert they approach the divine. In one way I suppose it's true, but people who think they know him really don't, and they don't own a piece of him. No one does. No one ever could. Anything anyone could know about Hubert is only the tip of the iceberg. The real treasure is kept locked up inside him, safe from opportunists, fair-weather friends, and selfish hangers-on.

The irony is, of course, that performing for people is what he does for a living and what makes him happiest. It's a delicious, enthusiastic, resounding "yea," not the everlasting "nay," that heals Hubert, keeps him going, and gets him back on track to recovery. And on the stage every night.

As I watch Hubert walk through the airline terminal, I know that tomorrow brings another show for which he must prepare. He's got another hotel room to stay in, another breakfast on the road, another late night at the venue with semi-acquaintances. But now, with a bag over his shoulder, guitar in hand, and off to catch a plane, Hubert is finally alone—at least for a few precious hours.

An Annotated, Selected Hubert Sumlin Discography

Hubert Sumlin Solo

Hubert Sumlin and Friends: Kings of Chicago Blues, Vol. 2 (Vogue 30175), 1973 (recorded 1971).

Hubert Sumlin's Blues Party! featuring Mighty Sam McClain, Ronnie Earl, Ron Levy, Greg Piccolo, and Jerry Portnoy (Black Top Records CD BT-1036), 1987.

Heart & Soul (with James Cotton and Little Mike & The Tornadoes) (Blind Pig BP7 3389), 1989.

Healing Feeling (Black Top Records CD BT-1053), 1990.

Hubert Sumlin/Willie Dixon/Sunnyland Slim: Blues Anytime! (Evidence ECD 26052-2), 1994 (recorded 1964).

My Guitar and Me (originally *Groove* on Disques Black and Blue; Evidence ECD 26045-2), 1994 (recorded 1975).

I Know You (Analogue Productions Originals APO 2004), 1998.

Wake Up Call (Blues Planet BPCD-1116), 1998.

Blues Guitar Boss (JSP Records JSPCD 2118), 1999 (recorded 1990).

About Them Shoes (Tone-Cool/Artemis TCL-CD-51609), release Jan. 25, 2005.
Over the last 15 years, there has been an attempt by mainstream rock stars to raise the profile of older blues and rock 'n' roll legends by teaming up with them on record. Call it the legacy of *The London Howlin' Wolf Sessions.* For example, Keith Richards was featured on longtime Chuck Berry piano man Johnnie Johnson's 1992 *Johnnie B. Bad* and on John Lee Hooker's *Mr. Lucky*—both of which were nominated for Grammy Awards. Jimmy Page, Eric Clapton, and Richards, among others, appeared on Jimmy Rogers All Star Blues Band's *Blues, Blues, Blues* (Atlantic) in 1998, just before Rogers died. It is conceivable that *About Them Shoes* will surpass these in critical and commercial success.

With Howlin' Wolf

1954

"No Place to Go"/"Rockin' Daddy" (Chess 1566).

"Neighbors"/"I'm the Wolf" (Chess LP 1512).

"Evil"/"Baby How Long" (Chess 1575).

"Forty-Four"/"I'll Be Around" (Chess 1584).

1955

"Who Will Be Next"/"I Have a Little Girl" (Chess 1593).

"Come to Me Baby"/"Don't Mess with My Baby" (Chess 1607).

1956

"Smokestack Lightnin'"/"You Can't Be Beat" (Chess 1618).

"I Asked for Water"/"So Glad" (Chess 1632).
> Some sources credit Hubert and/or Willie Johnson and Otis "Smokey" Smothers for writing. Hubert tends to play "I Asked for Water" live; rarely does he perform songs that he did not have a hand in writing and/or recording. Citing the closeness in structural composition to "Smokestack Lightnin'," Hubert says, "they are very similar. Just a little difference, you know?"

"Break of Day" (unreleased at time of recording).
> The Charly Records label would release this song on its 1993 *Complete Recordings 1951-1969* box set.

"The Natchez Burnin'"/"You Gonna Wreck My Life" (originally "No Place to Go") (Chess 1744).
> Possibly Hubert and/or Willie Johnson as writers; Hubert has often told the story of Wolf taking him to the spot in Natchez, Mississippi, where a nightclub had burned down, killing over 200 people in 1940. That tragedy inspired the song and the title.

1957

"Sitting on Top of the World"/"Poor Boy" (Chess 1679).
> This eight-bar blues starts with Wolf's honking harp. It's a song Hubert loves to play live, perhaps because it is in his vocal range and he was the only guitar player credited on the original recording. Wolf's track was based on the Mississippi Sheiks's song of the same name, recorded in the early '30s. Hubert's cascading guitar lines mimic and frolic about behind Wolf's sandpapery delivery. The killer twist? Hubert's slow, cathartic turnaround for the bridge.

1958

"I Didn't Know" (also re-recorded 1958)/"Moanin' for My Baby" (Chess 1695).

"Moanin' for My Baby" is a variant of Wolf's "Moanin' at Midnight" recorded in Memphis in 1951, with similar closed-mouth throat singing, and the same driving bassline. Hubert's notes glisten and rise to the top of this molten, rhythmic concoction of string and wind instruments. He also gets louder and louder and more adventurous with his playing—he extends and holds notes longer and even plays more notes, as the driving song, motored by Earl Phillips's drumming, moans along.

"I Better Go Now" (recorded 1958)/"Howlin' Blues" (recorded 1959), also known as "I'm Going Away" (released 1959) (Chess 1726).

"Midnight Blues"

Unreleased by Chess at time of recording. It was later to be included on a 1994 Chess Collectables compilation, *Ain't Gonna Be Your Dog* (currently out of print, but available as an import—Universal B0002J51QC 2004).

"I'm Leaving You"/"Change My Way" (Chess 1712).

"Change My Way" is similar to "Sitting on Top of the World," but Hubert's playing is far more atmospheric here, packed with searing reverb and echo.

"You Can't Put Me Out"/"Getting Late" (unreleased).

Another unreleased pair of recordings that would crop up on *Ain't Gonna Be Your Dog* (see "Midnight Blues," above).

1959

"You Gonna Wreck My Life"/"The Natchez Burnin'" (recorded 1956) (Chess 1744).

"I've Been Abused"/"Mr. Airplane Man" (Chess 1735).

Over a walking bassline, Hubert tangles with Wolf in a sonic duel during the harp solo on "I've Been Abused." As Wolf raises his voice and howls about being scared and "so mad I can shout!" Hubert ups the ante by strumming partial chords, making his high-pitched delivery a slippery, unresolved one. "Mr. Airplane Man" is a slower version of the one-chord romp "Smokestack Lightnin'"— the one-chord vamp is a well to which Wolf would return repeatedly. Why mess with a formula that works?

(**Note:** Songs like "Mr. Airplane Man" and "Smokestack Lightnin'" (both revolving around the key of *E*) are part of a cultural tradition that goes far beyond being based on a hypnotic, one-chord Delta feel. Western music tends to subdivide music and attempts to pinpoint precisely the absolute tone value of musical notes (and half-notes). It's impossible. The Western tuning system is compromised because our ears hear sounds/scales imperfectly. Secondly, the scope of those scales is limited. The blues, grounded in "blue notes" (African, Arabic, and Asian musical modes), plays into the gray areas of tunings at different intervals. There may be intervals smaller than half-tones used in an octave. In technical terms, the blue notes fall somewhere between a "natural" and half-notes on the C, G, E, and B scales. In blues, achieving a European or pristine tuning for guitar or piano is secondary to the emotional, vocal quality of the music. (Indeed, at times it seems as though Hubert plays his guitar without it being "in tune." He'll just pick it up and start playing.) More importantly, blues has always been about the space after a vocal stanza that was/is filled by instrumental accompaniment. This call-and-response is heard not only in blues but in gospel, and has roots in Africa. Vocal call-and-response predates vocal/instrumental call-and-response music. Some scholars even suggest that blues was somewhat influenced by Native Americans, whose call-and-response chants, derived from ritual ceremonies, could have fused with African polyrhythms and Asian/Arabic/European melody lines to create what is the blues today. It is not so far-fetched. Given all the intermarriage between African-Americans and Native Americans in the early part of this country's history, it would have been inevitable that some aspects of one culture would seep into the other.)

Moanin' in the Moonlight (Chess/MCA CD CHD-5908).

Wolf's first LP was comprised of his hit 78 rpm records. Its gray cover depicts a Wolf in mid-howl and is packed with such early hits as "Moanin' at Midnight," "How Many More Years," "Smokestack Lightnin'," "Evil," "Forty-Four," "I Asked for Water," and "I'm Leaving You."

1960

"Howlin' for My Darling" (recorded 1959)/"Spoonful" (Chess 1762).

"Wang Dang Doodle"/"Back Door Man" (Chess 1777).

There is debate in the industry as to who actually plays on these two tracks. Was it Freddie King or Freddy Robinson, or even Hubert Sumlin? If it was Mr. Sumlin, then here again, in "Wang Dang Doodle," written by Willie Dixon, Hubert can make a powerful statement with very few notes. He roughs it through the rhythm section for most of the verses, then lets his notes soar. It was a song Wolf supposedly thought sounded too old-timey because he is forced to call out a list of characters who inhabit the song, rhyming words with their descriptions. "Back Door Man" is perhaps the most menacing while also the most funny and over-the-top of any of the Wolf tracks.

"My People's Gone"/"Wolf in the Mood"

These two sides went unreleased at the time of recording, but *Ain't Gonna Be Your Dog* (see "Midnight Blues," 1958) includes "My People's Gone."

1961

"Little Baby"/"Down in the Bottom" (Chess 1793).

   The quivering, metallic lines of Wolf's acoustic slide on "Down in the Bottom" were straight from "Roll and Tumble," an old Delta song, and Robert Johnson's "Traveling Riverside Blues" that Wolf made his own. Muddy Waters, of course, also recorded this song, with the title "Rollin' and Tumblin'," in 1950 and made it one of his signature songs. "People don't realize that Wolf is playing on that track," Hubert says. "He plays slide. The old man could play, man."

"Shake for Me"/"The Red Rooster" (Chess 1804).

   "Shake for Me" contains some classic Hubert fills: distorted slides up the neck and a rhythm based on three beeping, horn-like notes—not a full chord. His solo is packed with vibrato and zigzag lines. Hubert also clicks his fingers across the strings to keep time when he is not playing full-on. "The Red Rooster" has been covered by none other than the Rolling Stones and Sam Cooke. Wolf plays acoustic slide throughout as Hubert follows sans slide.

"I Ain't Superstitious"/"Just Like I Treat You" (Chess 1823).

   While Hubert's remarkable playing can sit out front and lead the band with mastery and control, Hubert also has the countervailing ability to be the most sympathetic musician in the studio. On the classic "I Ain't Superstitious," Jimmy Rogers's warm, slinky, jazzy notes and Hubert's off-in-the-distance, near-whispery tone complement each other perfectly. A track like this has been influential in so many different corners of the blues and rock worlds. For example, both the Jeff Beck Group with lead vocalist Rod Stewart and headbangers Megadeth have covered the song. Beck outdoes himself with his wah-inflected, crybaby fills; Dave Mustaine and Chris Poland of Megadeth, as if to show reverence for the music, slow things down slightly and get bluesy—a rarity for that band in the 1980s.

"You'll Be Mine"/"Goin' Down Slow" (Chess 1813).

1962

"Mama's Baby"/"Do the Do" (Chess 1844).

Howlin' Wolf (aka the Rocking Chair Album) (Chess LP 1469).

   The Rocking Chair Album, so dubbed because of Don Bronstein's cover artwork, was released in 1962 and included a cherry-picked batch of Wolf keepers such as "Spoonful," "Goin' Down Slow," "Shake for Me," "The Red Rooster," "Back Door Man," and "Wang Dang Doodle." Similar to 1959's *Moanin' in the Moonlight,* this record had a profound impact on musicians and fans in America and overseas. These powerhouse records ignited the passion of serious-minded individuals who glued themselves to the speakers of their record-playing consoles to figure out the feel and timing of the classic tracks, often in vain. Both records were released on a single CD, Chess/MCA 5908, in 1990.

1963

"Sugar Mama"/"May I Have a Talk with You" (Argo LP 4031).
    Recorded at the Copacabana on July 26, 1963, for the variety album *Folk Festival of the Blues.*
"300 Pounds of Joy"/"Built for Comfort" (Chess 1870).
"Tail Dragger"/"Hidden Charms" (Chess 1890).

1964

"Shake It"
    This track was re-recorded later the same year with different personnel but was left unissued at the time.
"Dust My Broom" (Fontana TL 5225).
    Recorded live at the Musikhalle in Hamburg, Germany. The studio version of Robert Johnson's "(I Believe I'll) Dust My Broom" was recorded in 1967, but it is not as raucous as this live version. In both the 1964 and 1967 versions, Hubert's rapid-fire notes mimicking the original, and the conjoining, nearly jazzy noodling in the background, offer yet another example of how little—and how far—the electric blues roamed from its Delta folk-blues roots. "Dust My Broom" was initially covered by slide player Elmore James in 1951, and some critics suggest that version is the definitive one.
"I Didn't Mean to Hurt Your Feelings," "Rockin' the Blues" (instrumental), and "All My Life" from *Live in Europe 1964* (Sundown) and *Live Gold* (Fine Tune LLC); released 1998.
    These three tracks were recorded when Hubert and Wolf were overseas for the 1964 American Folk Blues Festival (AFBF). Willie Dixon's walking basslines are very prominent here, as are Hubert's searing tone and Wolf's sandpapery voice.
"My Country Sugar Mama"/"Love Me Darlin'" (Chess 1911).
    "Love Me Darlin'" was a recasting of Wolf's "May I Have a Talk with You" from the *Folk Festival of the Blues* LP. Stevie Ray Vaughan covered the tune in 1989 on his *In Step* album.

1965

"Killing Floor"/"Louise" (Chess 1923).
    Though uncredited, Wolf, it seems, is playing acoustic guitar on "Killing Floor," chugging along to Buddy Guy's rhythm guitar (it can be lost amid the clanking noises of Sam Lay's cowbell), while Hubert takes the foreground with a biting, rabid-dog tone. Wolf called in Guy, apparently because no one else could properly execute the rhythm guitar part under Hubert's lead.
"Tell Me What I've Done"/"Ooh Baby" (Chess 1928).

"Don't Laugh at Me"/"I Walked from Dallas" (Chess 1945).
> "I Walked from Dallas" was a rehash of 1957's "Walk to Camp Hall," which was not released at that time.

1966

"Commit a Crime" (released 1991 as part of *The Chess Box: Howlin' Wolf,* CHD3-9332).
> Another Sumlin smoker. If you had any doubt that Hubert could take command of a song and swap musical quips with Wolf, listen to this baby.

The Real Folk Blues (Chess/MCA CD 9273).
> To cash in on the coffeehouse folk craze that was sweeping the US in the early and mid-'60s, Chess released this compilation. Europe, at the time, was awed by the electric blues of Muddy, Wolf et al. Tracks include "Louise," "Killing Floor," "The Natchez Burnin'," "300 Pounds of Joy," and "Built for Comfort." Critics snipe that the title is deceiving: listeners may expect an acoustic set, while the album is securely planted in electric Chicago blues. Followed by *More Real Folk Blues.* Both records were released on one CD in March 2002, Chess/MCA 112820.

"Poor Wind That Never Change" (unreleased).
> See *Ain't Gonna Be Your Dog* (under "Midnight Blues," 1958).

"New Crawlin' King Snake"/"My Mind Is Ramblin'" (Chess 1968).
> If "My Mind Is Ramblin'" was a great take on an old Robert Johnson song—with some smokin', biting lead lines by Sumlin (the song fades as Hubert continues to vamp on a thrilling string of repetitive notes)—then "New Crawlin' King Snake" was a great follow-up to John Lee Hooker's 1949 acoustic, mid-tempo boogie written by Anthony Hollins for the Modern label. Hooker based his track on the sexually charged Blind Lemon Jefferson song "Black Snake Moan." Hubert decimates the song to where it is nearly devoid of connection to the Hooker version, with horn leads, courtesy of Eddie Shaw, and sonic dips and peaks. Hubert releases himself from the grounded, dense complexity of Hooker's polyrhythmic trance and, again, rips a lead that is a game of hide-and-seek with Wolf's lines and Henry Gray's piano lines. The difference between the two versions is self-evident, like day and night. The listener will decide which is day and which is night. However, Hubert does reprise Hooker's trembling vocal line in his solo. (Apparently the original still holds charm for Hubert. While driving with me one day, Stevie Ray Vaughan pumping out of my car stereo, Hubert noticed a Hooker tape that happened to include the 1949 Hooker version. He sheepishly asked me to play the cassette. "I saw it, sticking out of your rack," Hubert said, "but I didn't want to just come out and ask." Of course, I obliged.)

1967

More Real Folk Blues (Chess/MCA CD 9279).
  See *The Real Folk Blues* above (1966); this follow-up includes "I'll Be Around."
"Pop It to Me"/"I Had a Dream" (Chess 2009).

1968

The Super Super Blues Band (Checker LP 3010, Chess/MCA CD CHD-9169).
  Features Howlin' Wolf, Bo Diddley, and Muddy Waters.

1969

"Mary Sue"/"Hard Luck" (Chess 2081).
  These songs are an odd pairing for the Wolf motif. Perhaps the theme is not as
  dismal or dark (even self-pitying) as Wolf's 1968 solo acoustic numbers "I Ain't
  Goin' Down That Dirt Road" and "I'm the Wolf." "Mary Sue" is a downer for
  other reasons: the New Orleans-like horns are reminiscent of a Big Easy funeral
  dirge. Perhaps Wolf was preparing for his exit from this world. But Hubert seems
  to play whatever comes into his mind here—as he often did and still does—stop-
  ping short in mid-run, about an inch or two away from total abandon.
"The Big House"
"Tired of Crying"
  Both released on *Ain't Gonna Be Your Dog* (see "Midnight Blues," 1958).
Howlin' Wolf (Chess LP 4543) or *This Is Howlin' Wolf's New Album. He Doesn't
  Like It. He Didn't Like His Electric Guitar at First Either.* (Cadet 319).
  The infamous electric psychedelic LP.

1971

The London Howlin' Wolf Sessions featuring Eric Clapton, Steve Winwood, Bill
  Wyman, and Charlie Watts (Chess LP-60008).
  Re-released in 1989 (Chess/MCA CHD-9297) and in 2002, deluxe ed.,
  (Chess/MCA 0881129852).

1972

Live and Cookin' at Alice's, Revisited (Chess/MCA CD 9339) 1992.

1973

The Back Door Wolf (Chess LP-50045, Chess CHD-9358).

1974

Howlin' Wolf/Muddy Waters: *London Revisited* (Chess LP 60026).
  CD reissue as *Muddy & the Wolf* (Chess 9100, 1991).

1975

Change My Way (Chess LP 418, CD 93001, 1990).
    A solid offering of tracks recorded from 1959–1963. I echo the sentiment of the
    late Cub Koda as he wrote on www.allmusicguide.com: "If you really want to
    hear Hubert Sumlin rip up the fretboard, this is an excellent place to start."

With Muddy Waters

1956

** "Got My Mojo Workin'" (Chess 1652).

** "Don't Go No Farther" (Chess 1630).
    The Muddy Chess box set released in 1989 credits Jimmy Rogers with playing
    on the "Don't Go No Farther" session; the Muddy anthology released in 2001
    claims the guitar could have been either Rogers or Pat Hare.

With Chuck Berry

1957

"School Days"/"Deep Feeling" (Chess 1653).

* Compilations and Other Wolf Records

Live in Europe 1964 (Sundown LP70907), 1988.

The Chess Box: Willie Dixon (Chess/MCA 16500), 1990.

The Blues, Vol. 1 (MCA 31262), 1990.

The Chess Box: Howlin' Wolf (Chess/MCA CHD3-9332), 1991.
    A three-disc set that covers Wolf's recording career from 1951 through 1973;
    includes 75 tracks plus splices of a 1968 Wolf interview.

Howlin' Wolf: *Live in Cambridge, 1966* (New Rose 5082), 1992.

Chess Blues (box set) (Chess/MCA 9340), 1993.

Howlin' Wolf & The Wolf Gang: *Evil: Live at Joe's 1973* (Wolf Records 120.100), 1995.
    After Wolf survived his car accident, he and the Wolf Gang (so called since 1972
    and consisting of Hubert, Detroit Junior, Eddie Shaw, S.P. Leary, and Andrew
    McMahon) performed in Inman Square in Cambridge, Massachusetts. His
    health failing, Wolf does not appear until the fourth song (and exits after the five-
    minute "Blind Love.") Extended versions of "Evil," "The Red Rooster" (listed here
    as "The Little Red Rooster"), and "Goin' Down Slow" are blasts from the past.
    Wolf's voice on "Goin' Down Slow" is the old stuff. Check the great interplay
    between Detroit Junior's piano phrasings and Hubert's guitar on "Blind Love."
    The song illustrates a thumping, rockin' band in high action, improvising on a

single concept. Hubert's twangy twists do often get drowned out by Detroit's electric keyboard and Shaw's squawking sax (think angry seagull), but this is still a fascinating document of a band playing in full force—even though its legendary leader is near the end of his life. When Wolf doesn't sing, other band members front. It is very nearly a non-Wolf show, until, of course, the big man takes his seat center stage. The band played an entire week at Joe's, which had been open for only a year at the time of this recording. Three of these tracks (three on which Wolf sings minus "The Little Red Rooster" [sic]) are reissued on another label, Fine Tune LLC, for its *Live Gold* compilation.

Howlin' Wolf: *Ain't Superstitious* (Eclipse Music Group 64732), 1996.

Howlin' Wolf: *Bluesmaster* (MCA Special Products 20939), 1996.

Howlin' Wolf: *Highway 49 & Other Classics* (Masters Intercontinental 1124), 1996.

Mean Old World: The Blues from 1940 to 1994 (Smithsonian Collection Recordings/MCA Special Markets & Products, RC/RD 110, RB0003/RB0004, MSC4-35974/MSD4-35974), 1996.

A four-disc compilation with detailed liner notes in accompanying booklet.

Midnight Blues (MCA Special Products MCAD-21005), 1997.

A specially priced single-CD compilation with Wolf's "Baby How Long."

Howlin' Wolf: *His Best: The Chess 50th Anniversary Collection* (Chess/MCA CHD-9375), 1997.

Chess Blues Classics: 1947–1956 (Chess/MCA 9369), 1997.

Chess Blues Classics: 1957–1967 (Chess/MCA 9368), 1997.

Chess Blues-Rock Songbook: The Classic Originals (Chess/MCA 9389), 1997.

Repackaged double-disc set of older Chess material that is designed to show the influence Chess blues had on the birth of rock 'n' roll and rock music.

Howlin' Wolf: *Masters* (Cleopatra 364), 1998.

Howlin' Wolf: *The Great Howlin' Wolf* (BCD), 1998.

Howlin' Wolf: *Live Gold/The Gold Collection* (Fine Tune 2212-2), 1998, 2002.

See songs included above (1964).

Howlin' Wolf: *His Best, Vol. 2* (Chess/MCA CHD-12026), 1999.

Howlin' Wolf: *Electric Blues* (Delta Entertainment-LaserLight 17 192), 2000.

Howlin' Wolf: *Goin' Down Slow* (Classic World 9954), 2000.

Muddy Waters & Howlin' Wolf (Retro Music 4015), 2000.

Two-disc import.

Howlin' Wolf: *The Red Rooster: 14 Blues Greats* (Mastersong B00005JSPM), 2000.

Howlin' Wolf and Muddy Waters: *Back to Back* (Edel America 18215), 2000.

Howlin' Wolf: *The Collection* (Universal/Spectrum B00004WMXL), 2000.

Howlin' Wolf: *Legendary Blues Recordings* (Direct Source 1420), 2001.

** *Muddy Waters: The Anthology 1947-1972* (Chess/MCA 112649), 2001.

Screamin' and Hollerin' the Blues: The World of Charley Patton (Revenant Records 212), 2001.
A warts-and-all, seven-CD set that covers everything Charlie Patton did in his life—and even some songs he didn't record (go figure!). The set traces the major impact Patton had on artists such as Wolf (an interview with Wolf about Patton is featured), Son House, and others. It also includes a 112-page book written by John Fahey in 1970, not to be confused with the liner notes (it's an actual book, separate from the liner notes).
Patton certainly was influential beyond his locale, race, and generation. British rockers Led Zeppelin, having paid homage to Wolf and Hubert many times during their career, copped (either consciously or unconsciously) a line from Patton's "Jesus Is A-Dying (Bed Maker)" for the band's "In My Time of Dying." It was altogether appropriate for alpha-frontman Robert Plant to have sung this song, given the turmoil in his personal life in the mid- to late '70s. Not surprisingly, he lops off the final would-be mumbled, agonized word "bed" in his closing rambling rant, just as Patton did throughout his song nearly 50 years earlier.

Howlin' Wolf: *Chicago Blues* (Tomato Music 2103), 2002.

Howlin' Wolf: *Killing Floor* (Blue Moon/Tko Mag), 2002.

20th Century Masters: The Millennium Collection: The Best of Howlin' Wolf (Universal-Chess/MCA 000035802), 2003.

Howlin' Wolf: *Rockin' the Blues: Live in Germany* (Acrobat 4010), 2003.
See *Live Gold* above.

Alan Lomax: Blues Songbook (Rounder Select 1866), 2003.
Includes "Dust My Broom."

Martin Scorsese Presents The Blues: Eric Clapton (Polydor/PGD 000079602), 2003.

Martin Scorsese Presents The Blues: Godfathers and Sons (Hip-O Records 000062702), 2003.

Martin Scorsese Presents The Blues: The Road to Memphis (Hip-O Records 000070502), 2003.

20th Century Masters—The Millennium Collection: The Best of Blues Guitar (Universal/Chess/MCA 000037702), 2003.

Blues Classics: Millennium Collection: 20th Century Masters
(Universal/Chess/MCA 00003602). 2003.
Includes cuts by B.B. King, Koko Taylor ("Wang Dang Doodle"), John Lee
Hooker, Muddy ("Got My Mojo Workin'"), Little Walter ("Juke"), Wolf ("I Ain't
Superstitious"), and others.

Best of Howlin' Wolf (Master Classics 8014), 2004.

With Various Artists

Various Artists: *Ann Arbor Blues & Jazz Festival 1972* (Atlantic Records SD 2-502),
1973.
Although online record stores and record collector/dealer Web sites have made
this once hard-to-find double LP more available, it remains a highly sought-after
live collection containing tracks of the Wolf band, Sun Ra, Muddy Waters,
Bonnie Raitt, Bobby "Blue" Bland, Junior Walker & His All Stars, Koko Taylor,
Hound Dog Taylor, Luther Allison, and others, recorded at Otis Spann Memorial Field in 1972.

Elmore James: *Street Talkin'* (Muse Records MCD 5087), 1975.
Features Jimmy Reed and Eddie Taylor. Hubert backs Taylor and accompanies
Reed for two songs—"Do You Want to See Me Cry?" and "I'm Sitting Here."
Both tracks were recorded in 1964 for the Vivid label and re-released on this
mid-'70s compilation.

Louisiana Red: *Reality Blues* (L+R Records 42.011), 1980.
Of this record Red says, "It was a pleasure to play with Mr. Wolf's guitar player.
I was glad to be with musicians that I knew from Chicago. I knew Hubert a lit-
tle bit from Chicago, but we became closer friends after this session."

Various Artists: *The First Blues Sampler* (L+R Records 42.006), 1980.
Contains Hubert/Carey Bell's "Brought Up the Hard Way," which appears on
L+R Records' *Gamblin' Woman!*

Various Artists: *American Folk Blues Festival '81* (L+R Records 42.022), 1981.
A cast of characters including Hubert, Carey and Lurrie Bell, Louisiana Red,
Sunnyland Slim, and Margie Evans were recorded on March 10 and 17, 1981,
in Kamen and Siegen, Germany.

Various Artists: *Chills and Fever: Chicago Bluesmasters, Vol. 4* (Charly 1080), 1985.
Hubert's sole contribution to this compilation, "Tators and Mators," works on
two levels. It could be another example of Hubert's food fetish and/or a twisted
inside joke about the Mighty Wolf being shot in the backside by his first wife,
Katie Mae. Under the mistaken impression that Wolf had been unfaithful, Katie
Mae fired a shotgun at the bluesman, who at the time was carrying "tators and

mators" among other items he had just bought at a local West Memphis, Arkansas, food market.

Various Artists: *Antone's 10th Anniversary Anthology, Vol. 1* (Antone's Records ANT-0004CD), 1986.

Recorded live in July 1985, this record commemorates the legendary Austin nightclub's tenth anniversary. Appearing are Otis Rush, Albert Collins, James Cotton, Pinetop Perkins, Buddy Guy, Calvin Jones, Luther Tucker, Snooky Pryor, Derek O'Brien, Jimmy Rogers, Jimmie Vaughan, and, of course, Hubert.

Eddie Taylor: *Still Not Ready for Eddie* (Antone's Records 0005), 1988.

Hubert, Snooky Pryor, Jimmy Rogers, Sunnyland Slim, and Luther Tucker support Jimmy Reed's great foil/"sideman" on this posthumous release.

Various Artists: *Antone's Anniversary, Vol. 2* (Antone's Records ANT-0016-2), 1991.

This record contains nearly the same personnel as the first installment. Cotton and Hubert perform "Moanin' at Midnight" and "Evan Shuffle."

Lonnie Brooks: *Sweet Home Chicago* (Evidence ECD 26001-2), 1992 (recorded 1975).

Luther Johnson: *Lonesome in My Bedroom* (Evidence ECD 26005-2), 1992 (recorded 1975).

Eddie Shaw & The Wolf Gang: *Have Blues, Will Travel* (Rooster Records), 1977.

Buddy Guy and Junior Wells: *Live in Montreux* (Evidence 26002), original release 1977, reissued 1997.

Evidence reissued these tracks that were once distributed by Black and Blue and available only overseas for a while. Originally released as a live record of only Wells and Guy (the duo were making regular appearances with the Rolling Stones, recording with artists like Eric Clapton, and touring Europe and the US), the reissued CD has five bonus tracks. One of these, "When I Feel Better" (an electric, slightly different version of the acoustic song Guy recorded for L+R during the 1964 AFBF tour that is, oddly, not as electrifying or dynamic), features Hubert and Jimmy Johnson on guitar, Dave Myers on bass, and Odie Payne on drums. Check the nod to Wolf's version of "Dust My Broom" in the opening vamp.

Living Chicago Blues, Volume Number 1 (Alligator AL 7701), 1978.

In 1978, having finished recording *Have Blues, Will Travel* (produced by Wolf's widow Lillie Burnett), Eddie Shaw & The Wolf Gang were playing at Shaw's club (Eddie's Place—the New 1815 Club) plus the Kingston Mines and Biddy Mulligan's when they took time out of their busy gig schedule to record this compilation released by Bruce Iglauer's Alligator label. The Gang appears on five songs: "It's Alright" (in which Hubert is largely relegated to the background—

even when it sounds like he'll let loose, he seems stifled), "Out of Bad Luck" (a
Magic Sam tune on which Hubert returns to his mid-'60s, take-charge attacks),
"Stoop Down, Baby" (a live favorite of Eddie's), "Sitting on Top of the World,"
and "My Baby's So Ugly" ("she may be ugly, but she know just what to do").
Hubert, along with frontman/saxophonist/singer Shaw, keyboardist Johnny "Big
Mouse" Walker (his first-ever session—and gig—with the band), bassist
Lafayette "Shorty" Gilbert, and Chico Chism appear.

Willie Mabon with Hubert Sumlin, Eddie Taylor, Aron Burton, and Casey Jones:
Chicago Blues Session! (L+R/Optimism LR CD-2003) (recorded 1979).

American Folk Blues Festival '80 (L+R/Optimism Inc. LR CD-2013) (recorded
1980).

Hubert Sumlin and Carey Bell: *Gamblin' Woman!* (L+R Records LP 42.008), 1980.
The cover of this record, graced by what appears to be a glassy-eyed lady of the
evening complete with windswept hair, dangling turquoise earrings, and two gold
neck chains (someone a deep-pocketed man would take a chance on?), is just
one of its intriguing aspects. Recorded live in the studio with no overdubs,
remastering, or multi-tracking, this record is a true blues jam, albeit more from
the Delta/Mississippi angle than Chicago blues. In keeping with the country-
blues mood, Hubert mostly sticks with acoustic, as he did in 1964 with *Blues
Anytime!* He also plays an improvised instrument—a box with metal strings,
recalling his days with the diddley bow. Hubert plays electric guitar on only one
song here, the title track, and Sunnyland Slim accompanies on piano. Tracks
include "Blues for Chester" (guess who?), "Lonesome Blues," "Blues in My
Heart," "Blues on Blues," and "Hubert's 1980s Blues." These tracks are, once
again, an extemporaneous Hubert special, as he makes up lyrics and riffs right
on the spot. Bell injects some lusty harp playing that carries many of these tunes,
which are performed wholly as a duo. (Bell learned harp from Little Walter and
recorded with Muddy Waters until his solo debut in 1969.)

Eddie Shaw: *King of the Road* (Rooster Records) (R7608), 1988.
An Eddie Shaw career-spanning record—from 1966 through 1988—that features Hubert on a number of tracks with the Wolf Gang.

Zora Young, Bonnie Lee, Big Time Sarah: *Blues With the Girls* (EPM Musique), 1988.
The five-and-half-minute track "Well, I Love Ya" was written by Hubert and
speaks of Mojo and requited love. Zora Young, born in West Point, Mississippi,
just a few miles from Wolf's birthplace, begins a vocal call-and-response with
Hubert. In theory this seems to be a good idea: mix Hubert's weathered, weary,
Ray Charles–approximated voice with Young's Aretha Franklin/Gladys Knight–
influenced vocals. Sometimes the mixture of oil and water works well in music.
Here, the opposites only attract derision. Hubert seems to sing off-key for some
of the track. He elongates his lines so much that it's hard to know if he is aware

of the meters and timing. The word "loooooove" is held completely too long—a regrettable turnoff at best. One gets the feeling that Hubert is trying to sabotage the record. Why would he do that? Perhaps he thought he'd never get a call to do a similar guest appearance again, which may have been wishful thinking.

** *The Chess Box: Muddy Waters* (Chess/MCA CD 31268), 1989.

Little Mike & the Tornadoes: *Heart Attack* (Blind Pig BP 73990), 1990.

Guitar Player *Presents: Legends of Guitar: Electric Blues, Vol. 1* (Rhino Records 70716), 1990.

Jimmy Rogers: "Ludella" (Antone's Records), 1991.
   Rogers's song "Ludella" was the flipside of 1950's "That's All Right" (Chess 1435). It would be five years later that Chess spun Rogers off as a solo act, much in the same way they did Little Walter three years earlier, after he left Muddy's band.

Blues Masters (The Essential Blues Collection), Vol. 4: Harmonica Classics (Rhino Records R4 71124), 1992.

Little Mike & The Tornadoes: *Payday* (Blind Pig 4992), 1992.
   Little Mike composed 12 original songs in the style of 1950s Chicago blues. He called in Hubert to do the guitar honors.

Blues Masters (The Essential Blues Collection), Vol. 6: Blues Originals (Rhino Records R2 71127), 1993.

Chicago Blues Session, Vol. 22: Hubert Sumlin and Billy Branch (Wolf Records 120.868), 1993.

Sunnyland Slim Blues Band: *Decoration Day* (Evidence ECD 26053-2), 1994 (recorded 1980).

Sunnyland Slim Blues Band: *Be Careful How You Vote* (Earwig Records CD 4915), 1994.

Bill Hickey, Hubert Sumlin, and Jimmy Rogers: *Bill's Blues* (Atomic Theory ATD 1112), 1994.
   Recorded when Hickey was still a welcome member of the Hubert Sumlin extended family and the blues community at large. Hickey veered off the path of the straight and narrow after his surrogate mother, Bea, died.

American Folk Blues Festival: 1962–1965 (Evidence 26100), 1995.

Sonny Boy Williamson in Europe with Eric Clapton, Willie Dixon, Otis Spann, and Matt "Guitar" Murphy (Evidence 26071), 1995.
   Includes Hubert playing at the 1964 AFBF.

Eddie Shaw: *The Blues Is Nothing But Good News* (Wolf Records 120.866), 1996.

Blues Classics (MCA 11441), 1996.
   Three-disc box set that acts as a guide through the history of the blues starting with the year 1927 and ending with 1969.

** Muddy Waters: *His Best 1956–1964* (Chess/MCA 9380), 1997.

Pinetop Perkins: *Pinetop's Boogie Woogie* (Antone's Records 20), 1992; (Discovery/WEA 74210), 1997.

James Cotton: *Mighty Long Time* (Antone's Records ANT 0015-2), 1991; (Discovery/WEA 74208), 1997.

American Folk Blues Festival '62–'65: Highlights (Evidence 26087), 1997.
Still more from the AFBF.

Blues Guitar Duels (Easydisc 367049), 1997.

Hubert Sumlin and Pinetop Perkins: *Legends* (Telarc 83446), 1998.
Nominated for a Grammy Award in 2000.

A Tribute to Howlin' Wolf (Telarc CD-83427), 1998.
A two-year project involving Hubert, Sam Lay, Eddie Shaw, Calvin "Fuzz" Jones, and Henry Gray.

Sunnyland Slim: *She Got a Thing Goin' On* (Earwig Records CD 4942), 1998.
Recorded 1971, 1974, 1977, 1978, 1979, and 1983.

Various Artists: *Don't Worry Sing the Blues* (Atomic Theory 1131), 1998.

Bea & Baby Records, Vol. 2 (Wolf Records 120294), 1998.
Hubert appears on Sunnyland Slim's "Got That Jive" and Mack Simmons's "Help Me" and "Mother-in-Law Blues."

** *Best of Muddy Waters: 20th Century Masters* (Chess/MCA 11946), 1999.

Eric Sardinas: *Treat Me Right* (Evidence 26102), 1999.

Jim Liban Blues Combo: *Blues for Shut-Ins* (JLB 1001), 1999.
Featuring Liban, Dave Kasik, Matt Liban, Perry Weber, Ian Spanic, and Hubert.

Elliott Sharp's Terraplane: *Blues for Next* (Knitting Factory Records KFW-285), 2000.
Eric Mingus, son of jazz giant Charles Mingus, whether intentionally or not has the style if not the substance of Wolf's voice on this record. Between sets at a Hubert Sumlin show in early 2004, Mingus, who juggles two drinks (only one an alcoholic beverage), drapes an arm around me and says, "We should talk." His energy level is one notch below what it was onstage, and he appears restless and talkative, eager to tell me how much he is into the blues (undoubtedly because he thinks I automatically associate him with jazz). Being the son of a jazz legend—especially one known as a compositional genius—can't be easy. Eric has taken risks in his career, and critics have condemned him for it, perhaps unfairly, because they believe his musical choices should reflect his pedigree. Certainly, no one can accuse Eric of trading on his past. He never introduces himself as Charles Mingus's son. In fact, he seems totally divorced from his dad's legacy. He tells me how his dad introduced him to Wolf and Hubert when he was a small child. Eric grew up with Hubert and Wolf records, and tonight he gets the

honor of singing a string of classic Wolf cuts in an intimate setting with one of his lifelong heroes. "I was just a kid, maybe eight years old, and I was listening to blues records," Eric tells me. "My dad said, 'You like this stuff?' I said, 'Yeeeah.' I grew up with Wolf and Hubert."

Chuck Berry: The Anthology (MCA 088 112 304-2), 2000.

Jimmy D. Lane: *Legacy* (Analogue Productions Originals APO 2005), 2000.
Recorded 1997 at the same time as Hubert's *I Know You.* These were Jimmy Rogers's last recording sessions.

Peter Green: *Hot Foot Powder* (Artisan Records 10828), 2000.
Hubert, Buddy Guy, and David "Honeyboy" Edwards, a Wolf and Robert Johnson contemporary, guest. Green, who was one of the founding members of Fleetwood Mac and had played with the Godfather of British Blues John Mayall, has always maintained that Wolf's music—and Hubert's guitar playing in particular—has had a profound impact on the development of his style.

Blues Chicago Style: Guitar Stars (St. Clair Records 7232), 2001.
Hubert does "All I Can Do" and "Run Don't Walk."

Antone's 20th (Texas Music Group 307), 2001.

This Is Blues Harmonica (Delmark 746), 2001.

** *Muddy Waters: The Anthology* (Chess/MCA 112649), 2001.
Hubert is uncredited.

Chicago Blues Festival, Vol. 3: 1974–1976 (Black & Blue/Hepcat 603), 2001.

Little Mack Simmons: *Blue Lights* (Black & Blue/Hepcat 450), 2002.

Noah Witherspoon: *Buzz Me* (Analogue Productions Originals APO 2018), 2002.

In the Pocket: A Taste of Blues Harmonica (Telarc 83556), 2002.
Hubert sings "Rock Me Baby."

Luther "Snake" Johnson: *They Call Me the Popcorn Man* (Black & Blue/Hepcat 431), 2002.

Bob Margolin All Star Blues Jam (Telarc CD-83579), 2003.
Hubert appears on two tracks recorded at Margolin's house in North Carolina: "Goin' Down Slow" and "Last Time." He was given Margolin's 1930s Gibson acoustic for the session, while Margolin plucked a National.

David Maxwell: *Max Attack* (BlueMax 001), 2003.
Pianist and electric keyboardist Maxwell puts together a great crew here: Hubert, Pinetop Perkins, Ronnie Earl, Per Hanson, Michael "Mudcat" Ward, James Cotton, Kim Wilson, Duke Robillard, and Liane Carroll, among others. Hubert appears on three songs. Check the high energy of the guitar and harp—courtesy of Cotton—in "Thanks for All the Women" and Hubert's smokin' runs in "Handyman." One can really hear the intensity and conversational interplay

between Hubert and Maxwell in "Coming Home, Baby"—a variation on Hubert's "I'm Coming Home." We get a sense that Hubert likes what he hears, too: he screams into the mic as the song closes: "THAT'S what I'm talkin' 'bout!"

Chuck Berry: *Blues* (Chess/MCA 000053002), 2003.

Eric Bibb: *Natural Light* (Earthbeat 73830), 2003.

American Folk Blues Festival 1962–1966 (Hip-O Records 000103002), 2003.
Tracks recorded from the 1964 AFBF tour when Hubert accompanied Wolf, Sunnyland, and Sonny Boy Williamson II.

Best of Vee-Jay Blues (collectables box set 147), 2003.
Hubert with the Eddie Taylor band.

Bar Room Blues: A 12-Track Program (Telarc 83594), 2004.

Elliott Sharp's Terraplane: *Do the Don't* (Gaff Music GAFF 6731172), 2004.

Various Artists: *Lightning in a Bottle* (Columbia/Legacy C2K 92860), 2004.
Recorded as part of the congressionally mandated "Year of the Blues" in 2003. "Killing Floor," recorded at Radio City Music Hall, features Hubert with David Johansen. Johansen is quite a student of the blues. In a conversation I had with the singer-chameleon, he gave me historic pointers and expressed his love for the Honeyboy Edwards biography. "You have to read it," he said. "His voice comes through so loud and clear."

Eric Clapton: Crossroads Guitar Festival, DVD. (Warner Strategic Marketing/ Reprise/Duck 9703827), 2004.
Ron de Moraes, director; John Bueg and David Horn, executive producers; Mona Niemiec and Mitch Owgang, producers.

*The reader should be aware that many of the multi-artist compilations and Wolf titles listed here contain the same or similar material. They have been included to illustrate the breadth and depth of Hubert's recorded output.

** Per Hubert Sumlin.

Selected Bibliography

Books

Ammer, Christine. *HarperCollins Dictionary of Music.* 2nd ed. New York: Harper-Perennial, 1987.

Anonymous. *West Memphis 1927–1976.* West Memphis, Arkansas: Original research donated to the West Memphis Public Library.

Bacon, Tony. *The Ultimate Guitar Book.* New York: Alfred A. Knopf, 2002.

Berry, Chuck. *Chuck Berry: The Autobiography.* New York: Harmony Books, 1987.

Bordowitz, Hank. *Bad Moon Rising: The Unofficial History of Creedence Clearwater Revival.* New York: Schirmer Books, 1998.

Chipkin, Kenn, John Garwood, and Fred Sokolow. *Howlin' Wolf: Featuring Hubert Sumlin on Guitar.* Milwaukee: Hal Leonard Corp., 1996.

Cohodas, Nadine. *Spinning Blues into Gold.* New York: St. Martin's Press, 2000.

Cook, Richard, and Brian Morton. *The Penguin Guide to Jazz on CD.* 4th ed. New York: Penguin, 1998.

Dixon, Willie, with Don Snowden. *I Am the Blues: The Willie Dixon Story.* New York: Da Capo Press, 1989.

Erlewine, Michael, Vladimir Bogdanov, Chris Woodstra, and Stephen Thomas Erlewine, eds. *All Music Guide.* 3rd ed. San Francisco: Miller Freeman Books, 1997.

Gordon, Robert. *Can't Be Satisfied: The Life and Times of Muddy Waters.* Boston: Little, Brown and Company, 2002.

Guralnick, Peter. *Searching for Robert Johnson.* New York: Plume/Penguin Group, 1998.

Guralnick, Peter, Robert Santelli, Holly George-Warren, and Christopher John Farley, eds. *Martin Scorsese Presents The Blues*. New York: Amistad (HarperCollins Publishers), 2003.

Harris, Sheldon. *Blues Who's Who: A Biographical Dictionary of Blues Singers*. New Rochelle, NY: Arlington House Publishers, 1979.

Holley, Donald. *The Second Great Emancipation: The Mechanical Cotton Picker, Black Migration, and How They Shaped the Modern South*. Fayetteville: University of Arkansas Press, 2000.

Leadbitter, Mike, and Neil Slaven. *Blues Records 1943–1966: An Encyclopedic Discography to More Than Two Decades of Recorded Blues*. London: Oak Publications/Hanover Books, Ltd., 1968.

Lomax, Alan. *The Land Where the Blues Began*. New York: The New Press, 2002.

Moses, Charlie, and Alan Whitehead, Dennis Bouchard, Marla Cowie, Ethel Bibus, Donnie Whitehead, Sandie Tatum, Rubie Harrington, Elizabeth Collins, and Jim Cowie. *Williams Landing–Carroll County 1833–1983*. Greenwood, MS: Williams Landing Sesquicentennial, Inc. (in celebration of Williams Landing–Carroll County Sesquicentennial), 1983.

O'Neal, Jim, and Amy van Singel. *The Voice of the Blues: Classic Interviews from Living Blues Magazine*. New York: Routledge, 2002.

Palmer, Robert. *Deep Blues: A Musical and Cultural History, from the Mississippi Delta to Chicago's South Side to the World*. New York: Penguin Books, 1982.

Rowe, Mike. *Chicago Blues: The City & The Music*. New York: Da Capo, 1975.

Santelli, Robert. *The Big Book of Blues: A Biographical Encyclopedia*. New York: Penguin Books, 1993.

Segrest, James, and Mark Hoffman. *Moanin' at Midnight: The Life and Times of Howlin' Wolf*. New York: Pantheon Books, 2004.

Wardlow, Gayle Dean. *Chasin' That Devil Music: Searching for the Blues*. Edited by Edward Komara. San Francisco: Backbeat Books, 1998.

Woolfolk, Margaret Elizabeth. *A History of Crittenden County, Arkansas*. West Memphis, Arkansas: Original research donated to the West Memphis Public Library.

Wormser, Richard. *The Rise and Fall of Jim Crow*. New York: St. Martin's Griffin, 2003.

Wyman, Bill, with Richard Havers. *Bill Wyman's Blues Odyssey: A Journey to Music's Heart & Soul*. New York: DK Publishing, 2001.

Liner Notes

Alperin, Jeff. *Wake Up Call* by Hubert Sumlin. Blues Planet Records, 1998.

Bartolucci, Robert. *Evil: Live at Joe's Place, 1973* by Howlin' Wolf & The Wolf Gang. Wolf Records, 1995.

Blind Willie. *Hubert Sumlin: Made in Argentina 1993* by Hubert Sumlin. Blues Special Records, 1994.

Dahl, Bill. *Blues Anytime!* by Hubert Sumlin, Willie Dixon, and Sunnyland Slim. Evidence, 1994.

Dahl, Bill. *Heart Attack* by Little Mike & The Tornadoes. Blind Pig Records, 1990.

Dahl, Bill. *The London Howlin' Wolf Sessions* featuring Eric Clapton, Steve Winwood, Bill Wyman, and Charlie Watts. Deluxe ed. Chess/MCA, 2002.

Darwen, Norman. *Blues Guitar Boss* by Hubert Sumlin. JSP Records, 1990.

Guralnick, Peter. *Elvis Presley: The Sun Sessions CD* by Elvis Presley. RCA, 1987.

Hess, Norbert. *Gamblin' Woman!* by Hubert Sumlin and Carey Bell. L+R Records, 1980.

Hoffman, Lawrence. *Mean Old World: The Blues from 1940–1994* by various artists. Smithsonian Collection of Recordings/MCA Special Markets and Products, 1996.

Humphrey, Mark. *The Anthology* by Chuck Berry. Chess/MCA, 2000.

Humphrey, Mark. *The Back Door Wolf* by Howlin' Wolf. Chess/MCA, 1995.

Humphrey, Mark. *His Best: The Chess 50th Anniversary Collection* by Howlin' Wolf. Chess/MCA, 1997.

Humphrey, Mark. *The Very Best of John Lee Hooker* by John Lee Hooker. Rhino Records, 1995.

Koda, Cub. *Blues Masters (The Essential Blues Collection), Vol. 6: Blues Originals* by various artists. Rhino Records, 1993.

Kooper, Al. *Don't Say That I Ain't Your Man!: Essential Blues 1964–1969* by Michael Bloomfield. Columbia/Legacy, 1994.

Labbe, Randy. *A Tribute to Howlin' Wolf* by various artists. Telarc Blues, 1998.

Laredo, Joe. *The Best of B.B. King: The Millennium Collection* by B.B. King. MCA/Universal, 1999.

LaVere, Steven. *Robert Johnson: The Complete Recordings* by Robert Johnson. Box set. Columbia, 1990.

Lippmann. Horst. *American Folk Blues Festival '80* by various artists. L+R Records, 1980.

Loder, Kurt, and Robert Palmer. *Led Zeppelin [Box Set]* by Led Zeppelin. Atlantic, 1990.

Margolin, Bob. *All Star Blues Jam* by Bob Margolin and various artists. Telarc Blues, 2002.

Meltzer, Richard. *The Super Super Blues Band* by Howlin' Wolf, Muddy Waters, and Bo Diddley. Chess/MCA, 1992.

Milkowski, Bill. *In Step* by Stevie Ray Vaughan and Double Trouble. Columbia/Legacy, 1999.

O'Brien, Justin. *I Know You* by Hubert Sumlin. APO, 1998.

O'Brien, Justin. *My Guitar and Me* by Hubert Sumlin. Evidence, 1994.

O'Neal, Jim. *Living Chicago Blues: Volume Number 1* by various artists. Alligator, 1991.

Scott, Hammond. *Healing Feeling* by Hubert Sumlin. Black Top Records, 1990.

Shurman, Dick. *His Best, Vol. 2* by Howlin' Wolf. Chess/MCA, 1999.

Shurman, Dick. *The Chess Box: Howlin' Wolf* by Howlin' Wolf. Chess/MCA, 1991.

Templeton, Ray. *Charley Patton: Complete Recordings 1929–1934* by Charlie Patton. JSP Records, 2002.

Whiteis, David. *Bill's Blues* by Bill Hickey, Jimmy Rogers, Hubert Sumlin, and Friends. Atomic Theory Records, 1994.

Whiteis, David. *Decoration Day* by Sunnyland Slim Blues Band. Evidence, 1994.

Zeldin, Beverly. *Heart & Soul* by Hubert Sumlin, with James Cotton and Little Mike & The Tornadoes. Blind Pig, 1989.

Magazines

Bims, Hamilton. "Audiences Cried Wolf, and Chester Was a Star." *Ebony*, March 1972.

Blackett, Matt. "Learning Curve: The Blues Guitar of Hubert Sumlin." *Guitar Player*, December 2000.

Blandon, Jon. "Hubert Sumlin: Basic Blues with Style." *The Music Paper*, April 1987.

Blues Detective. "The Blues Detective Speaks with Hubert Sumlin." *DISCoveries*, September 1995.

[no author]. "The Blues Is How It Is." *Time*, Sept. 2, 1966.

Burr, Ramiro. "Antone's Founder Indicted." *Billboard*, July 5, 1997.

Cravatta, Michael. "The Beaten Path." *American Demographics*, February 1998.

[no author]. "Door Slammed for Obscene Reasons." *Rolling Stone*, Jan. 20, 1968.

[no author]. "Down Beat News." *Down Beat*, March 29, 1973.

Draper, Robert. "Clifford's Blues." *Texas Monthly*, October 1997.

Ellis, Andy. "Full Bloom: Mike Bloomfield's Ecstatic Chromatic Blues." *Guitar Player*, April 1995.

Ellis, Andy. "Hand Me Down Blues." *Guitar Player*, January 1999.

Forte, Dan. "Frank Zappa on…The '80s Guitar Clone." *Guitar Player*, January 1987.

Gifford, Barry. "Couldn't Do No Yodeling So I Turned to Howlin'." *Rolling Stone*, Aug. 24, 1968.

Goldberg, Michael. "MCA Buys Chess Catalog." *Rolling Stone*, Jan. 30, 1986.

Hoffman, Mark, and James Segrest. "Hubert at Home: Sumlin's Friends Keep Him Young." *Blues Access*, Fall 2001.

Isola, Gregory. "A Blues Legend's Wake Up Call." *Guitar Player*, July 1998.

Ivey, Ed. "Hubert Sumlin: On an Album Full of Superstar Guests—Eric Clapton, Keith Richards, Levon Helm—Wolf's Guitarist Finds That Muddy Changes Everything." *Blues Revue*, April 2001.

Knopper, Steve. "Star Guitars." *Rolling Stone*, Aug. 5, 2004.

[no author listed]. "Living Blues Interview: Howlin' Wolf." *Living Blues*, Spring 1970.

[no author listed]. "Mean Old Blues." *Newsweek*, Feb. 21, 1966.

Morgenstern, Dan. "The Blues Comes to Ann Arbor." *Down Beat*, Oct. 2, 1969.

Obrecht, Jas. "Hubert Sumlin: Legendary Chicago Sideman Releases Solo LP." *Guitar Player*, February 1987.

O'Neal, Amy. "Howlin' Wolf." *Living Blues*, January/February 1976.

Point, Michael. "Hubert Sumlin." *Down Beat*, December 1987.

[no author]. "Rebirth of the Blues." *Newsweek*, May 26, 1969.

Shurman, Dick. "Chicago…International Blues Festival." *Living Blues*, November/December 1975.

Sumlin, Hubert. "My Years with Wolf." *Living Blues*, September/October 1989.

Welding, Pete. "I Sing for the People: An Interview with Bluesman Howlin' Wolf." *Down Beat*, Dec. 14, 1967.

Wenner, Jann. "The Rolling Stone Interview: Mike Bloomfield." *Rolling Stone*, April 6, 1968.

Whiteis, Dave. "A Tender Heart and a Hustler's Soul: Sunnyland Slim's Long Life in the Blues." *Living Blues*, March/April 1990.

Newspapers

Chicago Sun-Times, "Chicago area hospitals ailing as much as their patients," Jan. 19, 1976.

Chicago Tribune, "Bluesman 'Howlin' Wolf' Chester Burnett dies," Jan. 11, 1976.

Christensen, Thor. "Development of rock 'n' roll's fuzzy side." *The Miami Herald*, June 8, 2004.

Elwood, Philip. "Red-hot evenings of Southside blues veterans." *San Francisco Examiner*, Nov. 31, 1996.

Fordham, John. "Elliott Sharp's Terraplane/Hubert Sumlin on tour." *The Guardian* (UK), Nov. 8, 2003.

Freedman, Samuel. "Hubert Sumlin: his blues are cause for cheer." *The New York Times*, July 5, 1987.

Harrington, Richard. "MCA to pay royalties to R&B greats." *The Washington Post*, Dec. 7, 1989.

Hoekstra. Dave. "Howlin' like the Wolf: saxophonist Eddie Shaw pays tribute to the late blues master." *Chicago Sun-Times*, Nov. 24, 1985.

Hoekstra, Dave. "Hubert Sumlin shows flash of Howlin' Wolf's genius." *Chicago Sun-Times*, July 3, 1988.

Johnson, Jeff. "Chicago blues festival at Grant Park." *Chicago Sun-Times*, June 15, 2004.

Joyce, Mike. "Cooling out with the blues." *The Washington Post*, Aug. 14, 1987.

Joyce, Mike. "Hubert Sumlin, backing up the band." *The Washington Post*, Jan. 2, 1989.

Joyce, Mike. "Piano player's boogie-woogie pair." *The Washington Post*, Jan. 8, 1993.

Joyce, Mike. "Taking blues bayou beyond the South." *The Washington Post*, July 12, 1991.

Pareles, Jon. "Blues innovator enters the spotlight." *The New York Times*, July 18, 1987.

Pareles, Jon. "Hubert Sumlin, guitar at the Abilene Café." *The New York Times*, June 18, 1986.

Philadelphia Tribune, "Saxman Eddie Shaw hits Warmdaddy's," July 21, 1995.

Seedorff, George. "Former Howlin' Wolf guitarist makes rare Michigan appearance." *Michigan Chronicle*, June 25, 1997.

Segaloff, Nat. "Cambridge filmmaker brings back the blues." *The Boston Herald*, Aug. 19, 1988.

Selvin, Joel. "The blues—Chicago's got it good." *San Francisco Chronicle*, June 8, 1987.

Stout, Gene. "A concert for the love of Hendrix." *Seattle Post-Intelligencer*, Feb. 20, 2004.

Tianen, Dave. "A quiet legend's rockin' years." *Milwaukee Journal Sentinel*, Nov. 19, 1998.

Web sites

www.allmusic.com

www.batesmeyer.com/jodywilliams

www.blues.org

www.gcvb.com

www.henrygray.com

www.hubertsumlinblues.com

www.louisamps.com

www.louisiana-red.com

www.nybluesandjazz.org

www.pbs.org/americanrootsmusic/pbs_arm_oralh_jamescotton.html

http://theband.hiof.no/

www.uark.edu/campus-resources/archinfo/parkin.html

www.wpnet.org/About_HWblues.htm

DVDs/Videos

Blues Story, DVD. Jay Levey, producer/director; Richard Foos and Jay Levey, executive producers. Los Angeles: Shout! Factory/SMV, 2003.

Eric Clapton: Nothing But The Blues, (unreleased). Martin Scorsese, director/executive producer; Stephen "Scooter" Weintraub, producer/writer. New York: CAPPA Productions, Inc./*In the Spotlight,* Thirteen/WNET/in association with Reprise Records, 1995.

Hubert Sumlin @ Abilene Café, NYC, (unreleased). Courtesy of Jon Paris, 1991.

Hubert Sumlin: Living the Blues, limited ed. VHS. Jim Kent and Sumner Burgwyn, producers. Boston: Juke Joint Films, 1986.

The American Folk Blues Festival 1962–1966, DVD. David Peck and Jon Kanis for Reelin' in the Years, and Janie Hendrix and John McDermott for Experience Hendrix, LLC, producers. Santa Monica, CA: Hip-O Records/Universal Music Group Recordings, 2003.

The Blues Guitar of Hubert Sumlin, VHS. Happy Traum, producer and director. Woodstock, NY: Homespun Tapes, Ltd., 2000.

The Howlin' Wolf Story: The Secret History of Rock 'n' Roll, DVD. Don McGlynn, director; Joe Lauro, producer, for Blue Sea Productions. New York: Bluebird/BMG Music/Arista, 2003.

Selected Original Interviewees and Personal Communications

Clifford Antone	Corey Harris	Richard Ramsey
Steve Arvey	Levon Helm	Keith Richards
Renee Austin	Ida Hicks	Paul Rishell
Cary Baker	Charlene Higgs	John Rockwood
Richard Barone	Donald Holley	Louis Rosano
Paul Barrère	Bruce Iglauer	Richard Rosenblatt
Richard Benson	Wayne Jackson	Bobby Rush
Jordan Birnbaum	David Johansen	Mark Sallings
Fiona Boyes	James Yancy Jones	Diane Sanders
Sam Burckhardt	(Tail Dragger)	Jesse Sanders (Little
Marshall Chess	Chad Kassem	Howlin' Wolf)
Chico Chism	Riley "B.B." King	Tommy Shannon
Tony Coleman	Bob Koester	Elliott Sharp
Paul Cooper	Jimmy D. Lane	Jay Sieleman
Andy Cornett	Steven LaVere	Hugh Southard
James Cotton	Sam Lay	Bob Stroger
Robert Cray	Colin Linden	Hubert Sumlin
Tom Cucchiara	Toni Ann Mamary	Otis Taylor
Jeff Dagenhardt	Bob Margolin	Susan Tedeschi
Bill Dahl	Mike Markowitz	Derek Trucks
Barry Dolins	Lucy Davis Marshall	Brad Vickers
Patrick Donovan	David Maxwell	Joe Vignola
Ronnie Earl	Doug McLean	Jimmy Vivino
Ben Elliott	Iverson Minter	Maggie Watkins
David Evans	(Louisiana Red)	Perry Weber
Rob Fraboni	Jeff Mitchem	Jack White
Michael Freeman	Kevin Murphy	Emery Williams, Jr.
Steve Freund	Charlie Musselwhite	(Detroit Junior)
Arnie Goodman	Curtis Obeda	Jody Williams
Henry Gray	Jim O'Neal	Kim Wilson
Col. Bruce Hampton	Jon Paris	
(Ret.)	Bob Putignano	

Other Interviews

Cotton, James. Video and print interview, *American Roots Music*, PBS, 2003.

Sumlin, Hubert. Radio interviews, WMBR (date unknown); WGBH, Oct. 19, 1985; WGSE, June 23, 1987.

Sumlin, Hubert. Q&A video documentary with Texas T-Bone, (date unknown).

Sumlin, Hubert. Audio interview, courtesy of Rob Fraboni, 2000.

Other Documents and Sources

Brookins Funeral Home, Chicago, IL. Obituary, Willie Bea Reed Sumlin, Oct. 30, 1999.

Christie's New York. Auction Guide and Calendar, Crossroads Guitar Auction, Eric Clapton and Friends for the Crossroads Centre, June 24, 2004.

Greenwood, MS Directory, 1910.

Greenwood, MS Directory, 1930.

Greenwood, MS "Heart of the Blues" Award, June 10, 2004.

MS State Department of Health Vital Records. Search report for Hubert Sumlin birth certificate.

Office of the Clerk, Cook County, IL. Statement of permanent real estate index number and legal description for 1815 West Roosevelt Road, Chicago, IL.

Acknowledgments

I
t has been quite a journey. I've traveled through a number of states, gone to late-night shows, met with complete strangers, old friends, and complete strangers who felt like old friends, and sparked stimulating conversations with fascinating specimens of humanity. This is the end of the road, but I couldn't have gotten here without plenty of help. There are lots of people to thank, so bear with me.

To the man "without whom"—Hubert Sumlin—I can't thank you enough for your kindness, time, trust, good nature, impossibly positive outlook, and presence on this earth. It's an overused cliché, but tailor-made for you: when they made you, they broke the mold. I'd say that you are one in a million, but, frankly, that probability is just too high. And to Toni Ann Mamary, thank you for allowing me the opportunity of a lifetime.

Given the vast expanse of musical territory Backbeat Books has covered in the last few years, and the high degree of talent on the company's author roster, I am honored to have been welcomed into the family with open arms. It is my absolute pleasure to renew professional ties with Backbeat Executive Editor Richard Johnston. (When Richard signed on to my idea for this book in 2003, I literally jumped at the chance to work again with the former *Bass Player* editor.) Thanks for your vote of confidence and undying professionalism, Richard. Your standard of excellence motivated me to be all I could be on a daily basis during the entire process. Others on Team Backbeat were instrumental in seeing this manuscript through to completion. Julie Herrod-Lumsden: thank you for your sharp eye, versatility, efficiency, and thorough editing. You turned my written words into *writing*. And special thanks go to Amy Miller, Kevin Becketti, Nina Lesowitz, Steve Moore, and Richard Leeds.

I would also like to acknowledge the musicians, researchers/historians, writers, photographers, music industry pros, esteemed colleagues, and friends who've joined me on this journey. Everyone on the list below has a love for the blues, blues history (or history in general), and/or Hubert, and it showed in the invaluable information they imparted and the tales they spun. Thanks to Clifford Antone, Chico Chism, Perry Weber, Jody Williams, James Cotton, Levon Helm, Henry Gray, Sam Burckhardt, Bob Stroger, Jack White, Riley "B.B." King, Robert Cray, Sam Lay, Curtis Obeda, Charlie Musselwhite, David Maxwell, Richard Rosenblatt, Emery Williams, Jr. (Detroit Junior), Maggie Watkins, Paul Cooper, Bruce Iglauer, Steve LaVere, Bob Margolin, Bobby Rush, Jon Paris, Richard Ramsey, Paul Barrère, Keith Richards, Chad Kassem, Bob Putignano, Ronnie Earl, Rob Fraboni, Michael Hill, Ida B. Hicks, Hugh Southard, Elliott Sharp, Andy Cornett, John Rockwood, James Yancy Jones, Jeff Dagenhardt, Fiona Boyes, Charlene Higgs, Bob Koester, Dan Beech, Col. Bruce Hampton, Tommy Shannon, Holger Peterson, Iverson Minter (Louisiana Red), Brad Vickers, Brian Smith, Colin Linden, Doug McLean, Jordan Birnbaum, David Johansen, Patrick Donovan, Wayne Jackson, Jimmy D. Lane, Arnie Goodman, Susan Tedeschi, Derek Trucks, Jimmy Vivino, Steve Arvey, Renee Austin, Paul Rishell, Carey Baker, Tony Coleman, Jay Sieleman, Jim O'Neal, Mark Sallings, Jeff Mitchem, Kevin Murphy, David Evans, Tom Cucchiara, Kim Wilson, Richard Benson, Marshall Chess, Mike Markowitz, Steve Freund, Michael Freeman, Corey Harris, Otis Taylor, Ben Elliott, Louis Rosano, Donald Holley, Jesse Sanders (Little Howlin' Wolf), Diane Sanders, Richard Barone, Bill Dahl, Sim Cain, Billy Hector, Tim Tindall, Eric Mingus, Teo Leyasmeyer, Joe Vignola, Pinetop Perkins, Jim Saley, Tom Compton, Steve Jordan, Randy Haecker, Terry Buckalew, Edward Chmelewski, Debra Regur, Dick Waterman, Beverly Howell, Tina France, Sue Schrader, Julie Doppelt-Boyer, and Marc Lipkin.

This book cropped up from fertile ground—the brilliant and tireless work of researchers who have paved the way for blues historians for years to come. Some of these trailblazers are Mark Hoffman, James Segrest, Joe Lauro, Jim O'Neal, Robert Gordon, Don McGlynn, Nadine Cahodas, Mike Rowe, Don Snowden (for his work with Willie Dixon), Hal Leonard, Robert Palmer, Alan Lomax, Robert Santelli, Gayle Dean Wardlow, Jim Kent, Sumner Burgwyn, Bill Wyman, David Whiteis, Dick Shurman, Mike Leadbitter, Neil Slaven, Jay Levey, Reelin' in the Years, The Experience Music Project, *Blues Revue* magazine, *Living Blues* magazine, Martin Scorsese, and all those who helped to raise the profile of the blues in 2003 (the "Year of the Blues").

I've had the good fortune to make contact with some incredible personalities throughout my career, but the following have been like beacons in a long, dark night: Brad Hamilton at the *New York Post,* Michael Molenda, Paul Schultz at the *New York Daily News,* Dennis Brabham, Tom Callahan, Michael Harrison, Barry Janoff, Adam Budofsky, Rick Van Horn, Christine Kreiser, Dana Asher, Mitch Gallagher, Steve La Cerra, Greg Loescher, Tom Bartsch, Sharon Korbeck, Michael Mazur, and the editors at EBM for their moral support. And to all those who erected roadblocks to my progress as an individual and professional (you know who you are), thanks for motivating me to work that much *harder!*

And last but not least, to my wife, Sharon. I've reached this point in my life because of your love, wit, wisdom, feistiness, inner strength, and boundless generosity. We've made it to this place together. This one's for you, babe.

About the Author

W ill Romano has written for such diverse publications as the *New York Post, New York Daily News, Guitar Player, Bass Player, EQ, Modern Drummer, Blues Revue, Goldmine, Military History, Popular Electronics, Dirty Linen, VH-1.com, Barnes&Noble.com, The Music & Sound Retailer, DJ Times,* and others. His writing also appears in *Writer's Digest's Handbook of Magazine Article Writing (All New Second Edition).* He is a working musician who has had the fortune to be a music columnist and beat reporter. He has taught media and marketing at Fordham University in New York and holds a degree in accounting. He and his wife Sharon live in Long Island, NY.

Photo Credits

© Ray Flerlage/Michael Ochs Archives.com: pages 40 and 75
Chad Kassem: pages 211 and 220
Jim Kent: pages 126 and 169
© Michael Ochs Archives.com: page 37
John Rockwood: pages 193 and 219
Sharon Bailey Romano: pages 203, 204, and 215
Will Romano: pages 19 and 21
Mary Rosenblatt: page 108
Brian Smith: pages 53, 56, 112, 167, 175, 187, and 195

Index